Education, Science and Truth

Routledge International Studies in the Philosophy of Education

1. **Education and Work in Great Britain, Germany and Italy**
Edited by A. Jobert, C. Marry, L. Tanguy and H. Rainbird

2. **Education, Autonomy and Democratic Citizenship**
Philosophy in a Changing World
Edited by David Bridges

3. **The Philosophy of Human Learning**
Christopher Winch

4. **Education, Knowledge and Truth**
Beyond the Postmodern Impasse
Edited by David Carr

5. **Virtue Ethics and Moral Education**
Edited by David Carr and Jan Steutel

6. **Durkheim and Modern Education**
Edited by Geoffrey Walford and W. S. F. Pickering

7. **The Aims of Education**
Edited by Roger Marples

8. **Education in Morality**
J. Mark Halstead and Terence H. McLaughlin

9. **Lyotard: Just Education**
Edited by Pradeep A. Dhillon and Paul Standish

10. **Derrida & Education**
Edited by Gert J. J. Biesta and Denise Egéa-Kuehne

11. **Education, Work and Social Capital**
Towards a New Conception of Vocational Education
Christopher Winch

12. **Philosophical Discussion in Moral Education**
The Community of Ethical Inquiry
Tim Sprod

13. **Methods in the Philosophy of Education**
Frieda Heyting, Dieter Lenzen and John White

14. **Life, Work and Learning**
Practice in Postmoderniity
David Beckett and Paul Hager

15. **Education, Autonomy and Critical Thinking**
Christopher Winch

16. **Anarchism and Education**
A Philosophical Perspective
Judith Suissa

17. **Cultural Diversity, Liberal Pluralism and Schools**
Isaiah Berlin and Education
Neil Burtonwood

18. **Levinas and Education**
At the Intersection of Faith and Reason
Edited by Denise Egéa-Kuehne

19. Moral Responsibility, Authenticity, and Education
Ishtiyaque Haji and Stefaan E. Cuypers

20. Education, Science and Truth
Rasoul Nejadmehr

Education, Science and Truth

Rasoul Nejadmehr

Taylor & Francis Group

LONDON AND NEW YORK

First published 2009
by Routledge
52 Vanderbilt Avenue, New York, NY 10017

Simultaneously published in the UK
by Routledge
2 Park Square, Milton Park, Abingdon, Oxon OX14 4RN

Routledge is an imprint of the Taylor & Francis Group, an informa business

First published in paperback 2012

© 2009 Taylor & Francis

All rights reserved. No part of this book may be reprinted or reproduced or utilised in any form or by any electronic, mechanical, or other means, now known or hereafter invented, including photocopying and recording, or in any information storage or retrieval system, without permission in writing from the publishers.

Trademark Notice: Product or corporate names may be trademarks or registered trademarks, and are used only for identification and explanation without intent to infringe.

Library of Congress Cataloging in Publication Data
Nizhad'mihr, Rasul.
 Education, science, and truth / by Rasoul Nejadmehr.
  p. cm.—(Routledge international studies in the philosophy of education ; 20)
 Includes bibliographical references (p.) and index.
 1. Education—Philosophy. 2. Truth. I. Title.
 LB14.7.N59 2009
 370.1—dc22
 2008041951

ISBN13: 978-0-415-99767-6 (hbk)
ISBN13: 978-0-203-88003-6 (ebk)
ISBN13: 978-0-415-64741-0 (pbk)

To Arta

Contents

Abbreviations		xi
Preface		xiii
	Introduction	1
1	Truth, Universalism and Relativism	17
2	Objectivism and Alienation	24
3	Relativism and Nihilism	45
4	Inclusive Notions of Science and Objectivity	68
5	Cognitive Pluralism	87
6	Plurality of Perspectives and Unity of Style	106
7	The Question of the Ground of Understanding	111
8	Education and Educators	119
9	Relations between Educators and Learners	129
10	The Educational Order of Truth	144
11	Education and the Problem of Authority	159
12	The Nature of Educational Renewal	166
	Conclusions	175
Notes		185
Bibliography		191
Index		203

Abbreviations

Nietzsche's works and essays are abbreviated as follows (textual references are in section numbers):

A	*The Antichrist*
BGE	*Beyond Good and Evil*
BT	*The Birth of Tragedy*
CW	*The Case of Wagner*
D	*The Dawn (Daybreak)*
DS	*David Strauss, the Confessor and the Writer*
EH	*Ecce Homo*
FE	*On the Future of Our Educational Institutions*
GM	*On the Genealogy of Morals*
GS	*The Gay Science*
HAH	*Human All Too Human*
NCW	*Nietzsche Contra Wagner*
P	"The Philosopher"
PHT	"Philosophy in Hard Times"
RWB	*Richard Wagner in Bayreuth*
SE	*Schopenhauer as Educator*
TI	*Twilight of Idols*
TL	"On Truth and Lies in a Nonmoral Sense"
ULH	*The Utility and Liability of History*
UO	*Unfashionable Observations*
UW	*Unpublished Writings from the Period of Unfashionable Observations*
WP	*The Will to Power*
Z	*Thus Spoke Zarathustra*

OTHERS

AAAS	American Association for the Advancement of Science
CPR	*Critique of Pure Reason*

Preface

This book is the product of a long educational journey, which started in the early 1990s in Stockholm where I began my studies in philosophy. It then took me to London, to London University's Institute of Education, to be precise, where I had my first experience of being a postgraduate student. Shortly after, I moved back to Stockholm and worked on a variety of art projects while doing my studies, utilizing the well tested email medium—what could we do without it?

It was in another port of call, Gothenburg, where the final draft of this book was completed. There I worked with Division for Art and Culture Development as a full time advisor on cultural diversity and cultural policy issues. The job involved daily interactions with artists and engagement with challenges facing art organisations, cultural policy-makers and cultural workers on the one hand, and with change processes, breaks, border-crossings and travels on the other. These interactions have informed my reflections on philosophical issues. Indeed, many of the ideas in this book have taken shape in train stations, airports, hotels, and on board trains and aeroplanes during my countless travels to conferences and cultural events in different cities, countries and continents. So the book is the product of a nomadic life in an age of global interconnectedness.

Through these enriching experiences, I become more and more convinced that the philosophical discourse on the relationships between education, science and truth, as traditionally conceived, is outdated and out of line with the educational needs of our time. My nomadic life experiences have also taught me over the years that these issues must be rethought in response to our need for cognitive democracy in an increasingly globalised world. I have developed the ideas in this book in response to our need to transcend national and cultural limitations and become engaged with challenges facing education worldwide.

During this long journey, I was inspired by countless correspondences, conversations and interactions with scholars, artists, colleagues, friends and anonymous interlocutors. I am grateful to all of them. In particular, I wish to express my most sincere appreciation to John White for his unreserved support during decisive parts of my journey. I have also learned much from

Dugald Murdoch. I want to address my thanks to him. Conversations with Helena Fårsos-Scott and Marie Wells provided encouragement for pursuing my research. I am grateful to them. I am also appreciative of Richard Smith, Paddy Welsh, Graham Haydon, Jan Derry and Michael Reiss whose encouragement and intellectual interest strengthened my ideas.

My special thanks go to my friends Abbas Faiz, Afsaneh Gitiforouz and Mehri Kashani for their immeasurable generosity, hospitality and support during my many travels to London. I also am grateful to Esfandiar Ahmadi and Kerstin Eiserman.

Finally, I would like to warmly thank Soudabeh Zahraei, who tolerates the inconvenience of living with a writer whose job as a cultural worker claims all of his daily hours, while he does not spare a moment of his free time to pursue his personal interests as a researcher.

Introduction

There is no topic more central to modern education than science. The need for education to be scientific is often unquestioned. My theme is that this unquestioned position of science is a main source of contemporary educational problems. There is of course a diverse array of well-intended efforts to resolve these problems. Despite good intentions, results have been poor, since their scope has been limited to science. Indeed, this has been a characteristic of the scientific thought style since Kant; he presented science as the paradigm of critical thought. Since then, science has been considered a critical perspective on other subjects as well as on itself. Faithful to this tradition, neither a scientific understanding of education nor criticism of this have been able to transcend the confines of the paradigm of science and see educational problems in a proper perspective.

In this study, I present a strong notion of education in order to avoid this dead end. My scope includes but is not limited to science, since an important development since Nietzsche has been the recognition that art as a perspective on science is a liberating force. Art is indeed a perspective we need not only to examine the problem of science and a scientific understanding of education but also to extend the scope of philosophical reflection. An examination of philosophy from the perspective of art is needed because when philosophy is used in education research it often loses its vitality, being reduced to a science of science rather than a critical perspective. Released from this burden, philosophy becomes yet another perspective on science. Thus science is considered from two perspectives, philosophical and artistic; these perspectives provide the broad context in which a scientific approach to education can be considered. In so doing, we go beyond the limits of each perspective and reach an inclusive understanding of the nature of a science-based education and its related problems. Using this inclusive perspective, I identify these problems as ones of alienation and nihilism.

Besides advocating a diversity of perspectives, each seen in the light of others, I suggest a shift of paradigm from the autonomy of science to an appreciation of its cultural character, from primacy of general forms of knowledge to the primacy of contextual knowledge, in order to reconfigure the educational field. However, my emphasis on context does not mean the absolute absence of transcendence, since I consider this absence to be a serious source of problems. Thus I try to suggest an educational model that enables us to deal with the paradox that emerges due to my emphasis on both contextual and universal aspects of knowledge.

THE LOCAL AND THE UNIVERSAL

This study endorses an education that is based, on the one hand, on the context-dependency of knowledge, and on the other, on understanding across differences in contexts. Such a view demands universally valid principles of thought and understanding. At the same time, it is equally aware that any educational activity takes place within a local context. Through emphasis on the notions of paradigm and life-world, I espouse the view that science is a cultural activity among other cultural activities and dependent on its contexts of production, justification and development. This means that science is produced in a complex world of various situations and points of view, each requiring its own due. Such a situation challenges the univocal application of universally valid principles of understanding, traditionally considered the foundation of true knowledge. Consequently, a one-sided establishment of a universal view of truth is marked by epistemological violence, since it has to forcibly push aside the plurality of perspectives in the name of a unified notion of truth. Indeed, to encourage individuals to submit to a universal will to truth regardless of context is violence. Besides, reification of the categories of thought and the social organisation of knowledge is the result of a view of knowledge based on general conceptions regardless of particularities like sex and culture. As a result, man becomes alienated from his knowledge and his world.

On the other hand, a monadic view of knowledge imprisons people within the limitations of local circumstances; it leads to a total lack of transcendence and this is the advent of nihilism. At the root of these extremes lies a view of objectivity as insensibility to contextual particularities. The one extreme confirms this notion of objectivity, while the other rejects it categorically. The position of the present study is that diversity of contexts is compatible with universalism; there are defensible universal aspects of truth as well as plausible local aspects. No doubt we must be sensitive to the uniqueness of individual contexts, but this does not mean a rejection of the universal aspects of truth. We need constantly to bear in mind the contextual limitations of our knowledge. However, these limitations do not constitute the whole of human knowledge. There is something else, namely, the possibility of communication through translation. Through the notion of translation, in its broadest sense, different contexts can constructively intercommunicate and engage in meaningful argumentation. This is the basis of agreements as well as disagreements to which we must attend when we investigate scientific education and related problems. These are non-violent forms of knowledge and learning, since acknowledgement rather than ignorance of contextual particularities is the presupposition of translation.

KNOWLEDGE AND "THE OTHER"

Regarding the source and nature of knowledge and its communication to the other, the position of this study is anti-Socratic. In *Phaedo*, Socrates argues that all knowledge is inborn. Indeed, Socrates is convinced that true knowledge is simply recollection. Seen in this light, the inclusion of the perspective of the other in cognition has no bearing on my knowledge, since I contain all the knowledge I need. According to this view, not only is knowledge considered ready made and closed, but also the source of knowledge is located outside the context of its production, organisation and dissemination. The knower is nothing more than a passive container of knowledge that emanates from a transcendental source; teachers are just transmitters of this knowledge. Pushed to its extremes, such a position justifies the exclusion of the other. It makes learning from the other obsolete, since it considers the knower as a self-contained entity. This position also becomes authoritarian, since it assumes access to true knowledge.

To include the other, on the other hand, means to lay emphasis on a participatory frame of mind, where participants are co-producers of knowledge. And this leads us to contextuality of knowledge; it means that knowledge is always knowledge of contingent human conditions. Hence, the source of knowledge is changing cultural contexts. Knowledge emerges through dialogical meetings between different individuals, since life, to refer to Bakhtin, by its very nature is dialogic (Bakhtin 1984: 293). This means that interlocutors are co-participants in producing knowledge; nobody can obtain knowledge without the existence of the other. As such, the other is necessary for my gaining new knowledge. Generally speaking, the other always knows something that I do not know and can thus contribute to growth of my knowledge. Hence, to be open to the other means the improvement of my own knowledge. Such a position does not try to exclude the other, or assimilate the perspective of the other into one's own perspective. To preserve the otherness of the other is a precondition of knowledge. Properly understood, the other cannot be reduced to a cognitively marginalised entity; rather he/she is an ontological entity on which my own knowledge depends.

To push for the domination of a single perspective, as traditional views of truth do, means to remain local forever. Indeed, universality presupposes the otherness of the other. To eliminate or marginalise the other means to destroy the very possibility of universality. It is through translation of one position into the other that universality emerges. The notion of universality used here is quite different from the problem-ridden traditional one. Traditionally, universality is considered to be something totally independent of all contexts; it is valid due to its rational purity and detachment from all cultural values. In this study, universality is considered an inclusive notion based on shared understanding, which in its turn is based on translation. Universality is then embedded in the context of translation. But, since translation always involves more than one context, it paves the way for transcendence; it creates dialogue and conversation across different contexts. In so doing, it goes beyond local contexts and creates shared zones of meaning and understanding that are common to a plurality of thought communities. These zones or spheres are universal in that they are shared by many thought collectives. Although different paradigms share these zones, they preserve their differences and contextual particularities; the very notion of translation depends on these differences. Further, these common zones are not free from values. These values, however, are shared by interlocutors, since they combine elements taken from different paradigms; they are inclusive values. Besides, interlocutors are active co-participants in creating them. In so doing, they transcend local contexts and become universal. Through these processes, participants in translation reach understanding although there is not a universality independent of knowers' sexual, ethnical and geographical affiliations. Indeed, what we need is not value-neutrality but understanding. Achievable through translation, this is a "creative understanding" in which interlocutors do not renounce themselves or assimilate the perspective of the other in their own in order to reach understanding. Rather they retain their "own unity and *open* totality" (Bakhtin 1986: 7). They reach understanding through creating meaning in the process of communication.

Having this view as a starting point means that if there is truth in knowledge and education it is to be found within these processes, not imposed externally upon them. This means that they are not to be submitted to the force of an external source of authority. In other words, and contrary to the old theological notion of truth, truth as used here is not a transcendental concept in the sense of existing outside the processes of education and knowledge that confer legitimacy on them. These processes do not treat truth as an external entity. Truth is, rather, immanent in them. Seen in this light, truth and untruth are aspects of the same process and in a perpetual interplay. Truths are produced and make sense through the process in which they emerge. This means that truth is relational and positional. It is never a totally abstract entity without any relation to the human world of contingencies.

Seen in this light, our need of truth is confirmed without the diversity of contexts being homogenised or alternatives being denied. Through considering life as dialogic and translation as the ground of dialogue and understanding, the question of why we should value truth finds it due place within our discursive practices. I consider the notion of a scientific conception of education in the light of a normative view of truth. This should guide and constrain our discursive practices, how we translate and communicate, and how these acts are assessed. It lends stringency to our reasoning and argumentations. Epistemologically, it constrains our methods of enquiry and claims to authority and knowledge. Lacking this principle, our discussions will become arbitrary and perplexed. At the same time, whatever truth is, it is human-made; we should control our truths instead of being controlled by them. I have had in mind this principle throughout this study.

THE PROBLEM OF THE GROUND OF KNOWLEDGE

The problem of the ground of knowledge, as discussed here, is symptomatic of a post-God world, where traditional models of truth have been discredited. The void that emerges after "the death of God" provokes demands for the inclusion of diverse views of knowledge, along with the idea of the dignity of all individuals and equity of perspectives. These demands have encompassed processes against homogenising, stability and control related to the traditional view of knowledge. They oppose totalitarian tendencies of universalism which want to take over the role of the dead God and educate people from the outside for their own good, conceived from above. The belief in plurality of interpretations regarding knowledge and the good life contests the universal logos, the basis of consensus about knowledge and education. The unquestioned and unquestionable logos is opposed and splits into competing discourses with immanent power mechanisms which work for the benefit of those who control these discourses. For our purpose, the most salient questions are: Can there be knowledge that respects a multitude of perspectives and is universal at the same time? Can knowledge really be universal when it fails to take account of our contextual particularities? In what sense do our perspectives as women, men, homosexuals and ethnic groups cognitively matter?

Regarding these questions, traditional ways of dealing with truth, knowledge and education take a one-sided position either for universality or for singularity. Consequently, they lead either into absolutism or relativism, to reified conceptual schemes or nihilism and lack of any meaning. I hold the view that a good education is neither relativistic nor absolutistic. Neither of these positions can address the issue adequately. I am trying to take from each those elements that are useful and that the other cannot offer. While not pretending to offer an exhaustive solution, the strong notion of education suggested in this study is designed to address issues discussed above. It is defined as strong in comparison with the prevailing scientific conception of education. This latter notion of education is weak because it presents truth as a primary educational goal without being able to resolve the resulting paradox, the paradox of the universality of truth and the particularity of educational practices. By denying cognitive values of the contexts of educational practices, it surrenders to truth as an external source of authority. Contrary to this, the strong notion of education encompasses truth as an immanent conception, with local and universal dimensions.

In summary, the notion of education suggested here questions essentialist views of truth as well as the thesis of incommensurability. It is opposed to uncritical taken-for-granted assumptions about representational connections between language and reality as well as the unconditional refutation of truth. The discussion not only engages with the notion of truth, but also covers a wide range of associated notions like those of reality, objectivity, fact, communication and translation. These notions, in their turn, are connected with the idea of educational exemplars, where truth, through its manifestation in people's lives and conduct, becomes educationally important. I use these conceptions in order to find a way out of the philosophical impasses caused by polarising absolutism and relativism.

THE PROBLEM OF SCIENTIFIC EDUCATION

Educational problems of our time become easier to grasp if we subsume them as the problem of scientific education. This problem arises due to several conceptual and methodological confusions. The first one is the confusion between (a) science teaching or science education and (b) scientific education. While science teaching refers to methods and procedures according to which science is taught in schools, scientific education signifies an education scientific in its form and contents regardless of its application to science or other subjects. Generally speaking, it designates overall educational efforts, methods and plans to transmit a complex whole of ontological and epistemological ideas as well as conceptual schemes based exclusively on science. This means initiation of young generations into a culture, where beliefs about what populates the world, methods of attaining knowledge about these entities and the language through which this knowledge is communicated are exclusively based on science. As a consequence, learners internalise the belief that it is only "within science" that reality can be "identified and described" (Quine 1981: 21). Embedded in this type of initiation is the idea that other perspectives on the world, like those of art and philosophy, should be continuous with science or they are baseless fancies and useless speculations. All we need is "the global science to which . . . we all subscribe" (Quine 1981: 21). Consequently, not only is the cognitive value of the arts denied (Beardsley 1958), but also excessive endeavours are made to reduce philosophy into science(Quine 1969).

To make it clear, while in science education, (a), education exclusively considers sciences, scientific education, (b), can be applied to other subjects as well as science. For instance, art, religion and philosophy can be taught scientifically.[1] Besides, these subjects are not only thought of scientifically, but also evaluated from the perspective of science. Although there are references to science teaching in this book, the overall focus is on scientific education (that is, a scientific notion of education), since the latter covers a wider range of issues and encompasses the former. As a result, claims about the latter bear on the former. Bearing in mind this distinction helps us understand the genealogy of the current educational paradigm and related problems. This distinction also sets scientific education apart from other kinds of education, such as religious education, and enables us to examine whether or not contemporary problems depend on education being scientific. This way of considering the issue is in line with the radical educational changes suggested here; these changes are not limited to improving particular teaching methods of science. Rather, the suggestion is a transformation of the basic principles of education.

The other confusion is related to the problem of considering scientific education from the perspective of science itself. Currently, much educational research is not only confined to science teaching, but also limited in scope. To be fair, it recognises a crisis in science education (Duckworth, Easley et al. 1990: 19). It also emphasises the need for reforms (Abell and Lderman 2007) and changes (Black and Atkin 1996: 1). These reform efforts are, however, disturbingly narrow; they are merely focused on enhancing science teaching and learning. Researchers focus mainly on a wide range of issues, such as ways to teach science effectively, with reference to useful teaching strategies, lessons, teacher education and education agencies. Generally, these researches are designed to stimulate student interest and involvement in science and the science curriculum. As a result, they are rarely concerned with scientific education as the framework of our educational practices. Neither do they go outside the perspective of science to shed light on problems caused by science's exclusive dominance over education; instead, they are focused only on recognising problems and their solutions within the perspective of science. As a result, they remain limited to the scope of science and use science as the judge of an education based on science itself. This is not to underestimate self-corrective efforts of science. They are necessary however not sufficient. Bluntly, science's capacity for critique reaches a limit when confronted with itself. Hence, it is, I want to argue, more apt to focus on scientific education on the one hand and to look at it from a perspective outside science on the other.

Finally, a third dimension of the problem of scientific education, which results from the factors discussed above and is complexly intertwined with them, involves the perception that "scientific literacy" is the solution to problems that result from science being the exclusive form and content of education (for example, Harding 1993). Again, this encloses us within the boundaries of science as the single perspective on the world.

To come to terms with these inadequacies, I shift the focus from science teaching to scientific education. My concern is with such issues as what happens to us as human beings at a time when so much is taught scientifically, when scientific principles are taken for granted, when we are not aware of these principles being taken for granted. These issues go far beyond science teaching. By distinguishing science teaching and scientific education and making the latter a matter of critical scrutiny, I am trying to redirect the critique toward science as the form and content of education. And this has to be done from a perspective outside science. By engaging art and philosophy, I try both to offer ways of practicing such a critique and to investigate the possibility of other forms of education than the scientific one. To be clear, my position should not be seen as hostile towards science or the results of scientific enquiry being taught in schools. Nor do I mean to propose that these results have no bearing on art and philosophy. Such a position is not sane. What is at issue here is scientific education's much stronger claim that science is the only unproblematic form of knowledge of the world worthy of being transferred to the young generations as well as its claims about science being the only viable foundation, form and content of education.

Basically, scientific education is based on acquiring certain, durable and presuppositionless knowledge about the external world through employing methodological principles of the natural sciences. This is a Cartesian legacy. Through emphasising methodological doubt, Descartes not only established a philosophical framework for modern science in its childhood, but also tried to lay down certain basic principles as the firm basis of what human beings clearly and distinctly perceive as true knowledge. These methodological principles were considered as true without any doubt. They are not only the unshakeable foundation of true knowledge on which all knowledge of the world is supposed to be based, but also rational tools by which reason can distinguish truth from falsity. Concern with methodology became then a main feature of science. The belief has not only been in a single scientific method, but also in this method as being a reliable criterion of demarcation, a criterion that can answer the question of whether any form of knowledge should count as true knowledge. Scientific education reveres this intellectual heritage and transfers it to the young generations through presenting science as the only genuine perspective in matters of knowledge, methods of enquiry, ontology and our discursive practices. Indeed, rather than being aimed at bashing science, my attempts are aimed at extending science's possibilities by freeing it from these dogmas.

In this study art and philosophy, like science, are used as perspectives on the world rather than just school subjects. To consider art, science and philosophy as equally important perspectives leads to an epistemological pluralism. Each perspective is used to make the grounds of the others transparent without any of them marginalising the others. There is a tension as well as productive interplay between them and they are translatable into each other. There is no need to put science, art and philosophy in an incommensurable relationship. They are different domains of thought and cover different spheres of experience. Each covers aspects of experience that fall outside the others. As a result, they cannot be substituted for each other. Furthermore, none of them can be an ultimate ground of knowledge; they are open and complementary perspectives. They have to be considered in the light of their advantages and disadvantages for the improvement of knowledge and enhancement of life.

I am not going to be engaged in any specific subject of scientific enquiry or a specific teaching method. As mentioned above, what is at issue here is science as such and scientific education in its totality. Moreover, when I am talking about science, I refer to both social and natural sciences, because it is the spirit of science that is at issue, rather than a specific scientific discipline. Seen in this light, the kind, character and motivation of science is much more interesting than science itself, for knowledge is historical and is inevitably going to change or vanish, but the effect it has on our lives lasts for generations.

I feel the relevance of this study to educational practices could be considered either extensive or limited, depending on the reader's interpretation. The changes advocated here are not minor modifications in subjects or methods of teaching; rather, I argue for a radical reshaping of educational grounds, a radically new type of science and a paradigm shift in our notions of education and mode of understanding. The character of the work is such that it cannot prescribe straightforward practical recommendations. But, it is not merely theoretical speculation either. Once the process of change which I am proposing has started, the practice of education acquires its distinct form and content, thanks to that process of renewal.

POLYPHONY

In this study I have drawn into conversations thinkers and philosophers across philosophical traditions and differences, across the traditional division between analytic and continental philosophies. It has been a demanding task to get the philosophical discourse going despite differences in idioms and discourses. In this connection, the notion of translation has been helpful; I have tried to translate from one philosophical discourse to another, from one idiom to the other. The pedagogical point has been to push for an educational ideal which educates people who can work fruitfully together and live a good life across philosophical, cultural, religious and social differences. I have sought to move away from the misunderstanding that the notion of truth is a simple matter of consensus or reaching a common ground of agreement; rather, it is inseparable from differences, as mentioned above. As there is no way of eliminating differences—nor does it makes sense to do so—we must learn to work better across differences without entangling ourselves in thoughts about truth as a point of reference beyond these disputes, an Archimedean point by which we can move the earth. I have tried to raise questions regarding science, truth and education. My intention has not been to resolve these questions once and for all, but to discuss and highlight them in an interesting and meaningful way. This means that I am not going to construct systematic answers to them by starting with dogmatic principles.

Rather, I try to identify domains wherein the solutions can be sought. To emphasise that questions are more interesting than answers is a way to avoid dogmatism and absolutism.

This study is not primarily about any of the thinkers mentioned here, but it borrows methods and ideas from them. Far from resisting an acknowledgement of their importance in this study, I insist that their association with this field of enquiry should be taken seriously. The use of a host of different thinkers has been an attempt on my part to present a comprehensive and inclusive perspective on my subject and shed light on it from different angles. At the same time, it has been important not to fall into the trap of ending up defending one philosopher. To achieve this, I have borrowed the Nietzschean principle of showing sympathy with a thinker without necessarily sharing his or her ideas. My study uses Marx, for instance, in order not to naïvely accept Nietzsche. Nietzsche's genealogical method can, on the other hand, reveal the one-sidedness of vulgar Marxism by disclosing the shared behavioural patterns between apparently opposed groups and people. For instance, the life of a bourgeois individual and his proletarian opponents might be ruled by the same principle, they might share the same pattern of behaviour and mode of understanding without being aware of it. Thus the problems of current society will not disappear if we simply reverse the power relation between the bourgeoisie and the proletariat since principles informing patterns of behaviour and modes of understanding will continue to function, albeit in a new shape. Things can be different for us if we change our own style of conduct and understanding of things. And this demands huge educational endeavours.[2]

A "SUBALTERN VOICE"

Although this study is far from autobiographical, it is influenced by my personal experiences of being a political refugee, a teacher and a research student. Moreover, it may well be that my current personal concern with issues of cultural diversity helps to explain my perspective on the issues discussed in this study. As a proper refugee, one is expected to behave in a certain way and in accordance with a prearranged script. Such a demand brings to the fore the question of the relation between intellectual integrity and adjustment to an apparently rational command from above which knows one's good better than one does oneself. In my case, it seems to me, pursuing a research degree has not been considered a part of my status as a refugee. As a result, my research acquires an extra dimension. I have no intention of discussing the many visible and invisible barriers I have had to overcome. Instead, I choose to focus on the educational aspect of the logic of overcoming. I have done my studies outside the academic world. Being active outside this world places me in a borderland between the academy and a bureaucratic everyday world wherein I work as a professional. Not belonging exclusively to either, I not only have an outlook on both, but I can negotiate with both of them to create a breathing space. This third position enables one to resist the demands for conformity coming from both. At the same time, one becomes a "subaltern" being as two powerful voices predicate good and evil, right and wrong; they have the right to do so, since they are sanctioned by dominating regimes of truth.

I have tried not to let this situation lead me into resentment. On the contrary, I have tried to do justice to my profession as well as my research through actively engaging myself in research in both fields. Through this process, I have discovered that the same mechanisms of exclusion are at work in both fields, in the cultural life of a country like Sweden and in the academic world in general. These mechanisms do not depend on individual professors or bureaucrats, though they work through them; rather, they are immanent in the body of dominating cultures. In both fields, unfair barriers exclude people because of their sex, race and economic and geographic belongings. To work for a fair social order by contributing to inclusive mechanisms becomes then a main human undertaking. This undertaking has personal and social aspects, both meeting in education. Education becomes an open arena where logics of inclusion and exclusion collide and, if we are prepared for it, this collision can be used fruitfully.

I have taken Nietzsche seriously and tried to cure my own despair through education. I was disillusioned by the nihilistic insight that escape from one form of tyranny, religious fundamentalism in Iran, led me into another kind of tyranny, sophisticated mechanisms of exclusion in western societies. Instead of remaining in this nihilistic state of mind, I have tried to transform my negative nihilism into a positive view, into an emancipatory force freeing me from both forms of tyranny. Through a process of self-transformation, I have tried to educate myself in the face of a hierarchical will to power which has tried to violently exclude me from a sphere of knowledge reserved to people of certain economic and ethnic affiliations. Believing in education as a therapeutic process means not only learning how to overcome different internal and external obstacles, but also improving discriminatory mechanisms through making education an inclusive process.

If Nietzsche is helpful at an epistemological level, Nelson Mandela is an educational exemplar when it comes to being engaged with the same mechanism on a social plane, though this distinction is not always clear-cut. He shows the necessity of his vision of an all-inclusive society as well as the tortuous difficulties one has to go through when one becomes truth-teller and opposes truth regimes of one's own time (the same difficulties that led Nietzsche to madness). Through a high admiration for his person and struggle, I resist the same hierarchical will to power which violently tries to push me to the margins of the social life. I use these two men as mentors against the inhuman treatment of other people. Since the unfair treatment of the other, in the name of absolutes like truth, race, nation, and culture is a universal phenomenon, resistance to it is also universal. Contrary to the former, which relies on external or metaphysical authorities, the source of the truth of the latter is grounded in nothing more or less than the life of exemplars. Herein lies the interconnectedness of knowledge and action, epistemology and ethics. Being an educator nowadays demands engagement with both spheres.

REMARKS ON METHODOLOGY

Some words about the method used in this study are necessary. The character of this study is such that it makes use of genealogical analyses. Epistemological issues to do with science, objectivity and their relations to education are deeply rooted in the history of thought. They are not properly understood if they are detached from their original context. They must be seen not only as parts of a network of interconnections and interdependencies but also as historical results of past intellectual events. I use genealogy to focus not only on the historical nature of the established notions of science, truth and education, but also on the mechanisms that select and transform certain postulates into facts and bestow them with pedagogical value. My approach affirms the Nietzschean view of interdependencies between facts and human needs. Indeed, facts disconnected from our needs, broadly conceived, do not belong to human life and are thereby of no interest to philosophical scrutiny. Through a genealogical analysis we can trace the roots of the notion of fact in those needs that have constructed a sphere of pure reason and logic, the creation of a world of unchangeable forms by Plato and his identification of knowledge, virtue and the good. It was subsequent to this important historical event that pure knowledge, knowledge detached from human needs, was postulated as the highest educative aim. Seen in this light, the positivistic distinction between the context of discovery and that of justification is untenable. The past and history are at work in the present. Such a view of knowledge undermines the thesis of incommensurability.

Genealogical analysis is a polemical way of dealing with established truths. It reveals immediately that our established truths came to continue to be truths just because they were not questioned; they are based on some kind of passive acceptance. To take issue with them is not only to come into conflict with established opinions but also to show their changeability. Claiming this, contrary to writers like Kuhn, I emphasise the possibility of resistance to the dominant paradigm. And it is just this possibility that builds a basis upon which new educational ideals can be reached.

It would, however, present a one-dimensional image of genealogy if we only considered it as a polemical method. It not only makes the apparently unproblematic problematic, but also suggests solutions and alternative ways of understanding things; genealogy has a negative and an affirmative side.

Introduction   13

This dialectic between destructive and constructive aspects of critique goes through the body of this book.

CHAPTERS AND THEMES

In order for the present text to be accessible, I devote this section to a brief overview of the chapters that follow. As I mentioned earlier, a universal account of the notion of truth seems, at first sight, to exclude contextual aspects. Considered traditionally, this is indeed the case. A main concern of this study is to oppose this tendency; it tries to bring about a viable synthesis of universal and local aspects of notions of truth and knowledge. This interconnection of the universal and the contextual, which the notion of education I suggest should teach, runs throughout this study. I start Chapter 1 by presenting accounts of traditional views of universalism and relativism in order to reveal their inadequacy, each taken by itself. I also emphasise our need for a new approach to these notions.

My endeavours to bring together universal and local aspects of truth are aimed at underpinning an education that offers ways of coming to terms with problems of alienation and nihilism. This study sees alienation as the basis of nihilism. It connects alienation to a one-sided emphasis on universalism and nihilism to a one-sided emphasis on relativism. Indeed, universalism and relativism presuppose each other; interconnections of these phenomena are the basis of my connecting alienation and nihilism to each other as different stages of the same process. In my opinion, alienation precedes nihilism, being a result of contemporary mass educational processes. Indeed, nihilism is awareness of one's being alienated and the subsequent response to this awareness. As my starting point is an epistemological one, I consider alienation and nihilism against a background of knowledge systems to which we are introduced through contemporary scientific education. We either uncritically submit to these alienating cognitive systems or try to understand and question them. In the latter case, we become aware of alienation on the one hand and understand the alienating cognitive order of things on the other. Essentially, this consciousness is nihilistic, since it reveals the shaky basis of the traditional notion of transcendence. I study these phenomena through a genealogical analysis of scientific education, the objectivist account of science, and its critics, such as Marx, Nietzsche, Kuhn and Fleck. These issues are dealt with in Chapters 2 and 3.

Alienation, as the term is used here, is based on separation between the individual and her/his cognitive activities, where the individual does not identify herself/himself with her/his own knowledge. Accordingly, this study tries to find ways of overcoming alienation and nihilism through making clear the active part of the knower in the process of knowledge. A first step in this regard is a reconceptualisation of the notion of objectivity, since the current notion of objectivity denies the individual's active part in knowledge through overestimation of the role of repeatable methods of science. I lay down the basis for a new notion of objectivity partly through a genealogical account of processes that led to questioning of the traditional distinction between subject and object. Such an account will enable us to understand processes by which the traditional notion of objectivity was discredited. Using these insights, in Chapter 4, I attempt to suggest an inclusive notion of objectivity. Traditionally, objectivity is considered to be the independence of science from individuality, background beliefs and cultural values. These values are, however, crucial for our cognitive activities. The inclusive notion of objectivity not only takes account of the importance of these values for our cognitive activities, but also includes values and perspectives of marginalised social groups, on the one hand, and art and philosophy on the other. Such a position not only highlights the active role of the individual in cognition, but also offers a multiplicity of perspectives, where each is seen in the light of the others. This makes the individual aware of his/her responsibility regarding his/her knowledge and the kind of person he/she becomes. Taking this responsibility seriously, the individual is able of identifying himself/herself with his/her knowledge. My starting assumption regarding the relationship between knowledge and knower is that the kind of knowledge is related to the kind of individual. Creating an inclusive notion of objectivity based on cultural and cognitive pluralism demands educating individuals who are able to direct it. This is the main educational challenge of our time. Chapters 4 and 5 are devoted to these issues.

In order to enable the individual to create unity among a plurality of perspectives and approaches, I introduce the notion of style as a regulative tool. Properly used, this notion creates unity among our different perspectives; it enables us to direct our knowledge systems and organise them in accordance with a style of our own. As a result, we identify ourselves with our knowledge. This means that the notion of style functions in a disalienating way. Different aspects of this notion are brought to light in Chapter 6.

Contemporary education gives students a supposedly firm foundation of knowledge, independent of historical contingencies. Such an understanding of the nature of knowledge is a misconception of how things really work. And this prepares the ground for alienation and nihilism. Because whatever these foundations may be, they are human-made. As such they are contingent. In Chapter 7, I discuss a new view of the basis of knowledge based on the creative participation of the knower in presupposing the starting points of knowledge. This means that the cogniser is a constitutive part of cognitive processes and their end products.

Establishing manifold views of knowledge, education and truth puts a huge responsibility on the individual and demands special individual abilities. In Chapter 8, I attempt to show that although a demanding task, educating such an individual is not impossible. To underpin this claim, I connect the notion of education with that of educators. In so doing, I bring an extra dimension to education and open up the possibility of a strong notion of education based on both theoretical and practical exemplars. Generally, the inclusive position of this study goes beyond theoretical knowledge and encompasses aesthetic-practical dimensions of truth, knowledge, education and life. Thus it engages both dimensions in educating individuals. I try to present different types of educational exemplars, showing their strengths and weaknesses in order to develop a new notion of education. Such an education will prepare the ground for a strong type of individual able to manage a variety of social and cognitive perspectives.

Generally speaking, problems connected with knowledge and education derive mostly from conceptual confusions. While believers in transcendence try to overcome the limits of different contexts by denying the importance of the diversified human situations, its deniers or relativists do the contrary. The problem arises from each one excluding the other. They ignore the complex processes of translation at work everywhere and at different levels. Bringing together different contexts and forms of life, the notion of translation connects particularities of different contexts and offers a kind of knowledge that is communicable across contextual boundaries. This is the meaning of the notion of transcendence as it is used here. Taking the notion of translation as my starting point enables me to come to terms with problems of incommensurability and relativism as well as those of fundamentalism. Discussing these issues in Chapter 9, I prepare the ground for a discussion of the relationship between education and truth in Chapter 10.

Traditionally, truth is limited to its notional concept. As such, it covers a limited sphere of human life, namely, the domain of verbal communication. It also becomes abstract and detached from human life. Having these characteristics, it functions as a source of alienation and nihilism. I oppose these tendencies by bringing into play different aspects of truth, like those of truth as disclosure and truth as manifest in the life and conduct of educators. Indeed, one becomes an educator by becoming the place where truth manifests itself. However, the position of educators is not absolute; rather, it is subject to change and historicity. The overall emphasis of this study is truth as a normative notion that guides our practical and intellectual activities.

The notion of education suggested here has its own problems. For instance, decadent cultures or fanatics can become educators and corrupt individuals. Central issues in this regard are those of power and authority. In contemporary education, power and authority are centralised and absolute. As a result, they become authoritarian and oppressive. The overall interpretive and aesthetic approach of this study decentralises these notions and makes them a matter of negotiation and renegotiation; they become contextualised, relational and positional instead of being absolute. I discuss these issues in Chapter 11.

A recurrent theme of this study is the dialectical relationship between the socio-cultural and individual aspects of education and knowledge. The same can be said about the educational changes suggested here. My starting point in this regard is that we need to combine politically based or social changes on the one hand with educational changes on the other. In so doing, it should become possible to achieve a productive dialectic between sociocultural and cognitive-educational changes. In the long run, this approach will overcome respective deficits in the approaches mentioned above. While the former tends to neglect the role of the pedagogical and cognitive paradigm shifts, the latter tends to neglect the importance of changes in alienating social orders. In Chapter 12, I try to develop a view of education as a transformative process based on both aspects of changes.

1 Truth, Universalism and Relativism

Since the notion of truth is central to this study, I begin by discussing it. This brings to the fore a wide range of conceptions like reality, knowledge, communication, exemplarity, conformity and creativity, since the question of truth concerns these issues closely. There is no consensus among philosophers about truth. Besides different theories of truth, we can talk, as Paul Ricoeur (1965) does, about different "orders of truth"—scientific, ethical, religious and philosophical. In the present context, we can talk about an educational order of truth. The complex questions concerning truth cannot be explored here.[1] I discuss only the local and the universal aspects of truth, since these questions are of importance to the relationship between truth, education and science. The focus then will be on the value of truth as a cognitive norm that guides our educational practices.[2] Having this starting point, a tension arises between the local nature of education and the universality of truth. This tension has to be dealt with properly. In the context of this study, this means reconciliation between the local and the universal in the same phenomenon, education.

Traditionally, this issue has been considered from two competing points of view. One has been based on a universalistic view of truth represented by philosophers from Plato to Russell, Carnap, Tarski, Frege and Habermas, for whom truth functions as an absolute and unquestionable ground of knowledge. From this perspective, truth has no local dimension. In matters of science, this tendency believes in scientific realism, according to which scientific knowledge is knowledge of theory-independent phenomena; true knowledge corresponds to entities in the natural world whose existence is not dependent on our beliefs and theories (Popper 1972, Putnam 1975). As different versions of this notion of truth are informed by the principle of correspondence—correspondence of thoughts to objects or the like—I subsume them under the umbrella notion of correspondence theories of truth.

The competing view has been based on the relativistic theory of truth advocated by philosophers like Protagoras, Quine, Rorty, Kuhn and Feyerabend, for whom a variety of local paradigms and truths compete for the allegiance of thought communities.[3] According to this tendency, scientific observations and experiments are theory-based (Fleck 1979, Kuhn 1970).

Correspondingly, two different roles have been ascribed to philosophers and philosophical discourse. The dispute has been about the nature of knowledge, the relationship between philosophy and science and what philosophy is and what it should do. In the former case, philosophers are assigned the exemplary task and privileged position of determining the truth once and for ever. Or, as Rorty, says the philosopher is considered to be the

> cultural overseer who knows everyone's common ground—the Platonic philosopher king who knows what everybody else is really doing whether *they* know it or not, because he knows about the ultimate context (the Forms, the Mind, Language) within which they are doing it. (Rorty 1979: 317–18)

In this account, philosophy provides the firm foundation of scientific enquiry. As such, it is supposed to establish once and for all conditions, limits and scope of science, truth and related discourses. At the other extreme, this relationship is reversed and philosophy is subordinated to science. This conception of philosophy "simply falls into place as a chapter of psychology and hence of natural science" (Quine 1969: 82), as Quine puts it. As a result, philosophy loses its autonomy and becomes continuous with science; it is considered to be just another scientific discourse. This issue will receive due attention in Chapter 5.

UNIVERSALISM

Providing the ontological and epistemological foundation of science, in the former view, philosophy presupposes a notion of truth independent of diversity of contexts as the aim of our cognitive practices. Traditionally, discussions of truth have been focused on the notion of objectivity and a notion of knowledge independent of all contexts, be it the context of a culture, an era, a specific community of thought, or the cognitive condition of the individual knower. Seen in this light, truth is the suspension of historicity and contextuality. This notion of truth presupposes a universal standpoint valid for humanity as a whole and across time and place. In sum, truth is considered to be the agreement of minds on the one hand and agreement of minds and reality on the other. As a result, notions of consensus and correspondence are central to this view of truth. Language is considered to be an instrument which merely registers consensus and correspondence without distorting or changing them. This belief is based on the presupposition that there is a natural link between words and objects determining their meaning and that language users have no impact on it; words reflect the essence of things. Thus truth and meaning are constant and achievable only for those who search for them unconditionally. A devoted and true searcher for truth just discloses or discovers it, it is argued. In this way the notion of the adequacy of thoughts and reality or objective correspondence between thoughts and facts is established.

Traditionally, the relation between reality and thoughts is signified by the notion of fact. In the correspondence view of truth, for instance, a proposition is true if and only if it corresponds to facts and false if and only if it does not correspond to any fact. The genealogical basis of this perception of truth goes back to the Aristotelian definition of truth. He maintains that: "To say of what is that it is, or of what is not that it is not, is true" (*Metaphysics*, 1011b25). In contemporary philosophy of science, different nuances of scientific realism continue to advocate this view of truth. A classical example in this regard is Bertrand Russell. According to Russell, there exists an objective relation between mind and the world of objects. For a belief to be true, according to this view, there has to be a correlation between objects and their relation in the world and the way these are represented in the propositions. Russell believes a proposition is true or false independently of minds. In other words, "minds do not create truth or falsehood" (Russell 1959: 129), they just reflect or represent them. Indeed, Russell belongs with those philosophers who consider true propositions constitutive of external reality. In the identity theory of truth, propositions do not merely correspond to facts, they are facts. According to this theory: "For every x, x is a true proposition if x is a fact" (David 2001: 684). Other defenders of epistemological realism, like Putnam, formulate similar theories though he considers truth talk internal to our world view. Accusing Rorty of a "phobia of objectivity", McDowell tries to keep the notion of objectivity. He relates our beliefs to reality and considers "the world as authoritative over our investigations". This means that contrary to relativists like Rorty and Feyerabend, he believes in the normative significance of truth for our investigations and judgements. Contrary to Rorty, for McDowell truth "transcends consensus". As a result, he makes us "answerable not just to the verdicts of our fellows but to the facts themselves" (McDowell 2005: 140).[4]

In these philosophical systems science is the paradigm of truth and enjoys a unique position; it is the "touchstone" of truth and "all truths", as Ricoeur puts it, "ought to be *of* science or at least *like* science" (Ricoeur 1965: 170). Formulated differently, science is considered not only as an activity with a fixed essence, which distinguishes it radically from other cultural activities, but also as the pattern and paradigm of other truth-seeking activities. Rather than being one sort of social activity among others or being a part of culture, it is viewed as high above cultures and their differences. Science is considered "the only unproblematic . . . kind of knowledge that there is" (De Caro and Macarthur 2004: 7), whose method of enquiry provides us with an exhaustive and reliable account of the world.

The universal notion of truth is related not only to a universal notion of science, but also to a universal notion of education, where scientific literacy is a "central goal of education" (AAAS 1989: 3). Such a notion of education is thought to bring up a universal kind of knowers who act for the benefit of humanity and whose perspective coincides with that of humanity. Embedded in this order of things is the presupposition that this universal type of knower is capable of creating the good life, a universal social order that is good for human prosperity (AAAS 1989: 12–13). Indeed, universality of truth is used to establish the context-independency of science, scientific education and the scientific social order. This homogenous world with homogenous relationships between its components would be a comfortable place to live in, provided that things work in the way they are outlined to do. However, problems emerge as soon as we ask questions about the nature of truth, knowledge, facts, education and the relationships between them.

RELATIVISM

To begin with, a major problem emerges as soon we relate the historical conditions of education and scientific practices with their changing truths to the idea of truth as correspondence and consensus. Philosophers like Rorty, Quine, Kuhn, Wittgenstein, Feyerabend and Margolis relativise truth to particular contexts and highlight their importance in the constitution of truth. They challenge philosophers like Habermas, Russell and Frege, who try to find ways to transcend paradigms and reach unconditional agreement on what truth is.

Relativists see universalism as an "authoritarian approach" based on the perspective of the Platonic philosopher-king or "super-experts". They also accuse proponents of the universal view of truth of wanting "the power to reshape the world in their own image" (Feyerabend 2005: 151). Relativism advocates the view that "different cities (different societies) may look at the world in different ways" (Feyerabend 2005: 151). To Feyerabend's mind, philosophers have no privileged position and anybody can function as a "wise man". Like Margolis, he overtly advocates Protagoras and his doctrine of: "Man is the measure". Feyerabend calls his brand of relativism "democratic relativism". It is democratic, he argues, because all citizens of a society are engaged in decisions upon and debates about basic assumptions, principles and disputes concerning truth. He defends a notion of science based on rejection of the distinction between the context of discovery and the context of justification. He is a critic of scientism and objectivism and their claims to a universal truth. Refusing intellectualism, he trusts "public opinion", "citizens' initiatives" and common sense as the bases of his view of truth and knowledge (Feyerabend 2005: 53–54). According to this view, truth is totally local with no universal aspect. According to Feyerabend sciences are divided into different regions that are unable to communicate with each other or equip us with an objective truth about the universe. Rorty also places the Western metaphysical tradition and the normative "we" connected to it against the "other". To his mind, transcendence is illusory and any claim to truth is dependent on a context.

Philosophers' destabilisation of old bounds between reality and truth was deepened by historians of science like Kuhn. Through his notion of scientific revolution, Kuhn showed the rise and fall of competing paradigms in the history of science. These studies confirm the relativistic assumption that we inevitably belong to a form of life that determines the boundaries of our cognitive activities and their results. Thus, questioning as well as establishing truth occur within the horizon of a paradigm. As a result, these activities are not universal, this line of argumentation goes. Generally, these theories argue that truths are produced by human agents in different thought collectives, like that of the scientific community, rather than being given, agent-independent and community-transcending forces. The questions to be discussed are then can we identify the "we" of particular paradigms with humanity in general? Is there any possibility of overcoming the limitations of paradigms and reaching a universal view of truth? Have we good enough grounds to base truths on human practice rather than general and abstract ideas?

Universalism and localism are both based on weak notions of truth, their apparently strong claims notwithstanding. Universalism is not able to explain local aspects of truth adequately and localism is unable to overcome its local limits and present a satisfactory account of the universal aspect of truth. They limit us to a choice between relativism and absolutism. Absolutism demands consensus and assimilation of all perspectives into a single one and relativism disperses humanity into scattered paradigms incapable of communicating and agreeing on things. In both cases, perspectives that fall outside one's own become inconceivable and are excluded. Both lead to philosophical dead ends. An inclusive notion of truth has to explain both aspects of truth, its singularity and universality, in an adequate way. As will be discussed in the coming chapters, to replace abstract definitions with notions like family resemblances is helpful in connecting truth to human practices and to the ways we do things.

To break down impasses of relativism and absolutism, discussions of truth have to change direction. Indeed, contemporary philosophy offers more alternatives than only universalism and localism. This is thanks to the destabilisation of the traditional metaphysics of truth based on dichotomies between notions of true/false and reality/appearance. A main source of this destabilisation has been the questioning of the representational notion of language. As a result, concepts of representation of and correspondence to reality, cornerstones of traditional views of truth, are strongly disputed. While objectivism tried to establish a notion of truth based on a language- and mind-independent world, the increasing tendency has been toward the contextualisation of truth. Truth is considered to be a process rather than a closed and pre-given entity to be discovered. Truth as proposition-thing correspondence and representational relations between language and the world are either rejected or at best are, as in Putnam's new Platonism, modified and limited to the representational activities that take place within specific linguistic communities. Traditional notions of representation and correspondence are replaced by notions like life-world or common traditions. In all these cases historico-cultural horizons shared by a community of users of a single language are the focal point of scrutiny. Philosophers like Nietzsche, William James, Heidegger, Wittgenstein and Derrida, to name some of the most famous ones, have contributed to changes in our perception of truth. Through their works, the discourse of truth has changed character, direction, form and content. Our need for truth remains, however, as acute as it was before. We cannot therefore dispense with truth or declare it redundant. Rather, we need a new notion of truth based on the reconciliation of its universal and local aspects.

The question Why truth? can be answered differently depending on our philosophical stand. One possible answer is: because "truth . . . today gives us a measure and a stand against the confusion of opinions and reckoning" (Heidegger 2005: 243). This is however, as Vattimo puts it, not to consider truth "as the ultimate point of reference beyond which we do not pass and which silences all questioning" (Vattimo 2005: 173–4). The logic of questioning, well established after the Nietzschean radical "school of suspicion", is nowadays at work everywhere. And this contributes to our understanding of truth and the nature of human knowledge, its relation to the world and social order. The lesson we have learned from philosophers like Nietzsche and Wittgenstein is that truth is not an unquestionable foundation or unmediated "brute fact". It is unquestionable while nobody questions it. The process of questioning the traditional foundation of truth, to mention one example, can be discerned in Wittgenstein's philosophical life and career. The Wittgenstein of the *Tractatus* and his view of the relation between language and the world do not need any explanation. In this period, he considered true propositions as images of reality. Rejecting this theory in *Philosophical Investigations*, he presents forms of life as the final ground of thought. But in *On Certainty*, he gains the insight that we cannot have any such firm foothold whatsoever. We are, rather, living in a foundationless world and have to learn to live in it without anything functioning as a final ground. Like Nietzsche, he recommends that we acquire such a foundation "in order to later free ourselves" (Stickney 2005: 304). Such a position not only signifies the loss of the old comfortable constant ground, it places that ground within human reach and makes it available for critical appraisal. This means encouraging the individual to take seriously his/her active participation in establishing and destabilising truth; this brings an ethical dimension to truth.

Questioning established truths is a good characteristic of thought, but, as will be explored later in this study, we have to make a distinction between different types of questioning. True, we realise the world within some conceptual frameworks, but we also need to break out of the confines of paradigms and reach general human knowledge, without collapsing into dogmatism and fundamentalism. In order to question, we have to accept some sort of reason. Our claims have to be based on a sense of reasonableness. And for that we do not need recourse to the traditional notion of truth. We do not need to possess the world or have a transparent comprehension of it via a first principle, God or a transcendental world of ideas. We can, however, make a distinction between historical aspects of truths and trans-historical aspects of life. As Wittgenstein says, we have to "distinguish between the movement of waters on the river-bed and the shift of the bed itself" (Wittgenstein 1969: § 97). He immediately adds, however, that "there is not a sharp distinction of the one from the other" (§ 97). We can ask anyway what this "bed itself" is. The question is quite warranted, since this distinction is not thoroughly illusory. Wittgenstein himself believes in something "common" to humanity beyond different cultural circumstances. To my mind, this is enough to make truth talk meaningful. In the case of unknown languages, Wittgenstein writes: "The common behaviour of mankind is the system by means of which we interpret an unknown language" (Wittgenstein 1968: § 206). Truth thus acquires a performative aspect and becomes connected to our discursive practices and to the way we do things. There is, in other words, a context of behaviour that is local and particular to any action. At the same time, there are universal aspects that are common to human behaviour as such. These two aspects go well together and the one becomes conceivable in the light of the other. They become inconceivable whenever we confine ourselves to either universalism or localism. The notion of translation or the way we "interpret" the language of the other, as Wittgenstein puts it, is the link between universal and local aspects of thought. Together with the notion of life as dialogical, the notion of translation conceived as the ground of understanding, the inclusive notion of objectivity and cognitive pluralism, the Wittgensteinian notion of "the common behaviour of mankind" provides a new basis for education and knowledge acquisition. Having this starting point, we are not limited to introducing students into frames of mind, where bivalence between True/False is used to exclude the others. There are indeed ways of educating which enable learners to develop intercollective and intercultural communicative abilities.

Relativism and absolutism are ideologies based on distorted understanding of how things really work. They reduce the whole issue of knowledge and education to either universalism or localism without disclosing the connections and borderlines. Education does not, however, need to be either relativist or absolutist. There is a range of nuances in between. We can make use of the advantages of both without subscribing to either. This is the paradoxical logic of truth used here. The paradoxical nature of educational truths will be thoroughly discussed in Chapter 10. For the moment, it is more urgent to focus on the problems caused by basing education either on objectivism or relativism. The next step will be to suggest an alternative education as solution to these problems.

2 Objectivism and Alienation

In the preceding chapter, I argued that traditional epistemologies present science as a universal account of the world and scientific development as a progress toward *the* truth. Formulated differently, a universally valid truth is considered to be the primary goal of science. For epistemologists like Marian David, knowing in general means to possess truth. To his mind, "We can possess truth by *knowing* it" (David 2005: 279). As this truth is universal, this line of argumentation claims, it is independent of individual scientists and their contexts of action; the individual scientist is to be subjugated to this truth. This view of science has far-reaching consequences for the individual, knowledge, education and the type of social order based upon them. Indeed, as will be explored later in this study, science currently appears to be independent of the individual scientist, and individuals are dominated by science. However, science does not occupy this position as a result of its being universally true; the source of this authority lies elsewhere. In reality, science is subordinated to the needs of the powerful "funding agencies", "private foundations, public-interests groups, and . . . government" as well as scientists' "personal, corporate, institutional, or community interests" (AAAS 1989: 30–31). Considering scientific education in this light reveals interesting points about the qualities of thought and life it gives birth to. A comprehensive analysis of all these aspects of the issue is not within the scope of this study, however.

As my focus is an epistemological one, I base my analysis of science on analysis of the notion of objectivity, since objectivity is considered to be the main characteristic of modern science. The privileged position that science and scientific education enjoy originates mainly in the common belief that scientific enquiry is objective. This means that scientific beliefs, unlike other beliefs, are exclusively determined by the facts. Within the operating paradigm, objectivity concerns partly scientific method and partly scientific knowledge itself. This is to claim that the outcomes of scientific processes are objective or independent of cultural contexts, since the processes by which these products are generated are objective. Scientific realism's account of science tells us that science is an accurate report of the facts of the world of objects. Further, it claims that scientific theories are true because most of their terms refer to processes and properties in the real world. Scientific method, this line of argumentation goes, guarantees the correctness of the processes of choice, rejection and development of scientific hypotheses. It guarantees that these processes are not influenced by arbitrary and subjective criteria and data are obtained and assessed in an unbiased manner. Anyone wherever and with any set of background beliefs and values can repeat an experiment and reach the same results, this line of argumentation goes. Consequently, science is declared to be totally independent of the subject and its context of action. Context-independency is therefore considered as something unscientific. This notion of science is the basis of the operating educational paradigm; the aim of scientific education is thus presented as the pursuit of truth and value-neutral knowledge. I think that this account of objectivity, science, education and their relationships is simply flawed. In fact, cultural values are constitutive of science. The knower also has an active part in the construction of scientific knowledge. To make these points clear, in the coming chapters I undertake a genealogical analysis of standard accounts of the notion of science as well as scientific education. Such analysis not only reveals misrepresentation of notions of science and objectivity but also highlights the creative part of the human subject in cognition. It also reveals the context-dependency of scientific education.

THE GENEALOGY OF THE OBJECTIVIST ACCOUNT OF SCIENCE

A genealogical account of the objectivist notion of science leads us back to Plato, his two-world ontology and the view of knowledge based on this ontology. Such an analysis helps us to understand the prevailing image of science and its importance for education. Famously, Plato reduced the reality we perceive to the realm of mere appearance and made its objects subject to opinion rather than pure knowledge. By so doing, he commenced indeed a process of belittling the world of contingent human practices and the role of the individual in constructing knowledge. Despising the contingency of the knowledge of the world of human senses, he ascribed to philosophy the task of attaining pure knowledge of eternal ideas through making use of reason. Since then, Western philosophy has undertaken the project of transcending the world of appearance and achieving pure knowledge of an ultimate reality. This undertaking has resulted in a variety of conflicting theories about ways of envisioning reality and attaining pure knowledge. Despite the alleged radical break with traditional philosophy, modern philosophers have also followed the same project; as one of the most influential educators of modern humanity and the father of modern philosophy, Descartes attached great importance to methodology and its central place in all acts of knowledge acquisition. He taught unconditional doubt as a method in order to establish an unbiased and certain basis for knowledge of reality.

Faithful to the essence of Platonism, he wanted to educate humanity in presuppositionless and pure knowledge. To reach this kind of knowledge, he replaced all kinds of theological dogmas with a critical analysis. He recommended emphatically that nothing had to be presupposed as the source of true knowledge. However, his Cogito Argument, *Cogito ergo sum* (I think therefore I exist), is not the self-confirming and presuppositionless proposition that he intended. It contains, rather, the presupposition of a unified knowing subject, a rational I, divorced from the world of extension, and a normative concept of knowledge is embedded in it.

However, Descartes' emphasis on methodology continued to influence scientists and the kind of science they produce. The leading idea has been that there is a single Scientific Method that determines whether an activity should be considered scientific or otherwise. In other words, the idea of unity of scientific method has been used "as a criterion of demarcation" (Dupré 2004: 42). One of the most influential defenders of the unity of scientific method is Karl Popper. Although strongly questioned, different versions of his theory of falsification are still supported by a variety of philosopher and scientists. Popper maintains that "in science, only observation and experiment may decide upon the *acceptance or rejection* of scientific statements, including laws and theories" (Popper 1972: 54). Accordingly, a theory is scientific in so far as it tries to falsify hypothesis within its domain in the light of new "conjectures". Using this as a criterion of demarcation, Popper identifies psychoanalysis and Marxism as standard examples of unscientific or pseudoscientific theories. They are not produced in such a way as to be subject to falsification, he argues. However, as will be explored, thinkers like Kuhn (1970) and Dupré (2004) have revealed that scientific activities like problem-solving are conducted in a variety of ways rather than being exclusively guided by falsification attempts. Hence, it has to be mentioned from the outset that objectivity of science cannot be based on the thesis of unity of scientific method, since as Dupré observes, "a unitary account of scientific method" is a myth (Dupré 2004: 43). By referring to the variety of scientific activities and diversity of ways in which scientists investigate the world, Dupré concludes that "methodologies have developed in wholly different ways in response to different kinds of problems, and the methodologies we have accumulated are as diverse as those questions" (Dupré 2004: 46).

Descartes also based his account of science on the dichotomy between the subject and the object. He considered knowledge to be ideas or representations of the world of objects. Objectification of nature and its reduction to a set of regularities that are to be disclosed and reported by science were among the results of this view of knowledge. As will be seen, common historical origin of scientific method and bureaucratic rationality led economic gains and chasing after profit to become the defining features of human relations to nature in capitalist societies. Descartes and his notion of presuppositionless science have been extremely influential in shaping our concept of education; this notion of science is still functioning as the form and content of the current notion of education. As will be discussed, since Descartes science, encouraged by his method of enquiry, has step by step become the main stock of collective knowledge. This means that science in the first instance occupied the position of being collective knowledge; it became collectively accepted. In the second instance, an education based exclusively on science was established and enforced. This means, at the same time, the marginalisation of other forms of knowledge. Social and cognitive by nature, these processes will be discussed in the coming sections.

EDUCATIONAL REVOLUTIONS

Its different shapes notwithstanding, the objectivist account of science, as I argued in the previous section, is deeply rooted in the history of thought. Seen in a historical perspective, scientific education is a quite recent event. By scientific education I mean a subject-based education signified by the rational systematisation of knowledge and schematised and routinised methods of learning. Rational administration is another important feature of this education. The emergence of such an education needed a special cultural climate and style of thought that first emerged in the context of Western culture, a culture based on rational and technical utilisation of scientific knowledge for economic gain. In the same vein, we can claim that education will not remain scientific for ever. The Kuhnian notion of paradigm-shift is helpful in this regard. Using this model, we can argue that the history of education is characterised by the rise and fall of competing educational paradigms; there have been periods of consensus upon educational aims and procedures alternating with times characterised by disagreement upon these issues. After each period of disagreement, agreement has been restored through modifications and changes in educational ends and methods.

It is worthwhile mentioning that the complex nature of educational changes discussed here cannot be exclusively assigned either to scientific development or to socio-cultural forces like economic development, religious upheaval or political revolution. For instance, we cannot claim that it was the success of Newtonian physics that led to a shift in educational paradigms from the ecclesiastical educational model to the scientific one. Neither can we say that scientific education emerged exclusively because of social events like industrialisation, urbanisation or the dissemination of protestant ethics in the West; rather, a complex whole of these forces have been involved in preparing the ground for new educational ideals and consequently for radical paradigm-shifts in the notion of education. These observations imply that educational paradigms belong to forms of life and their changes can be explained by changes in forms of life.

The point I am trying to make is that connections between the historical and the educational offer valuable insight into the current educational paradigm. They also offer clues to understanding my insistence on educational changes; huge transformative powers at work globally demand fundamental changes in the current educational paradigm. However, the current educational model diverges from this urgent demand for inclusion of different social and epistemological perspectives. Neither religion nor science, both so influential in this current educational paradigm, can offer a basis for inclusion because they are based on the principle of exclusion. Scientific knowledge is based exclusively on the calculability of the world and religion on an idea of the salvation of believers. I suggest, therefore, an inclusive educational perspective based on science, art and philosophy on the one hand and philosopher-artists as educators on the other. I will return to these subjects later in this study. Here, I concentrate on a brief account of social and economical events that paved the way for a scientific paradigm-shift in education.

THE EMERGENCE OF SCIENTIFIC EDUCATION

As pointed out previously, the objectivist notion of science was extremely influential in making science the form and the content of education. It was also mentioned that this process has not been a straightforward or isolated one; rather, it has been an integrated part of a web of interconnected social and historical processes, like those processes that brought about the triumph of the Reformation, the subsequent development of puritan sects like Calvinism, the dissemination of Enlightenment ideas, to name but a few. It was also argued that the rationalisation, systematisation and schematisation of knowledge and education are among the main traits of scientific education. Historically speaking, this education first gained popularity when it became important for the living conditions of large groups of people. It also needed to be justified ethically and epistemologically. This means that scientific education became generally accepted when it was perceived, on the one hand, as a way to spiritual salvation. In this regard, it received support from religious groups. On the other hand, it was considered as a basis for social progress and for individual careers. Consequently, it also was supported by secular forces.

In this regard, we can take advantage of Max Weber's analysis of the notion of rationality as the spirit of our modern times. For the purpose of this section, the Weberian emphasis on the remarkable coincidence between "the rational capitalistic organisation of (formerly) free labour" and "the rational ethics of ascetic Protestantism" is important (Weber 2002: xxxiv). This means not only a coincidence of interests of secular and religious groups, but also a rationalisation of different spheres of social life. Consequently, the way was paved for a "rational, systematic, and specialised pursuit of science" (Weber 2002: xxx). This event, in its turn, led to the "capitalist practical economic application" of sciences and related technologies (Weber 2002: xxxvii). Together, these elements stimulated gigantic transformative powers that in the long run changed conditions of knowledge acquisition and the meaning of being educated in Western societies; education became rationalised and scientific.

Generally speaking, Weber connects the rise of rational planning to Protestantism, especially to Calvinism. He reveals a close alliance between Calvinism and the then growing bourgeois class; they both favored the rational pursuit of economic gain (Weber 2002: xxxiv–xxxix). Another central notion in Weber's analysis is that of calling. This notion, Weber argues, brought together divergent elements like puritan "this-worldly asceticism", religious salvation and the rational planning of the economy. Through this process, we can argue, boundaries between the sacred and the profane were blurred and religious affairs were related to "rationalisation of conduct within this world". Remarkably, all these elements were juxtaposed with the mundane discipline, calculable economic interests and entrepreneurial attitude of the market (Weber 2002: 100). The notion of calling, Weber argues, brought private earning into the centre of the Calvinist life. Brought about by the Reformation, this concept puts a moral obligation on the individual regarding fulfilling this-worldly duties. For Calvin, salvation and damnation were predestined by God. However, any individual had to consider himself as chosen by God, since lack of certainty would indicate insufficient faith. The individual could demonstrate faith by good work in worldly affairs. Success in worldly affairs was considered a sign of being one of the elect. If we take Weber seriously, the result of this view of salvation was the dissemination of rationality throughout the whole body of society; the profane and the sacred met in the notion of rationality. Since then, as a direct consequence of rationalisation processes, the idea of God lost ground, but the idea of calculable economic interests preserved its hold on minds. Durable and rational planning of economic activities became the main concern of modern societies. Spiritual salvation was also pushed to the background, but rational economic activities brought about unprecedented accumulation of wealth. In the last analysis, although motivated by religious ideas, economic gain kept its primacy; in the long run economic reason used religion in its service and created a this-worldly welfare that overshadowed the idea of salvation and other-worldly paradise. Considered genealogically, however, religious ideas continue to influence minds, though in a disguised shape.[1]

Taking advantage of Weber's theory, we can claim that rationalism in scientific pursuits, merging observation with mathematics and calculability, technical utilisation of science and the rational systemisation of education happened alongside the rational systematisation of government, administration and economy as well as the rationalisation of mass production of commodities. The point is that these processes cannot be motivated by the rise of scientific rationality; rather, scientific rationally coincided with and was strengthened by economic and ethical rationalities; it became a powerful instrument for their ends. And education was the field in which science could meet demands of economy and religion.

The Reformation's idea that all spheres of life, spiritual as well as profane, are sacred, provided that they are dedicated to God, extended the influence of religion to all spheres of life. It also affected the growth of rational economical planning and, consequently, the development of capitalism, processes crucial for establishing mass education based on the rational organisation of education and the rational use of the sciences. This means that Protestantism not only directly and indirectly encouraged rational planning, but also contributed to education becoming scientific; it conferred positive spiritual significance on scientific education.

These observations can find support in White (2006), who also locates "the subject-based school curriculum . . . in Puritanism" (158). His observations also show the puritan origins of a further aspect of science and scientific education, their emphasis on the notion of method. Using White, we can assert that the Cartesian emphasis on methodology had a forerunner in the puritan logician and educational reformer Petrus Ramus (1515–1572). Indeed, as White maintains, Descartes' philosophical discourse can be placed within the Christian frame of mind. Famously, Descartes derived the truth about the world from the existence of God. Thus, modern philosophy was not free from religious values as is usually claimed.

According to White, Ramus was a pioneer in the systematisation of knowledge. He "provided a systematic map of the whole range of human knowledge and detailed guidance on how the items that constitute it can be transmitted from teacher to learner" (White 2006: 92). In this system, knowledge was organised "from the most general categories to the most specific" (114). Combined with the rational systematisation of economic life, Ramist logic and his systematisation of knowledge prepared the ground for an educational paradigm-shift. Epistemologically considered, Ramist ideas contributed to enhancing the idea of correspondence between thoughts and the world of objects. According to this style of thought, having the same creator as the world of objects, human intellects are "attuned by nature to be revelatory instruments, able to lead their possessors, through reason, to an understanding of God and of God's world" (White 2006: 93). Further, White argues, being a revelation of God's world, this kind of knowledge was, of course, considered the basis of appropriate human behavior. Consequently, ethical, economical, scientific and educational rationality became parts of the same world view.

Considering positivism against a background of what has been said so far, we cannot but discern important recurrent elements in the history of science and education; overestimation of methodology and formal logic as well as reduction of a synthetic proposition into simpler observable ones are parts of a puritan heritage taken over by positivism. A further point is that Weber's, White's and also Vattimo's (1988) observations show that religion and metaphysics, contrary to traditional views, are not necessarily the opposite of rationality. Famously, metaphysicians have persistently made use of rationality in the domain of theoretical philosophy and formal logic. Puritanism demonstrated a clear case of the rational pursuit of knowledge acquisition. White observes that puritans "saw no opposition between faith on the one hand and reliance on reason and the acquisition of knowledge on the other" (White 2006: 95). Considering metaphysics as the spirit of technology, Heidegger believes that "it presents the most extreme degree of rationalization" (Snyder in Vattimo 1988: xv). Thus, rationality is compatible with metaphysical thought; scientific rationality cannot be used as an argument for its being free from metaphysics. However, it has to be mentioned from outset that there is not only one kind of rationality; rather, there are rationalities. Hence, it is wise to ask "whose intellectual child the particular concrete form of rational thought" (Weber 2002: 38) is, whenever we talk of rationality. This means that rationality is contextual and historical rather than being absolute. Thus, to understand different types of rationality we have to determine what domain of life is rationalised, in what direction and what "ultimate values and ends" (Weber 2002: xxxviii) have been in view. Since scientific education is a child of masculine, Western, puritan and capitalist rationality, it is related to the specific interests of this type of rationality. This reveals our need for a rationality based on the inclusion of different perspectives, like those of women and marginalised people as well as those of art and philosophy. This means that rationality cannot be rejected or affirmed unambiguously.

In order, however, to avoid any misunderstanding, it may perhaps be useful to mention that scientific education was not merely a product of Protestantism. Neither did changes discussed above happen naturally or without conflicts; there were, of course, struggles to be fought and obstacles to be overcome. However, even in this regard, a coincidence of profane and sacred interests contributed largely to the establishment of scientific education. The religious notion of "salvation through education" (White 2006: 49) strengthened the idea of progress through education so central to modernity. Although the one aimed at the kingdom of God and the other at an enlightened classless society or the like, they shared the idea of using reason and knowledge acquisition as a means of reaching these aims. We can rightly claim that religious influences have contributed to authoritarian aspects of the current view of knowledge, since in a religious style of thought reason as well as knowledge is related to God and His created world. As a result, knowledge is considered as pre-given and unquestionable.

The interconnectedness of religious and economic interests and their impact on educational development has already been discussed. Here, I focus on another aspect of this development, namely, its connections with secular intellectual movements. In this regard, the rise of the Enlightenment and subsequent intellectual developments are decisive. Famously, the Enlightenment not only declared a strong opposition to authorities external to humanity, but also demonstrated a strong support for rationality, objective knowledge and empirical sciences. This means that the Enlightenment opposes Puritanism in the first regard, but shares the interest in objective knowledge with it. Contradictory as they are, these tendencies have been the source of an inner tension in modernity. The Enlightenment's opposition to external authorities led to the death of God, while its interest in pure knowledge demands the existence of such a source of authority, since this kind of knowledge demands a context-independent source of legitimacy. As a response to this need, God was replaced by a mind-transcendent reality. However, this reality, it came to be thought, cannot function as a source of authority, since the existence of such a reality is highly questionable. Consequently, this intrinsic paradox functions as a perpetual source of nihilism in the modern age. I will return to this issue in Chapter 3. Here, it is enough to mention that what we need is truthfulness to a new notion of objectivity and an ever changing reality, if we are to avoid nihilism.

The important point in the context of this section is that, inspired by the Enlightenment, decisive educational changes took place in the nineteenth century. This century was the climax of a struggle over the redefinition of the notion of education; at the centre of this struggle was the idea of making education scientific. Pioneers in this area were leading figures of the Enlightenment like John Locke and other scientifically minded thinkers like Pestalozzi, Huxley and Spencer in Europe and J. M. Rice and Charles W. Eliot in the United States, to name but a few. In order to shift the form and the content of education, they had to surmount the then established educational paradigm based on ecclesiastical scholasticism and classical studies. Together with factors mentioned above, the rapid growth of scientific knowledge and technologies and the powerful increase of their importance in daily life made the arguments in favour of basing education on science more and more compelling. As scientific progress continued and science penetrated more and more in the body of social life, "scientific literacy" became "necessary for everyone, not just a privileged few" (AAAS 1989: 14). Science became a concern of all instead of scientists alone. This point deserves further attention.

SCIENCE AS "SUPERADDRESSEE"

As mentioned above, in order for science to become the form and content of education, it first has to be accepted as collective knowledge within a form of life. As such, it becomes the basis of cooperative social practices as well as theoretical argumentation. Once this occurs science becomes implicit in any and each discourse and knowledge claim. This means that being educated in science becomes a necessary condition for any individual to be able to take part in language games. Expressed differently, science becomes "the superaddressee". For Bakhtin, "life by its very nature is dialogic" (Bakhtin 1984: 293). In his world, the notion of the superaddressee refers to an invisible third person implicit in any dialogue, an invisible person in addition to two interlocutors in a dialogue, the first person, who speaks, or the self and the second person, whom we address. The important thing for the purpose of this study is that the superaddressee is a generally agreed authority who stands above particularities of different dialogues and language games (Bakhtin 1986: 126). Taking the position of collective knowledge, science stays above particularities of different discourses. It becomes not only the judge of everybody and everything, but also its own judge; it becomes self-sufficient and self-contained. As Wilfred Sellars bluntly puts it, science becomes "the measure of all things, of what is that it is, and of what is not that it is not" (Sellars 1997: 83). This happens when we support our arguments by referring to their being scientific. In modern societies, science is implicit in every dialogue and decides the rule of the game. Hence, it becomes the content and the form of education, as it is implicit in all other discourses. Not only science itself, but also other subjects like art, history, theology and philosophy are often taught scientifically; our view of the world becomes scientific. Not only does being educated in science become a necessary condition of knowledge, but also the world becomes "shaped by science and technology" (AAAS 1989: 11). These processes underpin each other. I use the notion of scientific education to signify this situation, with "science education—meaning education in science, mathematics and technology" (AAAS 1989: 12).

SCIENTIFIC EDUCATION AND COOPERATIVE SOCIAL ACTIONS

As discussed in the previous section, by becoming the basis of education, science becomes implicit in any meaningful discourse. This is, however, one side of the coin; the issue also has a practical aspect. Given science's position in the framework of our form of life, our cooperative social actions also receive meaning and significance through references to science. A reference to Wittgenstein sheds light on this issue. For him, education is initiation into forms of life. He was interested in "how 'we'", through initiation, "acquire forms of practical reason: a stabilizing *habitus* of rule-following behaviours, norms, and certainties" (Stickney 2005: 299) in order to take part in social actions within a form of life. To become a part of social life in contemporary societies we have to be educated scientifically, since there are few or no other alternatives available. However, Wittgenstein emphasises, contrary to Kuhn, not only our learning to partake in language games, but also our ability to contest and renegotiate forms of agreement. This means a sense of responsibility for what we are. Changes in education can be considered as part of a process of resistance, negotiation and renegotiation within any form of life.

Before leaving this section a few remarks on the distinction between science teaching and scientific education are necessary: Using the preceding discussions, I argue that while science teaching is preoccupied with the ways science is taught, the notion of scientific education signifies a specific mode of education, the rational systematisation of education or its industrialisation in contemporary societies for the sake of economic gain. Certainly, there are many ways of teaching science; they can be scientific or otherwise. Science was taught before education became rationalised and systematised. It will also be taught after such a systematisation is replaced by other modes of education. In other words, science teaching marks science as being taught either through a rational systematised method of education or otherwise; it just signifies science as a school subject. Scientific education, on the contrary, is concerned with science as well as with other subjects being taught scientifically. Here, science is considered as a perspective on all spheres of education rather than as a school subject.

The advantages of this distinction are several. It makes us able to consider education and its development in the broader context of a culture instead of being limited to teaching methods. To see science and education in the context of a culture makes evident the importance of cultural events for education. It also reveals the importance of cultural values for knowledge and education. Signifying an education systematised through the use of scientific rationality, scientific education reveals our need for an education based on the perspectives of science, art and philosophy. By enabling us to see each of these perspectives in the light of the others, such an education not only contributes to cognitive plurality but also underpins an inclusive view of knowledge; it helps us overcome the narrow-minded exclusive notions of knowledge and education. I push primarily for radical changes in scientific education, aware that changes in this field will lead inevitably to changes in science teaching. In the long run, scientific education will run down. As explored in Chapter 5, this running down means diversification of cognitive perspectives. To avoid misunderstanding, it should be stressed that the aforementioned distinction is not always clear-cut; there are certainly overlapping areas and grey zones.

To conclude, rationalised and systematised scientific education is based on the article of faith that there is a single world, the world of God or an absolute reality that is one and the same for all. There is also a single notion of rationality that is universally compelling. Using rational methods, science is going to provide us with a final true account of this world. The desirability of the scientific account of the world, it is argued, depends on its rationality, its being determined by objective facts; scientific method works independently of contingencies related to individual scientists. Based on this style of thought, the notion of scientific truth is conceived as universally valid. All other notions are an appearance of this universal truth; it is the universal equivalence of all true notions. Through this act of self-legislation, science determines criteria of its own truth.

This study challenges this notion of science and the concomitant notion of education. It undertakes the demanding task of presenting alternative notions of science and education. What makes the current image of science undesirable is its masking the involvement of the human agent and its context of action in all acts of cognition. As a result, what people "themselves constitute and which they are locked into, virtually eliminates all natural elements and becomes 'nature' to them" (Adorno 1998: 12). Traditional scientific consciousness is then a reified consciousness, since human ideas become objectified; they become objective facts and start to dominate the human mind. Such a human type is alienated from his/her world. To disalienate the individual we need to highlight his/her active part in the construction of knowledge. We do this by tracing the important role played by the human subject in all acts of cognition according to major philosophers from Descartes to Nietzsche. By highlighting human creative resources, we can reconceptualise notions like science, education and truth. Before doing this, it is necessary to focus on the relationship between objectivism and alienation as well as that between relativism and nihilism. I discuss these issues in the present chapter and Chapter 3.

OBJECTIVISM, EDUCATION AND ALIENATION

The objectivist account of science and the concomitant notion of education, as has been argued, are based on a belief in systems of knowledge related to higher authorities than contexts of life. These authorities, it is supposed, guarantee the purity of knowledge as well as knowing and acting rightly. The main assertion in this section is that an education based on such a view of knowledge functions as a perpetual source of alienation. This is because it establishes a non-participatory mode of thinking where individuals' active part in cognition is veiled and denied. Consequently, individuals do not feel that they are actively engaged in the process of producing knowledge. Neither are they aware of the process of knowledge being constitutive of its object. Students of science have to passively accept what is dictated by texts and teachers, since pedagogical science is presented as being based on universally valid methods, truths and rational rules. Neither are teachers and texts answerable to these truths since these truths transcend their particular cultural contexts. The more devoted, depersonalised and selfless the individual the better. Knowledge and conceptions of consciousness are not presented as the production of the human mind; rather, they are presented as emanating from a higher source of legitimacy and are accordingly predisposed to dominate the individual. The humanly constructed nature of this world remains veiled behind the mask of objectivity. The individual is thus placed within a world of reified truths and knowledge alien to him/her. The main contention here is that alienation is a provisional state of mind inspired by prevailing socio-educational circumstances. Hence, it will be diminished if these circumstances are replaced by new ones that are true to the real nature of knowledge and truth. This means a radical shift in our understanding of education and of what knowledge is and how and through what processes it is acquirable.

Alienation is a complex notion. In order to do justice to this notion, it is proper to talk of alienations rather than alienation. There exist a variety of competing theories and definitions of this notion, and none of them are able to cover the whole range of characteristics necessary and sufficient for a phenomenon to be signified as alienation. Thus it is fully warranted, as Felix Geyer (1996: ix) suggests, to use alienation as an umbrella conception that covers a variety of interconnected phenomena. For the purpose of this study, the common traits of all these phenomena are that they mask the active part of the individual in all cognitive activities and they objectify the results of these activities; they signify the lack of participation. As discussed in the previous section, due to needs external to the individual, results of individual cognitive activities are separated from the knower, rationalised and systematised into abstract knowledge systems. This separation means at the same time an objectification of knowledge systems. As a result, these systems appear as alien forces and start to dominate the cogniser. In the context of this study, I emphasise current educational and cognitive configurations as sources of alienation, without ignoring resulting psychological states of mind. Indeed, these aspects of the issue are interconnected; alienation encompasses both.

Richard Schacht divides alienations into two groups, subjective and objective alienations. The former group of alienations is related to psychological states of the individual, and the latter is based on alienating environments regardless of how they are perceived by the individual (Schacht 1994: 30). In the former case the individual feels alienated regardless of the kind of social structure. In the latter, social structures are alienating regardless of the individual's attitude toward them. At first glance this distinction looks warranted and helpful. However, further considerations reveal its questionable character; it creates more problems than it is able to resolve. It is based partly on the traditional distinction between subjectivity and objectivity. Indeed, this distinction is itself a main source of alienation. To use this dichotomy as the basis for an explanation of alienation creates a vicious circle. As will be discussed later, a solution to the problem of alienation should be a move away from traditional dichotomies like that of subjectivity and objectivity. On the other hand, and most importantly, there are no clear-cut boundaries between these types of alienation; they are mutually interchangeable. There are indeed overlapping characteristics and grey zones. Besides, a solution to the problem of alienation that focuses either on individual attitudes or on social structures is certainly a one-sided one. And as such it is a useless solution. Accordingly, the above-mentioned distinction is obsolete. Instead of categorically distinct kinds of alienation, there are family resemblances among groups of alienation. There are clusters of likelihoods and differences that either relate or disconnect types of alienation. Like the notion of alienation itself, these likelihoods and differences are contextual and changeable rather than being fixed. Indeed, Schacht himself reveals the problematic character of his distinction by writing that *"there is no such thing as alienation. Neither is there any such thing as [subjective] alienation, or [objective] alienation. But there are myriads of alienation . . ."* (Schacht 1994: 34). As a result of this insight, we can make use of the notion of alienation as an umbrella notion. Such a notion encompasses psychological aspects of alienation as well as alienations related to social configurations of knowledge. As a result of what has been said, it is wise to state precisely what phenomena and what relation we mean in each specific case. We have to determine what aspect of alienation is dominating in each particular case.

My concern is alienation as a transformative process rather than a static state of being. As I mentioned above, in the context of this study, alienation is related to scientific education and knowledge acquisition. This means that alienation depends on the kind of relations between the individual and the environment on the one hand and is historical on the other. My main contention is that scientific education is alienating regardless of individuals' attitudes toward it, since it imposes on the individual a system of knowledge based on an unviable separation between knower and knowledge. This is, however, one side of the process. The other side is the knower's awareness of her/his being alienated. This second aspect forms the basis of my connecting alienation to the notion of nihilism. As a result, alienation as a conscious phenomenon becomes important. In my view, nihilism is the awareness of knowledge systems being results of historical processes and social hierarchies of power. This means that disalienation goes through nihilism. While alienation can signify false consciousness, nihilism is a sign of insight into the nature of knowledge and its relation to the knower; it signifies self-consciousness. Encompassing actual alienating states of affairs as well as how people feel about their knowledge, this mode of analysis is aimed at shedding light on the disorder and lack of self-determination that signify the current relations between systems of knowledge and the individual. To be clear, this brings a normative aspect to the issue; separation of individuals from their creative resources is unnatural and leads to dehumanisation. It is thus desirable to bring back the unity between the individual and her/his knowledge by stimulating individual consciousness about cognitive processes.

Alienation is a relational notion. Generally speaking, it implies alienation of something from something. It can thus be used in a variety of contexts and relations. While I have things to say about different forms of alienation, I shall not enter such discussions. I choose instead to concentrate on alienation of individuals from their labour or creativity. To make this point clear sheds light on the notion of alienation as it is used in this study. Genealogically speaking, alienation has religious and juridical roots. But through philosophers like Kant and their examination of the source and function of the notion it entered philosophical discourse. For the purpose of this study, Marx's theory of alienation is helpful, since he discusses the emergence of alienation in modern societies; it can easily be connected with rationalisation processes discussed earlier in this chapter. Marx considers alienation a historical phenomenon related to the capitalist social order and economic gain. As in other theories about alienation, he presupposes a natural state in which humanity was not alienated and people lived in harmony with each other and with nature. This state was destroyed by the emergence of private property, which led, Marx argues, to alienation in human relationships. In a market economy, he maintains, people are reduced to saleable labour power and subjugated to an abstract entity, money. The productions of human labour are also reduced to saleable commodities. In bourgeois societies, money and commodities, though productions of human hands and minds, confront humanity as alien forces. As a result humanity becomes foreign to the world. But, since this state of affairs is historical, humanity is fully capable of overcoming this middle stage and entering a higher level of harmony with nature and with itself. The Hegelian style of argumentation and Hegel's view of human history are easily discernible here. Indeed, Hegel was among the philosophers who were preoccupied with this problem and influenced later thinkers. He believed that though people create culture, it confronts them as an alien force. It is important to keep in mind that according to Hegel history is a plan of the absolute spirit; the absolute spirit uses people as tools to realise this plan. This study is in agreement with Marx, who declares the Hegelian notion of the absolute spirit obsolete and expels it from history. By so doing, he provides a useful analytical tool, the notion of human labour. By concentrating on the emergence of alienation in capitalist societies, he maintained, against Hegel, that it is human labour that creates culture, not the absolute spirit. Thus, alienation can be understood in relation to human labour. Being historical by nature, Marx declares, human labour manifests itself in different shapes. Depending on socio-cultural circumstances, it can be manifested either as "a *free manifestation of life*, hence an *enjoyment* of life", or as "*alienation* of life" (Marx 1975b: 228). Applied to our intellectual activities and to the cognitive processes basic for knowledge acquisition, this double nature of human labour has great explanatory value. It demands a shift of focus away from the quantity of human knowledge to its quality. It also attaches the greatest importance to the impacts of each alternative on human beings, to the quality of life and thought each alternative gives birth to. I should mention here that I consider human labour in its broadest sense to be our ability to create. Thus, the Platonic hierarchy between intellectual-philosophical activities and physical labour is contested. This is a part of my inclusive view of knowledge, education and truth.

To return to our main line of argumentation, far from being reified, in the first case, labour is not only an inclusive manner of relation to the other, but also a manifestation of the "essential nature" of humanity. The important point here is that the notion of labour is presented as human nature. Instead of a transcendental nature, as is the case with essentialism, here a historical notion becomes the main characteristic of humanity. I will return to this issue in Chapters 3 and 12.

In a non-alienated state of being, any individual is not only at one with his/her labour, but also affirms himself/herself and others in an active and generous manner. As Marx writes, in this mode of being:

> each of us would have *in two ways affirmed* himself and the other person. 1) In my *production* I would have objectified my *individuality*, its *specific character*, and therefore enjoy not only *an individual manifestation* of my life during the activity, but also when looking at the object I would have the individual pleasure of knowing my personality to be objective, visible to the sense and hence a power beyond all doubt. 2) In your enjoyment or use of my product. (Marx 1975b: 227)

This is an active mode of understanding. Due to its being manifested in its activities, the human subject becomes one with these activities. It affirms human creativity as the source of our individual and communal identities. It is also an artistic mode of understanding the world because it affirms the uniqueness of each individual and his/her inner creative resources. Seen in this light, though the produced object can appear as an entity in its own right it does not appear as an alien force to humanity, as is the case with commodities in capitalist societies. Created values and objects are, rather, manifestations of one's individuality and creative resources. Freely manifested in her/his creations, the individual affirms not only his/her own individuality but also that of others. There is no claim to assimilation, elimination or domination, but the enjoyment of a creative interplay which forms the basis upon which human relationships develop. It is far from narrow and egoistic individualism, since the individual cares not only about her/his own natural needs but also about others' needs as well. Thanks to the artistic or creative manner of being, the fulfilment of one individual's talents corresponds to the satisfaction of the "need of another man's essential nature" and to the joy of being creative. Not only is humanity not subordinated to external abstract principle, be it God, truth or money, but any individual is in full control of his/her creative activities and essential needs. As Nietzsche points out in *The Gay Science*, to make a genealogical or "backward inference from the work to the maker, from the deed to the doer, from the ideal to those who need it, from every way of thinking and valuing to the commanding need behind it" (GS 370), it is not "hunger but superabundance", not "revenge", but "gratitude and love" that become creative in humanity.

In an alienated state of affairs, by contrast, "My work is not my life" or "my true nature", but separated from it and "an *alienation of life*" (Marx

1975b: 228).[2] Here, the human world becomes splintered into two separate spheres and the one takes control over the other; we create things which gain power over us. The joy of being creative is replaced by the torment of being ruled by one's own creations. In the long run, the man-made nature of this power relation is forgotten and it appears natural. In *On the Jewish Question* Marx discerns the origin of alienation in bourgeois society's turning everything

> into *alienable*, vendible [saleable] objects subjected to the slavery of egoistic need and to trading. Selling is the practical aspect of alienation. Just as man, so long as he is in grip of religion, is able to objectify his essential nature only by turning it into something alien, something fantastic, so under the domination of egoistic need he can be active practically, and produce objects in practice, only by putting his products, and his activity, under the domination of an alien being, and bestowing the significance of an alien entity—money—on them. (Marx 1975a: 174)

Here, selling is presented as the practical aspect of alienation. In order for human labour to become saleable it has to be separated from the human subject. This means that, in the first instance, labour has to be separated from the human agent. Such a split is of course unnatural, since human beings and their labour are naturally linked and unified. Once it is separated, human labour becomes objectified and transformed into an exchange value; it becomes saleable or exchangeable and put under the domination of money. This means, as Istvan Meszaros observes in *Marx's Theory of Alienation* (1975), that alienation is connected to "universal saleability", to anything and everything becoming saleable. Meszaros argues that alienation has historically been related to reification, where human beings are reduced to objects. Kant discussed this aspect of alienation long before Marx. Kant maintained that an object has to first be alienated from its original owner in order to be transferred to a new owner. A living person (a slave), however, according to Kant, must first be reified, converted into a thing before she/he can be transferred to a new owner (Meszaros 1975: 7). A full discussion of this Kantian position is not within my scope. In our context, the main point that can be learned from Kant is that human beings must be objectified, in the first instance, in order for them to become saleable, in the second. Together with the fact that in modern time this principle expanded and embraced everything, this point gives us a powerful analytical tool. In fact, the principle of "universal saleability" means that anything becomes a commodity and is thus reduced to an exchange value. Commodification is the basis of human relations in bourgeois societies; everything is exchangeable to money. Money, on the other hand, functions as such a principle because it is considered a universal entity high above all commodities. "The *essence of money*", Marx maintains, "is its abstract universality" (Marx 1975b: 213). The characteristics of being abstract and universal release money from specific contexts and singular situations and make it a general form.

ALIENATION AND KNOWLEDGE SYSTEMS

Separation of labour from the individual and reification are indeed presuppositions of the rational capitalistic organisation of labour, mentioned earlier in this chapter. These tendencies, as also mentioned, have parallels in the rational systematisation of knowledge and education. Analogous to what has been said about rational organisation of labour in general, there can be two modes of production and distribution of knowledge. Either knowledge is a manifestation of life and the joy of human creativity or an alienation of life. In the former case, human beings are one with their knowledge and knowledge is a manifestation of their individual and communal creativity. In the latter, knowledge is not only separated from knowers, but also reified and reduced to abstract facts. It is reduced to a formal/propositional notion of truth on the one hand. On the other hand, any proposition is reduced to a truth value or exchange value. Truth, like money, is introduced as a general form to be recognised; it is considered to be abstract, universal, context-independent and community-transcendent. At the same time, to interpret truth in this way means to transform it into an object; it becomes a universal exchange value, the universal equivalent of all other values; it forms the basis for exchangeability of all other values. In summary, in an alienated state of mind human knowledge is subordinated to abstract truths as human material productions are subordinated to money; the mechanisms behind them are similar.

It is possible to draw parallels between economic and cognitive processes regarding the notion of the individual. On a social level, individuals are alienated from their labour and made to function as saleable elements in the market economy. At the same time, the real mechanisms of the market are masked by the principle of universal saleability; this principle is presented as the condition of individual freedom. In theory, the individual is free to sell his/her labour or refuse to do so, while in reality universal saleability forms the basis for social coercion and destroys individual freedom. Any individual has necessarily to become saleable in order to be able to work and live in a capitalist society; life is subordinated to the principle of universal saleability. On an epistemological level, individuals are alienated from the processes of production and distribution of knowledge; by hiding the active part of the individual in the construction of scientific facts, the metaphysical notion of truth appears as an alien force and dominates the human mind. In both cases, people are alienated from products of their labour, from control over the labour process and from the creative resources of the human race. In the former case, the individual is reduced to a saleable element in a market economy and subordinated to money. In the latter, the notion of the individual is reduced to an abstract element in systems of knowledge, and references to abstract truths are supposed to make him/her independent of cultural contexts.

As a result of these processes, science appears as a sovereign power and starts to dominate minds. To shed light on this aspect of alienation, a reference to Nietzsche is helpful. In his early writings he investigates relationships between science, the Hegelian notion of rationality, the labour market, education and human enslavement. He opposes scientific education, since to his mind such an education leads to life becoming controlled by science. Concentrating on the control relation between science and life, he asks, in *The Utility and Liability of History*: "Should life rule over knowledge and science, or should knowledge rule over life?" (ULH, 10). In my opinion, this is a fruitful way to deal with the question of relationships between life, education and science. Education, based on each of these alternatives, prepares learners for qualitatively different ways of life and of understanding the world. The difference is between humanity mastering epistemic values or being ruled by them. Needless to say, the subject is not a matter of indifference; it is about true cultivation on the one hand and dehumanisation on the other. I am in agreement with Nietzsche about education's as well as science's need of "the supervision and surveillance" (ULH, 10) of life in its cultural and biological senses, if life is not to be destroyed by them. Gaining control over science, life flourishes in all its richness and employs science in its service. Science also flourishes through being incorporated in an inclusive outlook on the world. In a life ruled by science, science confronts humanity as an alien source of authority. As a result, humanity becomes alienated from the world. A life dominated by science is not only subordinated to established interests, since, as mentioned in the opening section of this chapter, science is subordinated to interests of funding agencies and states, but in addition it "is much less *life* (ULH, 7), as Nietzsche writes. This view reveals a basic point about the nature of the scientific understanding of life and the world. Here, I have in mind reductionism at work in the standard view of science and the rational organisation of life. This view of science is based on rationalisation, systematisation and the calculability of being. And this style of thought is basically Socratic, where he considers the language of truth as calculation or mathematics. Based on Socratic and Cartesian styles of thought, science dissects and reduces to its parts whatever it comes in contact with. Once things are reduced to calculable entities, it is easy to make them subordinated to and exchangeable with abstract principles. A life ruled by science then becomes ruled by these principles. It is this type of scientific understanding of the world that this study opposes. A world understood from the single perspective of science is misconceived. Nietzsche is right in claiming that any phenomenon "that is supposed to be understood scientifically through and through will be destroyed as soon as it reaches this goal" (ULH, 7). The same can be said of education and its being understood merely scientifically. As we will see in

Chapter 11, this study's opposition to scientific education led by scholarly educators is conceivable in this connection. Understood scientifically, the world loses its ambiguity and is reduced to science of the world or to a system of scientific facts. Translated into modes of human being, this means "human slavery", since we lose power over products of cognitive processes and these products gain power over us.

Employing a term from Nietzsche's *Schopenhauer as Educator*, subordinated to the interests of states, market and funding agencies, scientific education makes the individual "current" (SE, 6). He probably has in mind the principle of saleability when he uses this notion. To make individuals current means not only to make them saleable but also to make them servants of the daily needs of the market. It also means reducing human creativity to "alienated *labour*" aimed just *"to earn a living"* (Marx 1975b: 219). We cannot fail to discern the similarity between this kind of labour and what Nietzsche terms "bread winning" labour.

Aimed at economic gains, detached from human beings, objectified, calculable and saleable human "activities . . . appear to [humanity] as a torment" (Marx 1975b: 217). To refer to Marx once again, estranged from true human needs, products of alienated human labour are "simply a *matter of indifference* to [humanity]" (221). These tendencies are not unique to economic systems. The same can be said of the current educational system. Governed by needs of the market, this education cannot but lead to a state of being in which individuals are indifferent to their knowledge and to the world. They do not identify themselves with their knowledge and their life world; they yearn to escape this world. Nietzsche refers to an important aspect of alienation that illuminates this notion as it is used here. Making a distinction between two human types, romantic and tragic, he maintains that romantics are foreigners in the world they are living in. They always dream of a world located in the historical past or nowhere (GS, 370). This self-forgetfulness refers to the individual not being aware of his/her creative forces in the present. He/she is not an active participant in the drama of life.

Properly understood, education can function as a liberating cognitive power that encourages willingness to change. By so doing, it saves humanity from torment and indifference. Having this starting point, this study considers education as a transformative process leading to improvement in conditions of human physical and mental labour through shifts in our understanding of the notions of knowledge, education and labour. This emphasises the role of conscious activities as an important element in curing alienation. As will be explored in Chapter 12, I am trying to combine Nietzsche's view of individual redemption with Marx's view of social liberation in order to reach an inclusive solution to problems of alienation and nihilism. This means that not only any society but also any individual has to overcome alienation and nihilism to become liberated. As will be explored later, this requires an education based on a plurality of perspectives rather than on the single perspective of science. This means heading for a horizon of life where humanity "has again become master over the businessman" (GS 362).

This account of the relationship between scientific education and alienation would be one-sided if it was not connected with the notion of nihilism, since I consider that alienation and nihilism are not only based on scientific education, but are also different but interconnected stages of the same process. The next chapter is thus allocated to an examination of the relationships between scientific education, relativism and nihilism. As with alienation, my approach to nihilism is a philosophical and epistemological one based on two different modes of knowledge.

3 Relativism and Nihilism

As discussed in the previous chapter, alienation is an inevitable result of the current educational system—its rational systematization of science into reified webs of objective facts. The main contention of this chapter is that alienation is often followed by a stage in which we become aware that these systems of facts are products of cultural contexts, that they are historically conditioned. The scientific community reached this stage in a diverse array of relativistic theories. Thomas Kuhn's incommensurability theory is the most well-known and influential one. In this study, positivism is considered the basis of alienation due to its reified categories of thought. By questioning the objectivity of these categories, Kuhn gave rise to a crisis of values in science; through him scientific culture became aware of the shaky basis of its ground.

Considering scientific facts as detached from human needs and beliefs, positivism was mainly concerned with the justification of science within the context of justification; logical analysis of the structure of scientific theories was the main focus. Kuhn, on the contrary, focused on mechanisms of change, growth and development in science. Looking in a very different direction, he saw things that positivism was unable to see. While positivism took agreement on truth for granted based on logical analysis of theories' structures, Kuhn discerned a pattern of alternations between periods of agreement and disagreements, consensus and lack of consensus within the scientific community. Translated into the way science is done, he called these alternating episodes normal science and revolutionary science, respectively. While positivism solved disagreement by reference to logical argumentation, Kuhn saw scientific revolutions as the final outcome of disagreements. At the same time these revolutions pave the way for new agreements. Kuhn's theory deserves thorough attention, since it reveals important points about scientific education.

OBJECTIVISM AND NIHILISM

Kuhn's main achievement has been to make science's dependence on paradigms widely known. Since the publication of *The Structure of Scientific*

Revolutions (1962), the notion of paradigm has been widely and frequently used in a varied range of contexts and significance. Such an extensive use has contributed to the dissemination of the incommensurability of different paradigms and has undermined universally compelling accounts of knowledge. Since in traditional philosophy of science there exist only two options, relativism and universalism, the questioning of universalism by the incommensurability thesis has inevitably led to relativism and the redundancy of truth. My contention here is that such a view of truth amounts to a form of nihilism, since it questions the very possibility of transcendence. In this regard, I am in agreement with Heidegger when he writes: "Nihilism is that historical process whereby the dominance of the 'transcendent' becomes null and void, so that all being loses its worth and meaning" (1987: 4).

Indeed, what Kuhn reveals is the lack of transcendence in a traditional sense. And this is the advent of nihilism. The Kuhnian awareness is nihilistic, since it not only distrusts old standards of knowledge, but also shows indifference to the notion of truth; it announces the redundancy of truth and does not care about it. Besides its stemming from alienation, indifference to truth, lack of care and distrustfulness of old standards of knowledge are among characteristics of the form of nihilism I wish to discuss here. This is a passive form of nihilism described in negative terms. Overcoming nihilism requires transformation from this passive nihilism, in which awareness of the human nature of knowledge leads to resignation, to an active one, in which human creativity is stimulated by insights into the nature of knowledge. Obviously, these types of consciousness are different in kind. Paradoxically, the former tendency demonstrates an unconditional will to truth about knowledge systems. But this will to truth is based on truth for its own sake. As such, it is ascetic. Once it reveals the untruth of the old view of science, its creative drives are transformed into indifference; since it does not find any truth in science, it distrusts truth as such. Recovery from this indifference and distrustfulness comes in the form of the insight that truth matters after all. Our commitment to truth is then perpetual. As I consider nihilism against a background of alienation, where separation between labour and human agent is central, unity of the subject and object, knower and knowledge, deeds and the doer are parts of the solution to the problem of nihilism. In this case, the individual overcomes indifference to what he/she has become, to what she/he knows, believes, says and does. As a result, life becomes meaningful after all.

Nihilism can be conceived in different ways. Indeed, there is a diversified array of views and theories about nihilism. Seen in this light, we can talk of nihilisms rather than of nihilism. To enter these discussions is beyond my scope. However, some words about my approach to the issue are in place. As mentioned above, I study nihilism against a background of alienation. This means that nihilism is discussed in the light of a Socratic/Cartesian view of the objectivity of thoughts, of connecting thoughts to "the divine". This style of thought is based on a belief in the transcendental as the guarantor of our thoughts being true. This transcendental source of legitimacy can be God, the Platonic eternal ideas, the Kantian forms of intuitions or the absolute reality. In such a world the divine endows things with meaning and significance. This is, however, an alienating style of thought. Here, as in the case with commodities, human thoughts gain meaning and significance through "bestowing" on them "the significance of an alien entity—[the divine]" (Marx 1975a: 174). To distrust this "fantastic" source of legitimacy causes a crisis of value. This is the meaning of the Nietzschean announcement of the death of God. Such a movement means a void of legitimacy or nihilism. My connecting nihilism to alienation on the one hand and to scientific education on the other means that nihilism emerges on a real social basis; it is not just a psychological phenomenon. Economic gain, as was argued, is the basic drive to knowledge in contemporary culture. On the other hand, there are claims about value-neutrality and objectivity of science. These contrary tendencies form the basis for recurrent crises of value. As long as God functioned as the fundamental aim of drives to knowledge and profit, they were endowed with meaning and value. But upon His death, the crisis of value was inevitable.

The death of God can be understood differently, either as rejection of any kind of belief or as inauguration of a new belief. In the former case, life loses its meaning. In the latter, life attains a renewed meaning. This meaning lies in life being conceived as the most basic perspective on knowledge. As such, life endows things with meaning by employing them in the service of its flourishing. To claim that nihilism is to be understood as the traditional notion of transcendence being distrusted does not mean that overcoming nihilism is a matter of the reestablishment of the old notion of transcendence; rather it means a radical reconceptualisation of it. This means, as will be explored in Chapter 9, a reinterpretation of the notion of transcendence in the light of the notion of translation. Such an overcoming is a transformative process. It goes from a strong belief in the transcendental to disbelief and lack of transcendence in order to take the next step to belief in human creativity. This demands our taking command over and responsibility for our beliefs and values, for what we say and do; identification of the knower with knowledge and the doer with deeds.

Seen in this light, there is no need to be afraid of nihilism, since it is a stage on our way toward liberation. It signifies awareness of people being separated from their labour as well as awareness of the human-made nature of all values. As discussed above, given the modern educational system, alienation becomes inevitable. To this we can now add that given alienation, nihilism becomes inevitable. While alienation stems from reified social relations, nihilism is a result of these reified relations being unmasked. On one level, alienation can be considered as a cultural phenomenon and nihilism as an individual one. Although these distinctions are not clear-cut, one can claim that, whereas alienation occurs because of certain social conditions and on a collective plane, awareness that these conditions are alienating occurs on an individual plane.

SCIENTIFIC RELATIVISM

In order to relate the notion of nihilism to that of the current notion of science and the related notion of education, it is worthwhile to look at sources of the Kuhnian brand of relativism, because the crisis of value in contemporary science is related to this notion. An analysis of the Kuhnian notion of science has to start with the key notion of paradigm. Kuhn presents paradigms as holistic units of methods, problems, solutions, conceptions, norms, beliefs and certainties which make doing science possible. Indeed, Kuhn took over many of the ideas and much of the work done prior to him by philosophers like Quine and Wittgenstein. These philosophers paved the way by shifting the focus away from elements internal to science, like scientific method, scientific reasoning and science's use of mathematics, towards external elements constitutive of knowledge, like background beliefs and cultural values. Of paramount importance in this context are Wittgenstein's notions of "language games" and "forms of life" and Quine's introduction of "conceptual scheme". They generally questioned the authority of the traditional notion of reality conceived as external to knowledge and independent of language, context and background. Once such a reality is questioned and made dependent on language games and conceptual schemes, not only does the source of authority become decentralised, but also these elements become constitutive components of knowledge and reality. Since there is not just one language game or one set of conceptual schemes, but rather a variety of rival games and schemes, the universal account of reality, so characteristic of modern science, loses its authority and privileged position. While internalist epistemologies remain within the conceptual framework of science and consider internal criteria, criteria within the discourse of science, as adequate, this position demands a point of leverage outside different schemes and games in order to evaluate each conceptual framework's adequacy with regard to external reality. Since such a point cannot be accomplished, we have no reason to believe that any perspective corresponds to reality more than its rivals. Consistently following this line of argumentation, relativism becomes an inevitable outcome.

A classical text in this connection, originally written in 1951, is Quine's "Two Dogmas of Empiricism" (1998), in which he criticised and rejected basic empiricist principles, the distinction between analytic statements, statements true by virtue of their meaning, and synthetic statements, statements dependent on empirical "matters of fact" for their truth value. He also attacked reductionism, the doctrine that each meaningful synthetic statement is equivalent to some observational (experiential) sentences, which "refer to immediate experience" (Quine 1998: 280). By rejecting the analytic-synthetic distinction, Quine takes the crucial step toward making clear "the necessary link between all knowledge claims and actual lived experience" (Hank 2005: 225). Principally, this means that any belief could be abandoned or revised in the light of experience. Quine also made it clear, against reductionism and the verifiability principle of meaning, that "our statements about the external world face the tribunal of sense experience not individually but only as corporate body" (Quine 1998: 295). Quine's theory of holism and his rejection of a priori knowledge undermined the empiricist firm faith in conclusive connections between individual theories and the outcome of certain observations and experiments; any theory is logically consistent with any given body of evidence. Rejection and choice of theories are thus not determined solely by observation and evidence. Indeed, Quine defended a more radical thesis of underdetermination than Kuhn did. Quine espouses the thesis, as Curd and Cover formulate it, that "any theory can be shown to be as well supported by any evidence" (Curd and Cover 1998: 391). While Kuhn defends a local version of underdetermination, according to which each theory competes for the allegiance of the scientific community with its known rivals and at a given time, Quine defends a global underdetermination based on rivalry between all possible rivals and all times. Holism and underdetermination are two important notions in connection with scientific education. As will be explored later, scientific education should be viewed not in isolation but as a part of a culture and a form of life. It is just within the framework of certain forms of life that such an education makes sense. Thus, critique of scientific education has to be undertaken with critique of its related form of life.

Like Quine's, Kuhn's criticism of the methods and content of science and science education can be rightly understood against the background of his criticism of philosophy of science, especially the logical positivism of the Vienna Circle and falsificationism presented by Popper. For the purpose of this study, this is the right way to consider the issue, since the canonical image of science presented by the school texts is actually based on a view of science primarily established and protected by these philosophical mainstreams. To make things clear, I am not going to defend a Kuhnian notion of science. I just see these two notions of science in an antithetical way, since, as mentioned above, I connect alienation to the positivistic view of science, where knowledge is reduced to reified scientific facts, and nihilism to the Kuhnian view of science, in which a positivistic notion of science is contested without being replaced by an adequate one. There is a further step to be taken in order for us to reach an adequate view of science. This issue will be discussed in Chapters 5, 4, 6 and 7. Here, I concentrate on another aspect of the Kuhnian view of science, its historicity.

THE KUHNIAN IMAGE OF SCIENCE

Together with notions of holism and underdetermination, revelation of the historicity of science had an important role in destabilising traditional notions of science and truth. Kuhn made a major contribution in this regard. Quine and Wittgenstein were philosophers, and they were interested in logic, philosophy of language and epistemology. Kuhn, by contrast, was a physicist and initiated into the scientific world-view. He was interested in the history of science and the way scientific theories develop. Not surprisingly, his thesis about incommensurability concerns scientific theories and is supported by examples drawn from the history of science, especially the history of physics. Kuhn criticises the way in which historians of science present the historical development of sciences. Famously, positivism was mainly concerned with analyses of the logical structures of scientific theories. Historians of science, in their turn, presented a continuous story of scientific development as movement toward the truth. Starting from the history of science and actual scientific practices, Kuhn maintains that the sciences are far from the positivistic picture of the world. He emphasised that neither confirmation nor falsification is the main concern of scientists. Neither is scientific development linear and cumulative; it is marked by recurrent disorder, ruptures and disruptions. These episodes of paradigm shift in science history that he terms scientific revolutions have a decisive role in science's development; they make the cumulative view of science meaningless, Kuhn thinks. In this regard, Kuhn was influenced by Ludwik Fleck. Though not a subject for this study, it has to be mentioned that Kuhn was anticipated by Fleck in nearly every concern. Indeed, Fleck can be presented as Kuhn's educator and forerunner. The extent of Fleck's influence on Kuhn is much more extensive than Quine's and Wittgenstein's and is such that one can claim that Kuhn's theory is a successful implementation, though using different material, of Fleck's theory.

Starting from the general structure of the scientific community, its social and cultural circumstances and preferences, Fleck concludes that these elements are more telling about scientific theories and the nature of science in general than a theoretical analysis of the logical structure of theories. Scientific theories are integrated parts of a larger context, a culture, and in order to be endowed with pedagogical value they have to respond to collective needs. Seen in this light, the textbook image of science is not the result of merely logical considerations; rather, it corresponds to certain social needs. Encountering this image of science, students of science are thus confronted with the totality of the dominant culture and its values.

Kuhn's view of science is based on the basic distinction between revolutionary and normal science. While revolutionary science signifies extraordinary episodes in the history of science, normal science refers to normal scientific activities. Normal scientific periods are periods of consensus upon paradigmatic science and educational procedures. During these periods, scientists concentrate on the articulation and development of the paradigm and science education is consequently subordinated to these needs. The paradigm provides education with conceptual schemes and students learn to apply these schemes to nature. The talent of each student or scientist, his/her success and failure are judged by his/her success or failure in learning to organise nature in paradigmatic conceptual schemes. Science, education and paradigm become institutionalised. As in all other institutions and systems, there are always elements of disturbance and destabilisation. In trying to impose their conceptual schemes on nature scientists daily encounter counterexamples, or anomalies, but they ignore them as not being serious scientific problems worth any investigation. If an anomaly is stubborn enough to get out of hand a crisis is imposed on the scientific community. During this period, scientists examine extraordinary research and implement new ways of solving old problems (Kuhn 1970: 78–85). A really deep crisis is finally resolved by a scientific revolution. Such a revolution means radical changes in the basic presuppositions of all scientific activities. A new paradigm, incommensurable with the previous one, resolves the problems that the old one was unable to. The science community shows its conservatism even in this case; the problem-ridden paradigm is abandoned if and only if there is an alternative paradigm available. As in the case of religious believers, scientists continue to use theories despite the evidence that refutes them. Opposing Popper, Kuhn claims that the logic of falsification is not at work in the rejection of paradigms; scientists do not test their enterprise continuously. A paradigm is not rejected on the basis of its consequences or as soon as empirical evidence opposes it. In addition to observational counterexamples, a more capable paradigm that allows for the existence of the enterprise is also necessary for a paradigm to be abandoned (Kuhn 1970: 70). Scientific revolutions are by definition tradition shattering, Kuhn argues, because the succeeding paradigms are incompatible with their predecessors. Each paradigm gives birth to new educational ends and procedures.

Kuhn's theory is helpful in explaining the current practice of science teaching. It is right in claiming that changes in educational paradigms do not happen according to a rational plan. Indeed, the rationale is constructed retrospectively. However, the extensive changes in science and the notion of education cannot be, contra Kuhn, explained only by reference to consensus among scientists themselves. Kuhn rightly emphasises the primacy of the dominant scientific paradigm in relation to educational style. However, he neglects the importance of social changes in relation to changes in science. Kuhn concentrates on a display of consensus and disagreement within the scientific community as if these changes take place independently of the frameworks of forms of life. According to Kuhn, scientific education becomes paradigm-based as soon as scientists reach consensus and a paradigm is established and problem solving becomes then the main scientific activity. This is not the whole story, however. As argued above, educational changes are complex processes and are to be seen in the wider context of social changes. Bybee and DeBoer show connections between changes in social circumstances and in the goals, form and content of education. The concentration of scientific education on problem solving, for instance, was as an educational response to industrialisation and urbanisation of society at the beginning of the last century (Bybee and DeBoer 1994: 358). During the Cold War "national security and the training of a technically competent military" was a main focus (Bybee and DeBoer 1994: 358). Nowadays, environmental issues like global warming, infectious diseases like aids and global communication are at the centre of scientific and educational concerns.

THE THESIS OF INCOMMENSURABILITY AND ITS CRITICS

The previous section discussed Kuhn's view regarding the relationships between science, paradigm and education. Although Kuhn's theory makes clear connections between scientific and educational paradigms, it is unable to show connections between social and educational changes. Kuhn is also unable to take a further step to create new notions of science and education. We have thus to take the step beyond Kuhn in order to create an adequate view of science as the basis of a new notion of education. Before going that far, in this section I would like to discuss some of Kuhn's critics in order to examine whether they can offer any help in this regard.

Due to its categorical rejection of shared meaning between different paradigms, Kuhnian relativism, it was argued, leads to lack of transcendence and to negative nihilism. Ever since its appearance, this theory has been opposed by a diverse array of philosophers and philosophical tendencies which defend the universality of truth and the objectivity of science. It has been contested by philosophers of science like Laudan and McMullin; they criticised Kuhn for not being able to present convincing arguments about his sweeping claims about scientific knowledge and the irrationality of scientific revolutions. They have opposed Kuhn in several basic regards. The holistic character of paradigms is one. The other is the importance of cultural values and background beliefs for science. His denying the notion of progress as getting closer and closer to the truth has also been criticised. Kuhn has mainly been attacked by those who defend different nuances of scientific realism. Contrary to Kuhn, these critics argue that scientific revolutions can be explained rationally. They try thus to implicitly or explicitly cure Kuhnian nihilism. The adequacy of these solutions will be discussed in the coming pages.

In order to refute the Kuhnian model of holistic paradigms, Laudan compares two models of scientific justification: the hierarchical model and the reticulation model (Laudan 1998a: 146–47). Any paradigm, Laudan explains, is a closed entity comprising three different levels. The factual level or conceptual framework is an account of entities that, according to each paradigm, populate the world. The methodological level determines rules for theory choice and justification. The axiological level, finally, is concerned with the goals and aims of science. Disagreement between scientists at each level is resolved by appeal to higher levels. A dispute at the factual level, for instance, is resolved by appeal to the methodological, and disputes at the methodological level by appeal to the axiological. In this model, there is a dead-end, since the axiological level is the highest one; if scientists are in disagreement about axiological matters, the aims and goals of science, there is no way out of the impasse. This model is, Laudan argues, hierarchical, top-down, linear, and involves a one-way justification of theories. According to Laudan, Kuhn's critique of rationality of science and his holism are flawed because they are based on this model, according to which the aims of science are subjective and arbitrary; some scientists may argue that the basic goal of science is to provide plausible but fallible explanations, while others may aim at adequacy or infallible knowledge, as in scientific realism. Since there is no higher level to resolve disagreements, there is no solution either. Laudan rejects this model by presenting a reticulational model, a model based on an anti-holistic view of paradigms and a non-linear conception of justification. He maintains that "scientific change is substantially more piecemeal than holistic" and though interrelated, changes at factual, methodological and axiological levels "do not come as an inseparable package" (Laudan 1998a: 150). In Laudan's reticulational model scientists do not choose or reject theories as a whole, as is the case with holism, which is defended by Kuhn and Quine; rather, they choose from among the individual elements and parts of a paradigm. More directly, scientists are actively engaged in paradigm transformation. In Laudan's model, scientists can remain in agreement about science's aims, while they can revise their methodological rules (rules about what kind of technique and instruments to use in experimentation). This model is, he argues, non-linear, two-way and down-top. In my opinion, although Laudan's model emphasises the active part played by scientists in the transformation of paradigms, it does not present new cognitive values different from the crisis-ridden ones criticised by Kuhn and others; it cannot cure Kuhnian nihilism. A major problem with Laudan's theory is that in theory scientists act within a single paradigm, that of science. As a result, rejection or acceptance of ideas is determined by a single paradigm; scientists are not able to negotiate with the scientific paradigm from a perspective outside science. Consequently, scientists are never able to look at their own enterprise and judge it from a perspective exterior to it; science remains its own judge. Besides, as will be argued later in this study, changes at one level of belief systems do not leave others untouched. Thus, his critique of holism is untenable.

Laudan's refutation of the holistic character of paradigm (paradigms as indivisible wholes), which means that changes at one level do not necessarily mean changes at the other levels, is shared by McMullin, who also defends the rationality of science. McMullin rejects Kuhn's instrumentalism—the idea that scientific theories are merely useful instruments that do not necessarily depict reality. He defends scientific realism or the adequacy thesis of truth. According to this thesis, theories are true by virtue of their relation to a theory-independent reality. Contrary to Kuhn, McMullin tries to establish a notion of truth. He assumes that values such as simplicity and fertility are indicators of truth rather than merely being valuable for their own sake. For McMullin, they are subordinated to goals like explanatory power and predictive accuracy. Thus, they are rational bases for preferring true theories and refusing false ones. McMullin adopts the Kuhnian notion of scientific revolution, but makes a distinction between shallow and deep revolutions. Whereas the former notion does not lead to changes in standards of science, the latter involves such changes. McMullin also rejects the Kuhnian distinction between normal and revolutionary science. The differences between these two genres of science are, McMullin argues, of degree rather than of kind. Contrary to Kuhn, to McMullin's mind incommensurable disagreements are common even within paradigms. According to McMullin, only true theories, those which correspond to a mind and theory-independent reality, are successful in gaining the advocacy of the scientific community. This is to contest the importance of cultures for science. Laudan also shares the refutation of the importance of contextual values and cultural contexts for theory choices.

McMullin is probably right in one aspect of his critique of Kuhn; indeed, as McMullin says, Kuhn "maintains the rational character of theory choice" (McMullin 1998: 135). In fact, Kuhn singles out epistemic values such as simplicity and accuracy as common traits of all paradigms. McMullin appeals to this Kuhnian presupposition in criticising him for being essentialist. From this, he argues the inevitability of scientific realism. Although his criticism of Kuhn reveals an important shortcoming of the incommensurability thesis, McMullin's return to scientific realism and its associated theory of knowledge generates more problems than solutions. To take this theory seriously is to believe in a final ground of knowledge independent of culture and cultural values. But, as Nietzsche and Wittgenstein have shown, there is not such a natural ground. We create it time and again in order to frame our relationships with the world. The problem is not paradigms as such; paradigms are really indispensable. We need in any case a framework within which we organise our relations to the world and to each other. The problem lies, rather, in making paradigms incommensurable and independent of human agents. Thus, McMullin cannot explain the problem of paradigms, and his theory is as problematic as Kuhn's.

True, Kuhn's essentialism leads to the thesis of incommensurability. A return to realism also does the same. It shares an essentialist notion of meaning with the thesis of incommensurability. By so doing, it takes the discourse back to a pre-Kuhnian epoch. And this is to grant incommensurability a rationale. Indeed, the incommensurability thesis is a reaction against realism's demands on the univocity of human communication and uniqueness of meaning. By questioning realism Kuhn opens new possibilities for thought. The problem is his inability to pursue further the logic of questioning in a proper way. A critique of Kuhn has to have its starting point in a post-Kuhnian era rather than a pre-Kuhnian one; it has to take a step beyond Kuhn.

Laudan's indiscriminate refutation of the importance of cultural values for science is also problematic. According to this view, there is no difference between cultural values; they are all harmful for the growth of knowledge. However, a satisfactory solution to the problem of value has, to adequately explain differences between different cultures and cultural values. Unable to explain the important issue of relations between science and culture, Laudan's theory is unable to explain connections between science, education and context in a satisfactory way.

In order to do this, we need new analytical tools and a new view of science and objectivity. Such a view goes far beyond Kuhn and his critics mentioned above. I will return to these issues in Chapters 4 and 5. Here, I concentrate on the consequences of the Kuhnian view of science for individuals.

THE INEVITABILITY OF NIHILISM

As argued in the previous section, neither Kuhn nor his critics offer an account of science that can go beyond nihilism. Given the image of science they present, nihilism becomes inevitable.

A first point to be made in this connection is that although questioning of the established notion of science is necessary, we cannot endorse it indiscriminately. A distinction has to be made between two kinds of questioning. Genealogically considered, there are constructive and destructive ways of questioning, each with different practical implications. The Kuhnian questioning of science is destructive, since it creates confusion about science instead of clarity. He rightly questions traditional accounts of scientific knowledge, but he does not destroy in order to construct. As a result, he is unable to take on the task of providing the scientific community with tools to do science in a proper way. By stopping at the stage of negating the old values, Kuhn paves the way for nihilism; he negates the old notion of truth without replacing it with a new one. As a result, he perpetuates a state of non-belief, indifference and lack of care about the notion of truth. Nihilism becomes then the inevitable outcome. In addition, considering paradigms as entities independent of individuals, whereby the possibility of resistance is nil, prepares the ground for alienation, the basis of nihilism.

A liberating notion of science goes beyond nihilism. For such a notion of science, truth matters. It overcomes nihilistic indifference to truth and is committed to it. It is able to do so because it is based on a creative frame of mind; it uses nihilism itself against nihilism. Indeed, this is the proper way of dealing with the problem of nihilism, since nihilism cannot be overcome once and for all. In fact, nihilism is a recurring state of mind. We are never immune to crises of values, but we can use them as liberating cognitive forces to create new values time and again. As will be seen, such an ability demands a plurality of perspectives on the world, strong individuals as well as an inclusive mode of thought.

A solution to the problem of nihilism has to consider the issue in a wider context than scientific discourse. Nihilism, as discussed here, is rooted in reified systems of scientific knowledge. Hence, it cannot be overcome scientifically. It demands aesthetic and philosophical engagement. By providing perspectives outside science, philosophy and art can shed light on the nature of nihilism and function as liberating forces. On the other hand, nihilism has to be considered against a background of alienation; this is to consider nihilism in a wider context than nihilism itself. By so doing, we become engaged with alienating cognitive and social structures. Nihilism is indeed a kind of consciousness. It emerges as a result of the alienated individual becoming aware of his/her alienation. By so doing, he/she negates alienating knowledge systems and enters a nihilistic state of mind. This means not only that alienation precedes nihilism, but also that nihilism can offer a way out of both problems. For the purpose of this section, alienation amounts not only to social disorientations, but also to lack of identification with one's own knowledge. Nihilistic awareness can become a source of re-orientation through enabling one to reclaim one's own knowledge and values. This means that nihilistic awareness is a stage in the development of the alienated individual, in which she/he is in a position to re-orientate.

One can be alienated without necessarily becoming aware of her/his alienation, and thereby never enter the stage of nihilism. Using a Marxian terminology, we can call this mode of thought false consciousness or ideology. However, my interest is less in this kind of alienation than in one which develops into nihilism. This is mainly because alienation and nihilism are discussed against a background of education. Education, as used in this study, is a liberating process. It liberates through highlighting the active part of the individual in cognition; the individual then identifies with her/his own knowledge. As such education is a process of self-consciousness, it sheds light on alienating cognitive systems. Properly understood, education helps us to re-orientate by showing us a hopeful horizon of life. Through enabling the individual to reinterpret his/her environment, education not only stimulates individual creative resources, but also creates a sense of belonging to the world and to culture. The individual and the cultural thus meet in the notion of education. Individuality is affirmed together with a sense of belonging to the community. Thus, individualism does not develop into egoism. Neither does collective belonging become oppressive and authoritarian. New kinds of knowledge and meaning and new beliefs are created. This process is never-ending and perpetual. Through this process the individual becomes at one with his/her knowledge, actions and values.

He/she lives in his/her own world and together with others, without one excluding the other; this is an inclusive mode of being in the world.

To my knowledge, writers mostly study alienation and nihilism separately. As a result, connections between the two remain masked. Solutions based on this kind of interpretation are thus one-sided and inadequate.

Without alienation, there will be no nihilism. The individual experiences nihilism as soon as she/he becomes aware of the fact that so-called objective values which dominate her/his mind have no objective ground outside human needs. In other words, there have to be actual alienating cognitive orders for nihilism to emerge. These configurations of knowledge are either historical, like Socratism, Cartesianism, Puritanism and positivism, which continue to influence the present, or they belong to a contemporary form of life, like scientific education. Through becoming aware of the nature of these phenomena and negating them, the individual gains nihilistic consciousness. My contention is that human resources released by this nihilistic insight can stimulate human creative resources and liberate humanity from the hold of alienation. But this is not the only outcome. Nihilism can either lead to despair and passivity, whereby the individual is paralysed and unable to replace the crisis-ridden values with new ones, or it can stimulate creative forces within the individual and lead to liberation. Thus, while alienation enslaves, nihilism can function as a liberating force. My suggestion is that we, through unmasking connections between alienation and nihilism and making education a transformative process, can enable the individual to take control of his/her life and circumstances instead of being dominated by them; this is freedom or, as Nietzsche would say, a master mode of living. Being mastered by circumstances is to be oppressed; it is manner of being enslaved.

Alienation as it is used here belongs to modernity. It is a result of the systematization, schematisation and rationalisation of education, knowledge and human life. As a result, human knowledge and relations became reified. Indeed, these tendencies lay down the foundation on which alienation rests. As such, alienation is then intrinsic to modernity. The same can be said of nihilism, since it is based on the notion of alienation. Nihilism is a cognitive crisis originating in a thoroughgoing and one-sided emphasis on scientific culture as the total framework of human activities. Seen in historical perspective, by negating alienation nihilism negates modernity.

As we observed, the Enlightenment showed opposition to authorities external to humanity. By so doing, it destabilised the stable ground of authority based on sources outside the human world; authority became a power struggle instead of being naturally given or sanctioned by "the divine". This action was a crucial step toward liberation. But we were not able to enjoy the full consequences of this fatal deed because the modern individual was still educated in reified knowledge systems; scientific knowledge was still verified through reference to an absolute reality. Positivism replaced "the divine" with what was "the case". Although different in kind, the function of these notions was, however, the same; humanity was not able to do science without reference to metaphysical sources of authority. Had we done this, our cognitive actions would have become at one with our own nature, released from alienation and nihilism. The death of God, as Nietzsche termed the event, could mean the collapse of the hierarchic order of God, Reason and Reality. Destroying this hierarchy, however, is not liberating per se. On the contrary, if this destruction leads to lack of care about truth and to a sense of meaninglessness, it can function as a source of nihilism. A world orbiting around transcendental sources of authority provided a horizon of life against which everything received its distinct meaning and became understandable. By taking away this axis without replacing it with a new one, modern culture created a world without transcendence that was, at the same time, dependent on transcendence. Consequently, humanity is constantly vulnerable to crises of consciousness. Humanity can take a step beyond the boundaries of traditional thought by realising the ever-changing nature of the world and knowledge without there being a natural and stable point of reference. Knowledge production activities become, then, open processes in perpetual interaction with their environment.

By relating alienation to systematization and rationalisation of knowledge systems intrinsic to modern rationality, and nihilism to alienation, we can discern a genealogical continuity that increases our understanding of phenomena at work in the present. By so doing, we create a frame of mind which enables us to see events in an adequate context. In the previous chapter, I claimed that current systematization of science and education are rooted in certain puritan ideas. If we take the Nietzschean connection between nihilism and theoretical reason seriously, the contextual emergence of nihilism goes back to Socrates' dialectic and his overestimation of knowledge through definition or theoretical knowledge. Truth became, then, a general and abstract notion disconnected from the human world. Once this occurred, it was easy to separate the subject from the object, deeds from the doer, knowledge from the knower, and so on. On this reading, the Platonic heritage reached modern Europe through Christianity; it continues to influence us through tendencies like positivism. Seen in this light, nihilism has followed Western culture over two millennia. However, it has to be added that nihilism took on gigantic dimensions and has become everybody's problem in the modern age. Education has played a central part in this connection.

SCIENTIFIC EDUCATION AND NIHILISM

As I mentioned above, faith in abstract knowledge has been transferred to later generations despite shifts in educational paradigms. This means that this faith can take different shapes. Its function has been the same, however; it relates human knowledge to fantastic or transcendental sources like "the divine" or a context-independent reality. By so doing, it creates indifference to our responsibility for our knowledge, its kind and quality. It also causes indifference to our responsibility for what we have become, what we say and do.[1] Freedom from nihilism, in contrast, is characterised by clear connections between the kind of person we have become and our kind of knowledge; it takes our responsibility for our knowledge and for what we do and say seriously without becoming rigid. It also unmasks the active part of the knower in the process of knowledge without becoming uncaring.

In addition to the rational systematization of knowledge, the positivistic notion of science, the basis of scientific education, subjugated the individual to what is "the case". Being influenced by this notion of science, scientific education has been faithful to the idea of correspondence between thoughts and a context-independent reality. Having this starting point, it separates knowledge from the person; knowledge is related to what is the case. All the person can do is discover pre-given facts.

This is, however, not the whole story. As I discussed in Chapter 2, scientific education emerged as a result of alliances between economic and religious powers whose common concern was the rational organisation of science and society for economic interests. However, this education formally presents disinterested knowledge as its cardinal aim. One way to come to terms with the problem of scientific education is to not take it for what it claims to be; rather, we have to penetrate beneath its claims and unmask their true nature. An analysis of the content, goals and procedures of scientific education reveals that—its claims notwithstanding—its concern is not objective knowledge; rather, it is a function of the interests of the scientific community and historical needs of forms of life. Interdependencies between economic interests and scientific education are not limited to this education. The same can be said of scientific education today. A look at the aims of education in the United States, as an exemplary case, shows that scientific education is concerned with issues like "national security, which includes the development of a strong, technically able military, an internationally competitive work force" (Bybee and DeBoer 1994: 357). The same can be said of scientific education worldwide. None of these aims has to do with eternal truths. Indeed, other educational aims like "personal development, . . . social efficiency" and "the development of science itself" (Bybee and DeBoer 1994: 360) are subordinated to national economic and military needs, since the cardinal aim of scientific education is to train labour power to work for these needs. Thus, as will be seen in the next chapter, it is a condition of the objectivity of science to focus on cultural values instead of denying their importance for education and knowledge acquisition. An education with the abovementioned aim cannot but lead to nihilism, since individuals cannot identify themselves with it.

SCIENTIFIC EDUCATION AND TRUTH

To my mind, when the horizon of humanity and its educational ideals are reduced to military ability and economic competitiveness, to include the notion of truth in educational discourse is liberating; it is to move away from nihilism. One may object that the notion of truth is already included in the discourse of scientific education. I postpone a thorough discussion of what relationships between truth and education should be until Chapter 10. Here, I focus on the fact that the current relationship between the two functions as a source of alienation and nihilism. Let us focus on the characteristics of the current notion of truth. For the purpose of this section, I will consider the notion of truth in the context of our contemporary educational paradigm. Seen in this light, the educational notion of truth is scientific, dogmatic and exclusive; it is based on the single perspective of science and excludes perspectives of art and philosophy. It imposes its own dogmas on everybody. This is indeed the meaning of being universal in a traditional way, the global domination of a single perspective. This can be said of scientific education and its related notion of truth, since they are based on acquiring scientific knowledge, learning its methodology and applying science in all arenas of social life (Bybee and DeBoer 1996: 357).

Another characteristic of the current educational notion of truth is authoritarianism. Students are not in a position to be critical of the quality of life and thought that they are subject to. Neither are they in a position to be critical of their teachers and textbooks. Indeed, there is a power imbalance embedded in scientific education. Fleck sees analogies between scientific initiation, which is the prerequisite of entrance into the scientific community, and religious and mystical initiations; the motives and mechanisms behind them are the same. In science as in religion the novice must go through an apprenticeship period during which she/he is subject to a purely dogmatic transfer of knowledge (Fleck 1979: 96). Though working through much more sophisticated mechanisms, the influence of scientific textbooks can be compared with that of holy books. Rather than being subject to critical consideration, science education is an authoritative initiation that enables the older members of the community to exert power over novices. The comprehensiveness of the system of public knowledge makes any rational choice on the part of novices meaningless, the Fleckian line of argumentation goes.

The situation described above destroys students' individuality and leads inevitably to conformity. Indeed, mass education based on the rational organisation of education has already demonstrated cases of the "brute predominance of . . . collectives" and "blind identification with the collective", as Adorno observes (1998: 197). Reflecting on behavioural patterns behind the Holocaust, Adorno sees "people who blindly slot themselves into collectives" and "make themselves into something like inert material, extinguish themselves as self-determined beings" (198). He sees this as the basis of brutal and loveless behavioural patterns. The main concern of such a human type is efficiency and a desire to get things done, regardless of their substance. As Adorno observes, this human type is characterised by a "reified consciousness" (198) because he/she assimilates himself/herself and others to things.

No doubt, the effective and instrumental use of human beings in modern societies is impossible without the aid of modern education. Initiation into the scientific community means first and foremost an unconditional acceptance of its theoretical assumptions and practical procedures, its single perspective on the world. A typical student of science accepts the paradigm in its totality, as in a package deal without any negotiation. It means that she/he becomes initiated into a complex whole of ontological, epistemological and methodological issues and presuppositions. To be educated within a paradigm is to constitute the world in accordance with dictums of that particular paradigm. Education equips the individual with "the right answer" to the questions posed by the paradigm. The fact that the educational style is a function of the dominant paradigm means that the scientific paradigm is a framework for standard educational issues, methods and shared goals. There is no place for self-determination, love or individuality, but only for general rules and concepts that are insensitive to individual contexts.

Kuhn's studies reveal the exclusive logic at work in paradigm science and concomitant educational procedures. As will be shown in Chapter 8, the prevailing paradigm not only determines the general cultural climate of an age but also functions as a model educator. It presents itself as the single legitimate source of interpretation and excludes all other interpretations; it determines norms, rules and certainties.

Characteristics ascribed to scientific education and its related notion of truth remind us of the Nietzschean notion of the ascetic ideal, the basis of nihilism. Indeed, in *On the Genealogy of Morals*, Nietzsche tells us that science is the *"most recent and most refined form"* of this ideal (GM III, 23). It has to be mentioned that similarities between science and the ascetic ideal are about both the quality and style of thought; they are both exclusive. Nietzsche writes of the ascetic ideal: "it relentlessly interprets periods, peoples, men in terms of" its own goal. Consequently, "it allows no other interpretation, no other goal, it reproaches, negates, affirms exclusively with reference to *its* interpretation" (GM III, 23). Since science is the content and the form of current education, similar mechanisms are at work in the current practices of education. They share an exclusive and authoritarian notion of knowledge; their categories of consciousness are rigid and dogmatic. They mask actual states of affairs by reference to transcendental truths.

Much has happened since Nietzsche. Although not totally free from its positivistic heritage, science has moved away from positivism. Theoretically, it is known that the positivistic image of science has been illusory. Tendencies like constructivism affirm interpretive procedures in science.

However, constructivism is limited to the discourse of science and science teaching. Mitzes, Wandersee and Novak (1997) and J. Nussbaum (1997), for instance, propose that science teaching could benefit by combining three areas of research: research on students' misconceptions, developments in cognitive psychology and developments in the history and philosophy of science (J. Nussbaum 1997: 166). At nearly every point they are similar to Kuhn and Fleck. Thus what has been said about the Kuhnian view of science and education can also be said about these writers' view of science. As discussed above, the Kuhnian critique of science has led to nihilism instead of liberation. I tried to spell out some of reasons behind this process. Kuhn, as argued earlier, remained within the horizon of science. Thus his critique of science is scientific; science is seen from the perspective of science. As such, the Kuhnian critique of the traditional notion of science is just another scientific discourse about science, unable to present new principles of thought. As a result, science preserves its basic principles like value-neutrality and its directedness toward abstract truths and definitions, which function as sources of nihilism. Faithful to the Platonic image of knowledge, science has strengthened its alliance with mathematics and the calculability of the world. The current image of science is indeed "the union of science, mathematics and technology that forms the scientific endeavour" (AAAS 1989: 25). In fact, in our age the "world is shaped by science and technology" (11). As things are now, art and philosophy are either marginalised or used in the service of science. Being the single perspective on the world, science reduces the world to mathematical calculability and technological manipulability. Such a view of the world is a source of nihilism, since we sooner or later become aware of the world not being the same as the image presented by science.

To conclude, the current notion of educational truth is itself a part of the problem to be solved, since it is ascetic. It shares some basic principles of thought with the ascetic ideal; both of them are based on disinterested knowledge and a supposedly objective reality. The ascetic ideal is the ideal of priests. Obviously, the scholar is a this-worldly ascetic type; she/he manifests, however, just another form of asceticism as she/he shifts the focus from knowledge as related to cultural contexts to disinterested theoretical knowledge.

NIHILISM AND HUMAN NATURE

Genealogical analysis contributes to a growing understanding of operating knowledge systems not only by studying them within their context of emergence, but also by examining their development. In so doing, it brings insight to these systems and the consequences of our being committed to them; it shows that the prolonged hold of these systems of knowledge upon us is decisive for who we are.

Genealogical studies reveal that although characterised by paradigm shifts, the principal ideas of scientific education are deeply rooted in the history of ideas. In Chapter 2, we observed how cultural ideas such as asceticism, predestination and economic rationality conferred educational and cognitive importance. We also observed that fondness for method is a basic trait of the scientific thought style and its concomitant notion of education. Methodologically, scientific education is based on persistent repetitive behavioural patterns. It is important to say some words about the effects of these characteristics of science on us.

Aristotle's view of human nature holds a clue to understanding the relationship between human nature, scientific education and nihilism. He tells us that habits become a matter of human nature through prolonged repetition. Such a view of human nature teaches us two interrelated points: First, it is historical. Second, the boundaries between first nature and second nature are not as sharp as they might seem. Famously, Aristotle makes a distinction between features that are intrinsic to humanity, our so-called first nature, and features that are imposed on or external to us, but which in the long run become parts of our behaviour, our so-called second nature. Speech, for instance, is, intrinsic to humanity, while being athletic or otherwise is external.

The historicity of human nature becomes clearer if we consider it in the light of Marx's view of human nature, namely, his considering our nature as identical with our labour. We also see labour as human creativity in general. This view not only demystifies human nature, it also refers to its being changeable. This means that there is no fixed and eternal human essence. In this regard, I also draw on Nietzsche. Regarding second nature as related to the first, he writes, in *The Utility and Liability of History*, that "even the first nature was once a second nature and that every victorious second nature will become a first nature" (ULH, 3). In other words, what was at one time an external element becomes internal, or a first nature, at another time. As second nature encompasses habits that in the first place are not intrinsic to humanity, habits that can become first nature can be imposed patterns of behaviour. When we are initiated into a paradigm or belief system from childhood it seems natural to us.

Nowadays we grow up with science. Science educators consider the kindergarten years to be the ideal time to begin this education (Härnqvist and Burgen 1997: 5). Indeed, cognitive science studies show that "students construct explanations at very early ages" (Duschl 1994: 460). The same studies show that in doing this they are guided by dominating epistemological models. Also, studies in cognitive psychology show the importance of "Gestalt psychology" and "the role of general schemata in organizing and constructing the meaning of information" (J. Nussbaum 1997: 166). This is to emphasise the holistic character of meaning production by children. Together, these points show that children from an early age are led into a scientific paradigm. They are shaped by accepted axiological and methodological practices into a complex whole. Through these mechanisms and in a world shaped by science and technology, scientific behaviour becomes natural. On the other hand, as mentioned, given the conditions of scientific education, nihilism is inevitable.

Genealogically analysed, nihilism has become the nature of Western man, because patterns of behaviour have been repeated for a long time. A behaviour that happens once or twice has no significance, but if it is repeated time and again and across generations, it becomes history. As the basic principle of scientific methodology, repeatability goes along with truth as being reduced to general and abstract knowledge. Together they suppress personal engagement and subdue individual creativity to general repeatable rules. As a result, the world takes shape in accordance with repeatable scientific patterns of behaviour and general rules.

"Cognition", Fleck writes, "modifies the knower so as to adapt him harmoniously to his acquired knowledge" (1979: 86). Analogously, we can say that patterns of deeds modify the doer so as to adapt him harmoniously to his acquired patterns of behaviour. Seen in this light, in modern societies the human race becomes scientific, cognitively as well as practically. As such, we become dependent on changes in the quality of science. Scientific rules, patterns of behaviour, values, skills and habits of mind, as Kuhn and Wittgenstein show, are paradigm-based. Since paradigms are subject to change and recurring crises of value, they make us vulnerable to nihilism. If we suddenly become aware of the scientific-technological world not being as we perceived it, this may lead to distress if we are not aware of the historicity of knowledge. Hence, education should be aimed at changes in human nature, where humanity is not reduced to scientific man.

THE UNITY OF DEEDS AND DOER

Besides methodological repeatability, the distinction between the subject and the object is a basic principle of the canonical notion of science. This Cartesian dichotomy leads to separation between the individual and his/her knowledge. As argued earlier, this separation functions as a source of alienation. As will be argued in Chapter 4, Schopenhauer tries to bridge the gap between the subject and the object. Nietzsche does the same for the gap between the doer and deeds. Unifying the subject and the object and doers and deeds is a presupposition of our liberation from alienation and nihilism. If by setting knowledge against the individual, separation between the subject and the object leads to alienation, separation between deeds and the doer sets our actions against ourselves as alien forces. If the former relates human knowledge to transcendental sources of legitimacy, the latter relates human actions to authorities external to us. Consequently, the doer does not act from his/her innermost drive. Human actions then become reactions; the doer reacts to the external authorities' demands. As a result, our actions become imposed, since they satisfy needs outside themselves. Acting from innermost forces or love, by contrast, means the unity of human beings and their actions. This means that any individual is at one with his/her actions or work, as Marx would put it.

In my view, education involves a level of personification of knowledge on the part of learners. Properly understood, they are to internalise knowledge in a personal way and identify themselves with their knowledge. Such a knowledge does not stay at an abstract level. It leads rather to action. An educated person in this sense acquires a way of life and conduct of her/his own through internalising knowledge and acting accordingly. Seen in this light, not only what we do, but also how we do things becomes important. While "what" refers to people being able to do things, "how" refers to a specific quality of behaviour. Bringing together Schopenhauer's view of unity of subject and object, Nietzsche's view that man is not only an artist by nature but is one with his actions and deeds and Marx's view that human nature is based in our labour or our ability to create, not only can we argue that unsurpassable lines between the subject and the object, the doer and deeds are artificial, but also we can propose an education that enables any individual to manifest human creativity in his/her own way. Education becomes then an open-ended and transformative process of self-formation and re-formation rather than being aimed at fixed and pre-given aims and a fixed image of the individual.

Considering objectivity as the externalisation of us in our cognitive deeds means, on the one hand, that these activities become external and alien existences. On the other hand, they begin to confront us as sovereign and alien forces. As a result, we cannot identify ourselves with or confirm ourselves in our cognitive deeds. We have, rather, to deny ourselves; we are ourselves when we are not engaged in cognitive activities. To separate our identity from our activities and knowledge is to reify them. In reality, we are not formed and fixed first and act in this or that manner subsequently; rather, our identity takes its distinct form while we act and experience this action, identities are expressions for actions and experience of actions, of different ways of acting and acquiring knowledge. Formulated differently, we become aware of our identity, who and what we are, while we act. This means that our identity is not formed once and for all; rather, it is in the process of metamorphosis, acting through changes and changing through actions. The heroic picture of the acting and fixed subject as the origin and organiser of actions created by Descartes gives us a misleading image of the way humanity is and acts. Human life is indeed the experience of an unfolding unity of action and knowledge through and in time. The awareness and experience of this unfolding is at the bottom of the process of our becoming self-conscious beings. Indeed, to become engaged in the question of which was first, deeds or the doer, entangles us in artificial problems. We are at one with our activities, our labour, our knowledge, our view of the world and our view of ourselves. To lose sight of this unity leads us into alienation and deep intellectual and mental crises.

One source of separation between deeds and the doer is the traditional causal bond between the notion of will and our deeds. To call into question this bond between intentions and deeds, as Nietzsche, following Hume, does, is to overcome the metaphysical separation between doers and deeds, the subject and the object. It is also the basic step toward a questioning of the relation between intentions and absolute truth. We cannot reach truth by simply intending or willing it. On the contrary, this intention becomes an intention to nothingness, since truth in its traditional formal vein is beyond our reach. Seen in this light, the will to abstract and universal truth is the tyranny of the will regardless of human limitations and abilities, since it puts an impossible demand on humanity. Indeed, going beyond human possibilities means a denial of life as the horizon of human possibilities. Seen from the Aristotelian perspective, humanity is always a possibility. To actualise each possibility means to reach a higher level of possibility. The chain of possibilities, in other words, never ends and an absolute consummation of possibilities can never be reached. Against the background of this notion of life and will, we can, following Nietzsche, call into question conceptions like absolute free will, absolute truth and transcendence. We cannot become whatever we wish or reach whatever we desire. Indeed, we can claim that whatever is within human reach is a possibility by definition and humanity can never transcend the domain of possibility. The will to the absolute becomes then a nihilistic will to nothingness. A will to nothing or nothingness is the ground of nihilism. Such nothingness or void is the notion of correspondence between thoughts and the world of objects. As there is no correspondence between scientific ideas and objects independent of the process of knowledge, the will to truth based on it is a will to a void, to a non-existing relationship. Domination of such truths over knowledge produces and reproduces nihilism again and again; it is an intrinsic trait of the drive to pure knowledge. And to base education on this ground makes us vulnerable to nihilism.

To put it more clearly, this study does not try to resolve the problem of nihilism once and for all. Indeed, we can never be immune to the danger of nihilism. Alienation, the origin of nihilism, is based on conditions of human labour; it is a result of our ability to create objects distinct from ourselves. The important point is whether we are slaves of our own productions or can master them. Correspondingly, we can either be liberated or alienated. We cannot resolve the problem of nihilism once and for all; it will be with us and within us, overcoming it is thus perpetual. This study tries to suggest ways of overcoming the current form of nihilism.

To overcome current nihilism is an educative process of self-overcoming and self-formation. Through this process we become trained in a way of understanding and acting that provides us with mastery over the productions of our mental and physical creative forces. A renewed education takes the interdependencies between knowledge and the knower seriously. This means that good science demands a certain type of humanity and vice versa. Thus, education cannot simply concentrate on either knowledge or the knower. It cannot neglect concerns about the kind and character of relationships between the two. It takes on the challenge of creating a new type of knowledge, a new type of knowers and new relationships between them. Indeed, these are different aspects of the same process.

4 Inclusive Notions of Science and Objectivity

So far I have criticised the prevailing notions of science, truth, scientific education and related phenomena. I have also discussed critics of these notions and their inadequacies regarding solutions to the problems of alienation and nihilism. Applying the logic of this study to itself, this critique is nihilistic; it is destructive. This negative nihilism has to be followed by an active one in which through creating new meaning and significance we overcome negative or reactive nihilism. This educational task will be discussed in the coming chapters.

If the positivistic account of science paves the way for alienation and the Kuhnian one leads into nihilism, this new notion of science has to show a way out of these problems. A first step in this regard is to find the sources of the problem of science. This leads us to the notion of objectivity; this notion is the basis of meaning creating activities as well as of connections between science, alienation and nihilism. To reinterpret this notion becomes, then, a main task. Starting from this point, we also need to revise other basic notions like knowledge, individual, rationality and truth. These have to be seen as interconnected components of the same process. In so doing, we pave the way for a new notion of education.

Post-Kuhnian science studies are right in destabilising the traditional view of science. They also are right in assuming science as one cultural activity among many. In this regard, we can indeed use the Wittgensteinian notion of family resemblance to identify science. Seen in this light, science has no fixed essence. There are family resemblances between different cultural activities. This means that there are similarities that can be added to or deleted from a cluster of likelihoods. An activity has to satisfy a number of characteristics, not necessarily all of them, to be identified as science. Likewise, cultural activities outside science can satisfy a number of these characteristics without for that sake becoming science. These characteristics are not permanent, but contextual and historical. Thus boundaries between science and non-science are not always unsurpassable. These merits of post-Kuhnian science studies aside, they are unable to identify the source of the problem of science and scientific education.

THE SOURCES OF THE PROBLEM OF SCIENCE

We can thus argue that the main reason why Kuhn's solution to the problem of science is insufficient is his not identifying the problem properly. As a result, he searches for solutions in the wrong place. He identifies the source of the problem in the paradigm-dependency of science. Since there is no science without paradigms, he denies objectivity as such and throws out the baby with the bathwater. As the Kuhnian solution to the problem of science is itself a source of nihilism, it becomes itself a part of the problem to be solved. In order to identify the problem properly and find its proper solution, we need to follow the development of the critical consciousness of the nature of science from Descartes to Nietzsche. Once this is done, we can identify problems and evaluate suggested solutions by taking into consideration their practical educational implications.

Descartes' view of science was discussed in Chapter 2. His epistemic dualism and the dichotomy between the subject and the object were presented as sources of the problem. An important but neglected point in the context of this study is that Descartes indeed emphasised the role played by the individual subject in cognition; the Cartesian I or ego functions as a source of coherence. Descartes' irreconcilable dualism between the subject and the object, between the material world and our ideas about the objects in that world has its roots in his insistence on the certainty of his own self's innate rational capacity. Although Descartes believed that the rational subject, or I, perceives the material world, he emphasised that in the last analysis what I perceive is my own innate idea of objects. These objects may or may not exist in the material or physical world. He emphasised the inborn capacity of the subject by declaring that "the human mind has within it a sort of spark of the divine, in which the first seeds of useful ways of thinking are sown" (Descartes 1988: 4). What brings in an external source of legitimacy is his basing his philosophy on the certainty of one's individual consciousness. For this task, he trusts only a God's eye point of view. It is "the divine" that protects us against scepticism and relativism and guarantees the objectivity of thoughts. By concentrating on the subject's capacity for attaining knowledge of the external world, philosophy in Descartes' hands became epistemology, a philosophical discourse about science.

KANT'S COPERNICAN REVOLUTION IN METAPHYSICS

Although Descartes was an influential defender of the notion of objectivity and was strictly dualistic in the philosophy of knowledge, we found some indications in Cartesian philosophy of the active role of the subject in cognitive practices. Seen in this light, the subject is not a passive mirror of the external world. In Kant, this topic receives clearer contours.

In Kantian philosophy, two lines of development meet and merge. One is the Cartesian line of the certainty of empirical science. This style of thought counters speculative philosophy's promising true knowledge of a real world. It champions the notion of verifiability (or falsifiability, as Popper would put it). The other, also based on empiricism, is the sceptical line of Hume, who questioned the legitimacy of all scientific as well as philosophical claims for pure knowledge. The precondition for all science, Humian scepticism claims, is categories (causality, for instance), which themselves are not and cannot be empirically justified. Hume functioned as Kant's educator. Kant was awakened from his "dogmatic slumber" or rationalistic optimism by Hume, as Kant himself puts it. This Kantian "dogmatic slumber" refers to his faith in rationalistic philosophy and its claim of being able to attain objective or pure knowledge of the world through rational principles of thought. This conception of knowledge was based on the old presupposition that the world itself is reasonable and referred to as *logos*. The other side of this coin was the presupposition that humanity is able to represent the reason of being by thinking referred to as *nous*. In the tradition of Newtonian science depicting the "given" was considered the fundamental activity of knowledge. Thus, agreement or correspondence between understanding and things became the central assumption of all objective or true knowledge. The possibility of knowledge was the core of Kantian philosophy. He did not dispute pure knowledge, as claimed by Cartesian philosophy, but attempted to understand how this knowledge is possible. He wanted to educate humanity in a critical mode of understanding turned against rationalism and empiricism. Against the Cartesian rationalism, Kant argued that knowledge is impossible without experience. He also disputed empiricism by arguing that knowledge is also impossible if there is only experience. There has to be, Kant argued, a cognitive union between *a priori* elements of thought and *a posteriori* experience to give rise to true knowledge. Philosophy should show how this union occurs and is possible. "How are synthetic a priori judgements possible?" is, famously, the fundamental question in Kant's philosophy, by which he attempted to lay down the basic condition of human knowledge. Kant's answer to this question was also a mid point between rationalism and empiricism; without the categories of understanding and forms of intuitions there cannot be any knowledge or any reality at all. By this claim Kant made "objective" reality dependent on "subjective" elements of thought. He argued that knowledge is possible because our sensations are formed by intuition, space and time, which themselves are not sensations but forms of our mind. On the other hand, these structured forms comply with categories, which are not empirically justified.

In place of the old conception of knowledge, Kant imposed, in *Critique of Pure Reason*, the critical principle that "reason has insight only into that which it produces after a plan of its own" (CPR B xiii). In other words, he replaced "depicting" reality by "creating" it as the fundamental activity of our reason. The most interesting aspect of Kant's epistemology, in this context, lies in his emphasis on the structure of questioning as the possibility of secure science of nature rather than "factual" and objective observation. He maintains that reason must approach nature "not in the capacity of a pupil who lets the teacher tell him whatever the teacher wants, but in capacity of an appointed judge who compels the witnesses to answer the questions that he puts them" (CPR B xiii). This art of questioning is in sheer contrast to traditional claims about scientific explanations, predictions and discoveries as being true about reality. To put it differently, Kant reversed the idea that the knower conforms to reality. Quite the contrary, it is reality that conforms to the knower and just because of that it becomes experienced and known reality. The reverse will dissolve humanity in the unknown. To know, in strictly a Kantian way of speaking, is to schematise reality or impose a self-invented instinctive schema upon chaos. Kant's philosophical Copernican revolution alludes to his shift of focus from the external world to humanity and his cognitive faculties, from knowing the *logos* of the world to the moral activity of self-legislative universal law. Despite its radicalism the Kantian critical project retained the Platonic two-world model. The Kantian theory of knowledge is based on the dichotomy between two kinds of reality; the reality we experience is always a reality for the knower. It is known by a special kind of animated being with a special physiological capacity for knowledge. It is reality as it appears to us, so-called *phenomenal* reality, not reality as it is or *noumenal* reality. *Noumenal* reality is a reality without the knower; though it is the ground of our knowledge it remains unknown to humanity because knowledge of reality as it is, or things in themselves, is unattainable.

A useful point in this context is Kant's emphasis on the important role played by the imagination in the interpretation as well as constitution of experience. The role of the imagination in Kant's philosophy coincides with my longstanding interest in the imagination and interpretation; it will prove extremely useful in constructing a new image of science based on interpretation as the main cognitive activity. It is by the power of the imagination that we can overcome the limitations of experience. The main function of interpretation is to manage the limits associated with our discursive understanding. Both relate the directly given in experience to what is indirectly given.

SCHOPENHAUER AND UNITY OF SUBJECT AND OBJECT

As discussed above, Descartes was not insensible to the role of the subject in cognition. Kant's Copernican revolution established a subject-centred model of knowledge and made the spontaneous or active role of the subject clearer. It keeps, however, the dichotomy between subject and object. The next step, in the course of development we are following here, is taken by

Schopenhauer. He bridged the gap between subject and object and declared their unity. In the context of this study, the importance of Schopenhauer lies mostly in this point. He is also the link between Kant and Nietzsche, whose views of science, cognition and education are of paramount importance for this study. Nietzsche refers, in fact, to his indebtedness to Kant and Schopenhauer in his first published book, *The Birth of Tragedy* (BT). Schopenhauer learned from Kant that what we perceive is the world of representations, rather than reality itself. This means that through our knowledge of the phenomenal world, we know much more about ourselves than the world outside. According to Schopenhauer, knowledge is "illusion". In this way, Schopenhauer radicalised Kant's theory of the thing-in-itself. Here, the *noumenal* world becomes much more distant and unknowable than in Kant. On the other hand, there is, Schopenhauer tells us, immediacy in our knowledge of our own bodies. He maintains that, as knowing beings, we are not only knowing spirits for whom everything appears as representation. We are also bodies among other bodies. As a known entity, a body is only a representation, quite like other things, such as cars and trees. But there is a fundamental difference between the knower's own body and other objects of knowledge. Our bodies are not only given to us as mere representations, like other objects, they are also given to us immediately; the human body is "immediately *known*, is *immediate object*" (Schopenhauer 1910: 25). This means—and this is the important difference between Kant and Schopenhauer—that we know our bodies not just as representations, but also as the things in themselves of these representations. As such and in this immediacy the thing-in-itself presents itself as will, the inner essence of the world. In their immediacy our bodily movements present themselves as representations of will. To put it another way and plainly, we know ourselves in an immediate way and as such we are subject and object at the same time, willing to know and knowing this will at the same time. This means that in us the thing-in-itself becomes self-conscious and aware of itself. According to Schopenhauer, we reach the thing-in-itself, the world as will. Because of the act of willing we overcome the very basic distinction between subject and object. This view challenges the traditional notion of knowledge in a basic way. Subject and object do not belong to two different worlds. Rather, they are elements of the same context, the same culture and history. This means that context becomes constitutive of them and discussions of them must refer to this context. By inventing a mode of understanding based on the unity of subject and object, Schopenhauer prefigures the flaws of positivism and challenges its view of objectivity. His view of knowledge undermines the basic positivistic assumption, the distinction between subject and object. This also means an undermining of the basic principle of scientific education.

Schopenhauer takes a decisive step towards releasing humanity from the unknown world of ideas. His sceptical and pessimistic attitude is necessary in order to overcome the Cartesian aspiration to exactitude and certitude. Schopenhauer also challenges the exclusive position of science by presenting art as a way of envisioning ideas. This thought style was revitalised by Nietzsche and his view of art and its role in cognition. Such a notion of knowledge is liberating in that it lets our creative potential become manifest.

In summary, in Kant and Schopenhauer, we find a critical awareness of the nature of cognition and science. They highlight the active part of the knower in the process of knowledge. Together with Schopenhauer's dissolution of the sharp boundaries between subject and object, this point is extremely important for the purpose of introducing new notions of science and objectivity. However, after Schopenhauer and Kant, there was still a further step to be taken in order to highlight the place of science in modern culture and its relation to contemporary problems. And this step was taken by Nietzsche. The path-breaking step from Kant to Nietzsche is that in Nietzsche science appears as a problem and an alternative view of science is presented. While in Kant it is the paradigm of critique, Nietzsche considers that science cannot be used as a solution to other problems because it is itself the root of the major problems of modern times. The acute problem is rather to cure science itself. And Nietzsche considered this challenge his main task.

NIETZSCHE AND THE PROBLEM OF SCIENCE

Indeed, Nietzsche radicalised Kant's critique of knowledge and its possibilities and pushed it to its extreme limits. If Kant presented science not only as unproblematic but also as a powerful critical instrument and, as such, the constituting constraint of intuition itself, Nietzsche took a step further. By directing the critique to science, he revealed the limits of science as an instrument of critique and, consequently, our acute need of other critical tools. The importance of this crucial step in our context is that it signifies not only a questioning of science but also the possibility of scientific critique. The source of "the problem of science", as Nietzsche terms it, is that science itself has been its own judge and has set the critical standards for philosophical accounts of scientific theories, scientific practice and its progress. Other perspectives on science have been excluded, neglected and marginalised. As a result, science has been the supreme judge of the cognitive and social organisation of life. Consequently, science has not been able to uncover its own shortcomings and problems. Identifying the source of the problem, we have to present a solution at the same level as the problem. And this leads us to the notion of inclusion.

Nietzsche's solution to the problem of science has been a two-step one. At the first stage, he found that "the problem of science cannot be recognized in the context of science" (BT, Pref. 2). At the second stage, he transcends scientific context and suggests a perspective on science outside science itself, that of art. Such a solution takes a step outside the scientific discourse and is liberated from the limitations associated with Quine and Kuhn referred to above. Consequently, it can avoid the problem of relativism and nihilism. The first Nietzschean step questions science's self-sufficiency. By so doing he enters nihilism. However, he uses nihilism against nihilism itself by going beyond science. While Kant finds in science an adequate outlook on the world, Nietzsche questions the sufficiency of science as an outlook. To see science in this perspective is to provide a source of creative endeavours to find complementary perspectives, a basic step toward an inclusive epistemology. The second step presents this complementary perspective, art. The place of art in knowledge acquisition will be discussed in Chapter 5.

If Kant made clear the importance of cogniser and Schopenhauer revealed the unity of the subject and the object, Nietzsche sheds light on the importance of perspective and history. Put together, these three points of view are useful for the purpose of establishing an inclusive notion of knowledge.

KNOWLEDGE AND HISTORY

Basically, the dispute between Nietzsche and Kant is based on two points, both related to the importance of history. Nietzsche is in agreement with Kant that our experiences are the common products of empirical evidence provided by the physical world and that we use our cognitive faculties to organise this evidence. But he strongly resists the Kantian notion of the thing-in-itself as the utmost cause and underlying ground of the objects of knowledge. The other point of disagreement concerns the conceptions by which we express and organise our experiences in language. Indeed, Nietzsche demystified the Kantian world. As this is crucial in this context, it deserves more elaboration.

Although the thing-in-itself is central in his philosophy of knowledge, Kant considered that we are not able to know anything about it; insistence on knowledge of it leads inevitably to antinomies that we have to avoid at any price. This is metaphysical since, according to Kant's view, things in themselves have nothing to do with the world of senses; they are substances or "objects of the pure reason" (CPR A264, B320). Things in themselves are the proper objects of the complete conceptual description of the intellect and belong to the world of theoretical knowledge rather than the practical world. Hence, we have no power to make use of such self-subsistent entities. Although they are the underlying ground of the objects we know through experience, we lack the intellectual intuition to represent such objects. "In the case of the noumenon, there the entire use, indeed even all significance of the categories completely ceases" (CPR B308). Thus in trying to discern these objects we only reveal the limitation of our concepts. Frankly put, things in themselves are unknowable by definition.

Nietzsche directs a critique against the very Kantian distinction between a world of phenomena, things for us, and a world of things in themselves whose true nature and purpose must eternally remain hidden from us. Indeed, it was Hegel who had already put the question regarding the meaning and significance of the thing-in-itself. What is the use and point of retaining as a philosophical concept something of which we can never have any knowledge? In other words, if our cognition has no meaningful application to the thing-in-itself, then it also has no way of making sense of the distinction between the appearance of things, the reality which is posited for us by the mind, and things in themselves. Nietzsche endorses this Hegelian point by writing "We do not 'know' nearly enough to be entitled to any such distinction" (GS 345). From the very fact that it transcends the realm of the legitimate employment of our cognitive faculties, the apparently innocent notion of the thing in-itself is not only incoherent and consequently obsolete but also leads to human enslavement under the domination of an unknown world. In Nietzsche, philosophy reaches a crucial moment of awareness; it takes a decisive step toward human liberation by refusing to accept any transcendent realm. This reconciles us with our real conditions of life.

As already mentioned, a second point where Nietzsche criticises the Kantian view of knowledge is related to the concepts and categories we use to organise our experiences. In Kant these are reified notions since for him our categories transcend experience and are thus independent of its contingencies; categories are the prior condition of the possibility of experience and no cognition would be possible without them. Nietzsche's focal point was, on the other hand, the categorical insistence that everything human depends on history. Seen in this light, reason as well as categories are historical. It means that our intellectual faculties are not "pure principles of understanding" as they were for Kant; rather, they are means by which we represent and know our surrounding world in order to live securely in it. By appeal to the contingency of our concepts, Nietzsche rejects the Kantian claim about the necessity of a single universal conceptual apparatus and its authority over minds. We accept a set of concepts not because they are the necessary precondition of our experience. Rather, we adopt them because of our contingent needs, interests and values. These facts about us as human beings constitute the cognitive "situations" in which we find ourselves and which influence our particular perspective. Because the underlying features of our concepts are variable and contingent, our perspectives are continuously changing. As all too human beings we are embodied, prejudiced and historical knowers. Nietzsche thus preceded Kuhn, Fleck and others in emphasising the context and perspective-dependency of science and cognition in general. By taking the further step he makes this awareness a liberating force, since this view of knowledge stimulates human creative resources and makes us the creator and master of our values and conceptions.

Historically considered, contrary to Platonism, Nietzsche tries to bring us back to our world of the body and the senses. He not only tries to claim the dignity of the human body and the human world, but also puts a huge responsibility on humanity for creating values and conceptions. The Nietzschean awareness also anticipated the flaws of Kuhn and similar brands of thought and avoids them by going beyond the critical stage of the negation of Platonism.

Concerning the contextuality of cognition, Nietzsche's main educational concern was to correct and reverse an ancient error committed by the Platonic-Socratic rational philosophy that originated in ancient Greece and continued to dominate minds in different ways. On this plane, he presents the history of philosophy as the history of the genesis and development of this error. The essence of this error is the rationalistic dream of pure observations, objective knowledge, disinterested predictions and total control of nature. Science is signified by an illusory conviction that an objective account of laws of nature is possible. And this can be done only by using the perspective of reason, science and skilled scientists. This position of science was summarised by Nietzsche in terms of *hubris*, a term borrowed from the ancient Greeks:

> Our whole attitude toward nature, the way we violate her with the aid of machines and the heedless inventiveness of our technicians and engineers, is *hubris*; our attitude toward God as some alleged spider of purpose and morality behind the great captious web of causality, is *hubris* . . . our attitude *toward ourselves* is *hubris*. (GM III, 9)

This attitude was, Nietzsche exclaimed, the "greed of the moment". It manipulates nature and reduces humanity to labouring masses for the sake of the daily needs of the market and states. In Chapters 2 and 3, we observed how states and religious and economic powers use scientific knowledge as an organisational model to maximise economic gains. To oppose these tendencies, this study is in agreement with Nietzsche's educational project aimed at the liberation of humanity and science from the greed of the moment. It derives inspiration from Nietzschean endeavours to make us able "to press" upon our "experience the stamp of the eternal" (BT 23). In so doing, this study advocates inclusive qualities of thought aimed at the enhancement of life as the basis of humanity. Since life is interpreted as both a biological and cultural phenomenon, this position takes into consideration the cause of culture as well as that of environment. Such a position is trans-historical, since life is eternal despite our individual mortality and our historical embodiment. Internalising a trans-historical perspective enables us to reverse the relationships between the narrow needs of the market and the needs of life being eternally flourished. Such a shift in perspective demands a paradigm shift in our understanding of education. Being educated, then, means to see our individual needs as well as those of our time in the light of the needs of life and humanity across cultures and times.

Nietzsche called his version of science "gay" or "joyous" science. Based on reverence for nature, for humanity and gods and focused on eternal human problems, such a science overcomes the narrow perspective of current science. It is a new beginning and can function as the starting point of a new interpretation of science. The most important thing in this context is Nietzsche's taking a further step beyond presenting art as a perspective on science. In order to overcome the problem of science, he recommends that we "*look at science in the perspective of the artists, but at art in that of life*" (BT, Pref. 2). Thus, rather than from art or science, the utmost perspective from which all other perspectives are judged is life itself, in whose existence and primacy there can be no doubt. This view gives us a common ground of objectivity and a frame of reference in matters of cognition. The notion of objectivity defended here is based on the plurality of perspectives, since life, in its cultural and biological sense is not limited to a single perspective.

THE NECESSITY OF PERSPECTIVAL PLURALITY

To use a diversity of perspectives as the basis of objectivity is a necessary condition of a notion of knowledge free from nihilism. A notion of objectivity based on plurality of perspectives is not authoritarian. In the traditional view, science's authority is based on its being connected to the notion of reason. Reason in its turn is based on universal concepts. Famously, Plato reduced the sensory world to the realm of shadows of timeless ideas and subordinated it to these ideas. The source of authority has been a mimetic view of science and art based on rationalism. Indeed, rationalism, conceived in this way, is an ideology about the use of reason in an exclusive way rather than the use of reason as such. As mentioned in Chapter 2, in order to understand different types of rationality, we have to ask questions about their domain, direction, ends and values. Regarding the notion of knowledge, rationalism has been directed at an authoritarian view of the matter, where a single voice, the voice of a certain type of humanity, sanctions good and evil, right and wrong. It occupies the central position in the power hierarchy and marginalises all others; the principle of exclusion has been an ultimate value. The alternative view of knowledge is a polyphonic rather than monophonic one, to use two notions borrowed from Bakhtin. Bakhtin uses these conceptions in literary contexts, but they are applicable in other contexts as well. Bakhtin thinks that "Dostoyevsky, like Goethe's Prometheus, creates not voiceless slaves (as does Zeus), but rather free people who are capable of standing beside their creator, of disagreeing with him, and even of rebelling against him" (Bakhtin 1984: 4).

Tolstoy's novels, by contrast, are dominated by the author's authoritarian voice and are thereby monophonic, Bakhtin argues. A polyphonic notion of knowledge is, we can argue, an inclusive one, since it includes many voices. It means a decentralisation of intellectual authority and sources of knowledge. Contrary to the traditional world view, there will be no centre and periphery—neither in education nor in knowledge. In the current order of things, the monophonic notion of knowledge is based on the perspective of male Western reason. God, reason and teachers build a hierarchy of power against which the student has no possibility of "standing beside", showing "disagreement" or "rebelling"; the student becomes a "voiceless slave". Once this enslavement is established, it becomes a habitual pattern of behaviour and a habit of mind: it continues throughout the individual's life. She/he becomes subordinated to abstract and general rules of reason. The polyphonic or inclusive view of knowledge, on the contrary, builds up the horizon of life from several interconnected perspectives. This new kind of knowledge takes into account the perspectives of history, philosophy, art and science on an equal basis. This plurality of perspectives is completed by the equality of the perspectives of male, female, children and different cultures. In other words, perspectival plurality has two interconnected aspects. One is the inclusion of perspectives of art, philosophy and history, the other is the inclusion of perspectives of women, children and other marginalised social groups.

In a polyphonic education, it is not the amount of information imposed on students that is important, but the inclusive quality of their thought and knowledge. Such an education questions the dominant monopoly of science by widening the scope through including perspectives of art, philosophy and history. The question of intellectual authority changes character, since the educator is not trying to subjugate the learners to an authoritarian voice or systems of facts. Their relationship is based on mutual love and the perspective of pupils is included in the process of knowledge production and acquisition. Sophisticated mechanisms of manipulation currently at work will be replaced by ways of thinking that offer students the possibility of "standing beside" teachers, showing "disagreement" with collectives and "rebelling" against an authoritarian view of knowledge. Knowledge based on plurality of perspectives goes beyond the ideological economic and military interests of states and market. The authoritative and narrow-minded perspective of economic profitability is set aside by the requirement of the cultural flourishing of humanity.

The inclusive notion of knowledge is to be based on an inclusive notion of objectivity. A first step in this regard is to go beyond the traditional dichotomy between objectivism and subjectivism. In fact, we can find ways that do justice to both, but avoid problems associated with each. Objectivism is based on the value-neutrality thesis, according to which good science is objective in the sense of being totally free from all cultural values. According to this view, contextual values, like the background beliefs, interests and preferences of societies and social groups, are not related to the cognitive aims of science. These values should remain outside science, since they distort scientific judgement. There are characteristics internal to sciences that provide the basis of its objectivity. This means that science can be done in the same manner and scientific observations reach the same results regardless of cultural and historical contexts. Subjectivity is not necessarily coupled with an idealistic ontology. As was argued earlier, to bridge the gap between the subject and the object means to emphasise the due place of the individual and human embodiment in the process of knowledge acquisition. Human embodiment as a constitutive element of cognition has already been emphasised. The point to be added is that we are embodied beings within a cultural context. An inclusive notion of knowledge includes not only the perspective of the body—by giving human senses, drives and emotions their due place in the processes of knowledge production—it is also knowledge of the world from within, since man recognizes his being as an integrated part of nature.

Culturally and physically, our bodies are parts of a wider context. By trying to obtain knowledge of our own bodies, we consider them as objects of our knowledge. In such a cognitive act the body is an intentional object of itself. As a result, its knowledge is an immediate knowledge. In this sense, bodies become subject and object simultaneously. Since the body is a part of the world of objects, it becomes known in and through the world. More clearly, my knowledge of my own body is knowledge through my own body itself which, in its turn, is a part of the world. This notion of knowledge is, then, knowledge of the world from within. By including human embodiment in the process of knowledge acquisition, objectivity and subjectivity reach each other in the same phenomenon and become one. On the other hand, the human body is not an abstract entity; it exists in a particular place, time and culture. Our knowledge is thus interwoven with particularities of time, place and culture and cannot be value-neutral.

SCIENCE AND CULTURAL VALUES

As observed, culture and history are constitutive elements of science. This means that our cultural values and historical interests influence our knowledge. Philosopher of science Helen Longino contests the value-neutrality thesis. She starts from the "actual practice of science" and talks about "contextualist analysis of evidence" (1998: 174). Longino emphasises the distinction between epistemic and contextual values. To her mind, contextual values can not only be different in different historical and cultural contexts, they can also vary from individual to individual. In other words, and more clearly, they are not intrinsic to science. This means that science can be done with different sets of contextual values, under different socio-cultural circumstances. Epistemic values, by contrast, are intrinsic to science. They are permanent, universal and insensitive to the diversity of cultural contexts. Longino endorses the positivistic distinction between the context of discovery and the context of justification and focuses on the latter. In her theory confirmation and justification are dependent on background beliefs, and value-ladenness is compatible with scientific objectivity. Longino emphasises the social nature of science, but she chooses a line of argumentation that is in contrast with Fleck and Kuhn. While Fleck and Kuhn use the social nature of science as an argument against scientific objectivity, she emphasises the communality of science in order to argue for its objectivity. She relates objectivity to a social organisation of science that permits a plurality of perspectives and encourages critique. At the centre of the communality of science she sees a process of criticism at work. To her mind, communality of science makes possible shared collective standards, collective response to critique, shared venues of criticism and equality between qualified practitioners of scientific enterprise that safeguard the objectivity of science (181–85).

Indeed, several philosophers of science focus on the value-ladenness of science. While Sandra Harding insists on Eurocentric traits of science, Kathleen Okruhlik shows the sexist and androcentric biases of modern science. By discussing several cases, Okruhlik shows that "gender ideology has had deep and extensive effects on the development of many scientific disciplines" (1998: 192). Biology has been especially important, since it has been used to justify women's functioning "in a socially subordinate role" (Okruhlik 1998: 192). For example, until female scientists entered the field, studies of primates were entirely focused on the competitive behaviour of male primates. Through the engagement of female researchers the field widened and another pattern of behaviour was discerned, female community-building.

It is important to emphasise that sexual and ethnocentric biases are not confined to a single scientist or observation; rather, they are institutionalised in scientific culture and influence theory choice and the way observations are described. Contextual values are thus essential to science. In other words, science is culture-bound. Contrary to Longino, Okruhlik questions the sharp distinction between context of discovery and context of justification. She espouses the view that such a distinction cannot protect science from sexist biases, since the context of discovery inevitably affects that of justification. Her line of argumentation goes: If we agree that in the context of discovery theories are contaminated by sexist values, they continue to affect theories even in the context of justification, since theories selected as the best ones in the context of justification indeed originate in the context of discovery. Thus, the philosophy of science's one-sided focus on the context of justification hinders our understanding of the true nature of scientific knowledge. Indeed, by emphasising the interconnectedness of the context of discovery and that of justification and the inclusion of "theory generation" in the constituent elements of science, Okruhlik pushes for changes in the social organisation of science. She focuses on "science policy" instead of on individual scientists. In my opinion, this is the right way to consider science and its place in contemporary societies. On the one hand, historical origins of thought influence its development. A notion like "atom" is indeed a result of context and history, a link between antiquity and contemporary contexts. On the other hand, humanity, nowadays, has access to gigantic powers, like atomic power and microbiology, which makes an inclusive and responsible social organisation of science a much more acute issue than whether specific scientific theories are true or false for individual scientists. An inclusive and responsible management of science can protect us against global environmental and social dangers threatening life and humanity. Together with an inclusive notion of knowledge, such an organisation of science covers the whole spectra of human reality in an unprecedented way. Not steered by the perspective of a single group, science focuses on problems and research methods related to life as such.

Okruhlik rightly suggests a social arrangement of science based on the diversity of perspectives constitutive of science. This can be reached by including female perspectives in the social arrangement of science. Male science has in vain put trust in eliminating contextual values by methodological means, rules, criteria for theory choice and justification. The male perspective is also focused exclusively on individual scientists and their psychological make-up. Okruhlik emphasises, by contrast, the impotence of the social organisation of science and espouses the view that "social arrangements acquire *epistemic* significance" (205). Thus, there are no unsurpassable boundaries between cultural and epistemic values. Their becoming the one or the other is positional and relational. This means that democratisation of science's social organisation can attain epistemic significance and increase science's objectivity. Okruhlik pushes for women's participation in scientific research, equality between sexes in matters of science and taking seriously women's critical views of male science. According to Okruhlik, these factors contribute to the improvement of science and its objectivity. To view the notion of objectivity in the light of the inclusion of different perspectives or epistemic democracy is much more in agreement with the position of the present study than the traditional notion of objectivity, based on a single perspective. While the former is an inclusive and non-violent way of obtaining knowledge of the world and a responsible and inclusive way of organising it, the latter violently excludes other perspectives in order to enhance and sustain its own domination. While the former cooperates, the later exploits. Accordingly, in the former case, human intellectual labour is an expression of love and creative human resources; in the latter, it is an expression of violence and suppression. As a result, the former marks a non-alienated state of being while the latter results in alienation and nihilism.

AN INCLUSIVE NOTION OF OBJECTIVITY

Although extremely important, the inclusion of different perspectives is not to be endorsed unequivocally. Harding helps us nuance our image of objectivity. She terms objectivism or the traditional notion of objectivity "weak objectivity", since in this view, she argues, objectivity is considered to be identical to neutrality. According to Harding, the claim that science is free from cultural values gives a distorted image of cognitive processes, since there is no perspective that is outside culture. While Longino makes a distinction between contextual and epistemic values, Harding takes a step further and makes a distinction between different cultural values. To her mind, the main flaw of objectivism is that it "is unable to discriminate between . . . aspects of culture that enlarge our understanding and those that limit it" (Harding 1998: 136). Objectivism tries in vain to eliminate cultural elements as such. Harding refers to the fact that ways of life give rise to distinctive ways of thought. She writes: "What we do both enables and limits what we can know" (141). To deny this insight is indeed to limit the scope of knowledge, she argues.

Kuhn did not make use of feminism and post-colonial science studies. Thus he remains, on the one hand, within the male perspective, and on the other, within a conceptual framework of authoritarian science practices that favour only empowered Western elites. Harding, by contrast, makes use not only of feminism, but also of post-colonial and post-Kuhnian science studies. For the old or weak notion of objectivity, she substitutes the notion of "strong objectivity" based on standpoint epistemology. Standpoint epistemology is relational and positional and takes into account perspectives of marginalised people like women and the oppressed. Strong objectivity is based on two presuppositions. First, contextual values are constitutive of science, and second, there is a difference between values that are beneficial for the growth of knowledge and those that block such growth. Formulated differently, some contextual values are to be preferred since they ease the growth of science, while others are to be rejected since they block it. The question is, what contextual values and beliefs assist the growth of knowledge? No doubt, democratic values, environmentally friendly ideas, equality between the sexes, respect for the dignity of disadvantaged people are values that contribute to the flourishing of science and human beings. On the contrary, values like racism, sexism, Nazism and the like block not only human flourishing, but also the growth of science. Thus, there is an undeniable connection between the growth of knowledge and social relations. Inclusion and exclusion have to be based on the kind of ideas and perspectives.

To have diversity of perspectives as an epistemological standpoint is an important point. We also need men and women who manage this plurality. In other words, besides taking into account the cultural values beneficial for the growth of science and including the perspective of marginalised people in the social arrangement of science, we need to take into account individual characteristics favourable to the growth of knowledge. These characteristics are those which enable the individual to master a way of thinking beneficial for the growth of knowledge. More directly, there are individual characteristics that ease human understanding and those that block it. Thus, we should not stop at the level of collectives, as Harding does; rather, we need to connect progressive cultural values to positive individual characteristics. The Nietzschean notion of objectivity is helpful in this connection. Instead of being entirely intrinsic to science, objectivity is here connected to the individual and is conceived as "the ability *to control* one's Pro and Con and to dispose of them, so that one knows how to employ a *variety* of perspectives and affective interpretations in the service of knowledge" (GM, III, 12).

Gathering these two aspects of humanity together, we would not only, like strong objectivity, be capable of distinguishing between different types of cultural values and employing "a variety of perspectives", but also be individual agents of cognition in control of our arguments. This position demands not only positive cultural values, but also disciplined and rigorous individual ways of thinking, self-discipline and self-determination. This is not only to declare the conceivability of the natural world, but also to make "the other" conceivable. As Nietzsche puts it in *Ecce Homo*, to obtain knowledge in this way is to "delineate reality *as it is*" (EH XIV, 5), since, contrary to objectivism, this type of knowledge is, as mentioned earlier, knowledge of the world from within. On this basis, we can establish an inclusive notion of epistemology. Such an epistemology encompasses traits of strong and weak epistemologies without being limited to them. Like weak epistemology, it keeps the notion of truth. Like strong epistemology, it recognises the importance of contextual values. Unlike these two, it creates a synthesis of the two tendencies. It also highlights the significance of different individual characteristics for cognition.

By including perspectives of men, women, and different cultures, the inclusive notion of epistemology not only moves away from homogeneous metaphysical realities, but it takes its own heterogeneous reality seriously. Recognising the right of different social groups to actively participate in decisions about production, distribution and criticism of science is based on the fact that the life of these groups is affected by science—by the kind of science, its organisation and its use. In a world like ours all humanity is affected by the results of scientific research and related technologies. For instance, atomic research and research in biological sciences have huge impacts on a global scale. To give another example, global warming, caused mainly by the patterns of consumption and behaviour in Western societies, impinges on all human beings regardless of their gender, geographical or ethnic groups. Doing science is thus not merely an epistemological matter of improving knowledge and making certain technologies possible, it also has the moral responsibility of giving people an opportunity to have an impact on what is vital to their life. If the first aspect refers to conditions of good science, the second has to do with the fair treatment of others and justice. On the other hand, to be able to actually make use of possibilities that an inclusive notion of science provides demands a person's having access to education and financial resources. Epistemological/educational changes, in other words, are incomplete without social changes.

THE DEMOCRATISATION OF SCIENCE

Some might object, and rightly so, first, that marginalised groups do not share a single view of what knowledge is and, second, that merely being marginalised is not valuable in itself. It cannot function as a criterion of inclusion. Differences between marginalised groups as well as differences within categories like ethnicity, class, and gender deserve as much attention as differences between the dominating perspective and marginalised ones. Indeed, in some cases, differences between marginalised groups run deeper than those between centre and periphery. The same can be said of individual differences within groups. Members of these categories are indeed individuals, with distinct identities, interests and levels of intellectual development. Moreover, there are marginalised groups whose views are more exclusive and violent than empowered groups. In fact, these views are about trying to get power in order to exclude others. By so doing, the members reverse the power relations without resolving any problems. Where there is an attempt to eliminate the plurality of levels of truths and perspectives the same violence is at work; it does not matter whether it is taking place in the name of a majority or a minority, a centre or a periphery. Consequently, we need other validation criteria to guide our judgements, choices and decisions in this regard. This is certainly true and it is for this reason that there is a problem. But this should not lead us away from the main issue, namely, harm caused by blocking disadvantaged people's contributions to science. Of course, perspectives such as racism and sexism, which use scientific knowledge to prove sexual and racial inferiority, are not as good, valid and valuable as, say, feminism; they are, rather, inhuman. These ideologies certainly do not confer any virtue on their bearer. Neither do they deserve inclusion in scientific activities. Their exclusion harms nobody; rather, justice and ethical considerations require their exclusion, since there are neither moral nor empirical reasons that protect these ideologies. On the contrary, there is evidence of their distorted view of the world and humanity. Further examples are creationism and intellectual design. Despite strong claims about the origin of the world and humanity and its development, these ideologies are unable to present evidence and reasons that are publicly accessible and defend the claims. Consequently, they are indefensible empirically.

A qualified position is a position which respects the dignity of all human beings and shows solidarity with other social groups. As Charles Taylor says, such a position has to have something aesthetically and intellectually interesting not just for its own group, but also for humanity as such (Taylor 1994: 125–73). In addition to respect for human dignity, respect for a plurality of points of view, and recognition of the complexities of the various orders of truth, for a perspective to be included it has also to respect the autonomy of scientific research and defend progressive cultural values. The inclusion of such positions leads to the enlargement of human knowledge, while their exclusion harms humanity by depriving us of valuable insights. Another aspect of the issue is the role of cooperation in science. For instance, as Yu Xie and Kimberlee A. Shauman show, "The underrepresentation of women is a hallmark characteristic of science" (Xie and Shauman 2003: 1). The same can be said of other disadvantaged groups. While these groups' participation in science makes scientific issues relevant to them, the lack of relevance causes alienation and indifference. To recognise and encourage the contribution of women and disadvantaged people in scientific activities is not only a step away from alienation, it is also a step towards opening science to a wider range of epistemological and social issues. Thus, women's and marginalised groups' participation not only democratises science, it also increases science's resources. In summary, the inclusion of women eliminates androcentrism and the inclusion of marginalised groups eliminates ethnocentrism in science. This means a plurality of perspectives and a widening of the basis of choices, selection, judgement, decisions and priorities regarding scientific problems, methods and fields of research. New questions and problems like those related to women and the Third World would then receive more attention and resources, instead of those going to the requirements of advantaged classes. For instance, instead of the extreme concentration on the human genome, a profitable affair for multinationals, global issues like elimination of poverty, global warming, healthcare and pollution would get more attention. This would mean an improvement of knowledge in the service of human well being on the one hand and human liberation from reactionary ideologies and humiliating social situations on the other.

The scientific view of nature, masculine, Western and ethnocentric in character, is marked by violence. Support for the modification of genes, for instance, is a will to dominate and a blind will to power, since it involves limited knowledge and vast ignorance of possible harm to nature and humanity. Inclusion of women and other cultures would modify this view of nature and substitute for it a view of nature based on care. Another aspect of androcentric science is its relation to a masculine structure of power and the hierarchy of masculine authority. Multinationals and private interests are dominating scientific research more and more. This has made science just a saleable commodity among others. Seen in the wider context of alienation and nihilism, commodification of science sustains and enhances the reification of social relations. Inclusion of women and disadvantaged groups would be a decisive step away from nihilism, since it would lead to the increase of awareness of the active role of the human agent in the construction of scientific facts and values.

Kuhn tried to re-interpret the history of science. Although he took an important step, his endeavours remained within the limits of the western scientific tradition. A whole-hearted re-interpretation of the history of science has to take a further step and encompass the history of non-European sciences like Chinese science. To write the history of science anew will also reveal a history of oppression stemming from science's endeavours to reduce all perspectives to a single one. Western science indeed appropriated Indian mathematics, Islamic medicine and Chinese science and made them invisible by writing them out of history. Colonialism also destroyed local knowledge through forbidding or making difficult education for indigenous people. Properly understood, the participation of women and marginalised groups and the inclusion of non-Western sciences means radical changes in scientific discourse, its social organisation and methods of enquiry. Such a science can function as the basis of a universalism grounded on a variety of social and cognitive perspectives. It is truly universal, since it covers a wide range of perspectives and a variety of problems, research areas, analytical tools and research methods. It also resolves the paradox of truth by using a range of perspectives to transcend the limits of different contexts and horizons of interpretation. This kind of argumentation is indeed based on an inclusive notion of rationality.

Last but not least, inclusion is not to be governed by the needs, norms and conditions of those already empowered. It has, rather, to demolish the asymmetrical power relations by taking into consideration norms and needs of the empowered and the disempowered. Inclusion is, in other words, a transformative process. It negates the old exclusive values and creates new inclusive ones. It is an educational process through which the empowered and disempowered meet, understand each other, and change their view of science and themselves accordingly. Knowledge becomes, then, an open and perpetually changing process of negotiation and renegotiation of what knowledge is.

5 Cognitive Pluralism

Views and theories discussed so far, including that of Harding, emphasise the participatory roles of marginalised social groups, colonised people and women. All these perspectives are focused on scientific knowledge. They also push for the inclusion of socially marginalised perspectives. In order to widen the scope a step further, we have also to talk of the inclusion of the marginalised perspectives of history, art and philosophy as possible perspectives on science. In the prevailing scientific paradigm, science rules art and philosophy. Science is the perspective in which all other kinds of knowledge must justify themselves. This is the basis of a weak view of knowledge, whereby science is considered the only unproblematic knowledge of the world. It is based on epistemic exclusion, since science is considered the only unproblematic perspective on the world; as Quine puts it, "it is within science . . . that reality is to be identified and described" (1981: 21). Furthermore, it is an authoritative view of knowledge. Knowledge is reduced to the domain of "the global science", on the one hand, and "we all" are expected to "subscribe" to this science, on the other. Beardsley, in his turn, excludes the arts from the domain of knowledge and truth by writing: "Painting and musical compositions are not, and do not give, knowledge about reality" (1958: 391). While Descartes talked of the First Philosophy as the ontological and epistemological foundation of the sciences, Russell reversed this relationship by talking of "scientific philosophy", a philosophy based on the methodology of science (Hylton 1990: 15). Such influential views paved the way for the reduction of philosophy to epistemology. On this conception, philosophy has accepted the servitude of science. Art, in its turn, has been marginalised to entertainment and the ornamentation of life. As has already been shown, science, which stays on the top of the hierarchy, has, in its turn, accepted the servitude of everyday politics and lost sight of eternal human problems. Thus, in our age, philosophy, art and science have fallen prey to the everyday interests of politics and lost sight of what is eternal in humanity. Instead of liberating humanity, they enhance human servitude. These relationships have to be reshaped in order to give things their due. And this will be a process of human liberation from alienation and nihilism. In this chapter, I concentrate on relations between science, art and philosophy.

PHILOSOPHY AS CRITICAL THOUGHT

Polyphonic knowledge is an inclusive notion and has different components. Philosophy is the overarching perspective of an inclusive understanding of the world, on the one hand, and the framework of a life lived philosophically, on the other. It is a horizon of interpretation. Nowadays, philosophy is mainly reduced to a profession related to academic positions or to an academic discipline continuous with science. This is mostly the case within the analytic tradition of philosophy. Indeed, this reductionist tendency has been at work since Descartes and reached its culmination in Quine. If Descartes talked of a First Philosophy as the unquestioned foundation of science, Quine questioned this notion by replacing it with a "scientific epistemology". He prescribes "abandonment of the goal of a first philosophy prior to natural science" (1981: 67). As Barry Stroud observes, Quine introduced this thesis against Carnap's thesis of "rational reconstruction" (Stroud 2004: 24–25). Indeed, Quine is in agreement with Carnap about reducing philosophy to epistemology. Carnap maintains, however, that the main task of philosophy is to show how all propositions and beliefs about the world can be justified by reference to sense experiences. Quine maintains that this "cannot be done" (Quine 1981: 23). In Carnap's conception, rather than being concerned with the actual practices of science, philosophy was concerned with analysing the logical relationships between principles and conceptions employed by the sciences. In other words, analytic philosophy, or epistemology, was focused on science's logic rather than on how it is done, develops and is learned. Philosophy was then considered to be *a priori*. Quine's analysis of the distinction between *a priori* and *a posteriori* knowledge showed the shaky foundation of this distinction. Consequently, Quine declared that "there is no place for a prior philosophy" (1969: 26). He shifted the focus away from the logic employed by science to the everyday practices of scientists, the way science actually is contrived and how language is learned. Having this starting point, his thesis of holism maintains that the human mind, the knowledge we acquire and the meaning we base our truths on are all interrelated components of the same world that is the subject of our enquiries. This is one side of Quine's dyadic theory, its ontological aspect. When it comes to its other aspect, its methodology, or epistemology, it maintains that this single world is to be recognised "within science". Accordingly, rather than being subject to philosophical scrutiny, notions like truth and meaning "are to be studied in the same empirical spirit that animates natural science" (26). Conceived in this way, philosophy is reduced to epistemology. Epistemology, in its turn, is assimilated to "empirical psychology" (Quine 1981: 72). In other words, philosophy is reduced to just another scientific discourse. More succinctly, Quine believes that "the epistemological question is . . . a question within science" (72). Seen in this way, science becomes the only knowledge proper of the world as well as the only reliable basis of judgement about this knowledge.

Consequently, science is not only exempt from being "answerable to any supra-scientific tribunal" (72), but also becomes its own judge as well as that of philosophy and art. This is the meaning of what is called Quine's "naturalistic turn", so influential within analytic philosophy.

Obviously, a notion of philosophy as First Philosophy, where it authoritatively decides once and for all principles regarding foundation, attributes, limits and the domain of scientific discourse is not tenable. The same can be said of an *a priori* conception of philosophy, whereby philosophy is concerned with analysis of scientific theories' logical structure. Quine's critique of these tendencies is thus a step in the right direction. However, from the untenability of both the Cartesian First Philosophy and an *a priori* notion of philosophy, we cannot conclude the redundancy of philosophy as such. It is nihilistic, since it negates the old without replacing it with the new; it stagnates in negation. We need a notion of philosophy that encompasses aspects of old notions of philosophy, but is not limited to them. Philosophy as used here not only embraces some features of old notions of philosophy, like critical concern with the foundation of science and consistency of its principles, but also is connected to our life and conduct as human beings. A philosopher is, then, one who lives philosophically rather than just having theoretical knowledge about a subject. To live philosophically means to be a free-minded and active human being with an inclusive view of knowledge and life. Such a philosopher is able to use a variety of perspectives regarding knowledge and values and organise them in accordance with a personal style. Seen in this light, philosophy is not a privilege of the few; anybody can live philosophically. Being at one with her/his knowledge and deeds, the philosopher does not just persuade others of what is true; rather, she/he exemplifies a life lived philosophically by means of her/his own practical life. This is to mistrust "self-sacrifice" and "self-mortification" related to the behavioural pattern of alienated human beings, as Marx (1998) would say. Rather, the individual lets his/her own creative resources become manifest and links them with those of humanity as such. This means coincidence of intellectual and physical health, since the person acts from her/his innermost drives instead of being splintered between knowledge and action. Seen in this light, philosophy becomes engaged with and gains relevance to education. This task is immanent in the process of one's living philosophically, a process of creative resistance, struggle and overcoming, rather than of being informed by some transcendental truth.

The need of our time is thus to rethink philosophy and its relationships with science rather than to reduce it to epistemology or displace it by science, as Quine does. Such a reductive approach harms both philosophy and science. The non-reductive approach suggested here is an attempt to bring together philosophy and science in a way that suits the education proper of individuals whose knowledge and action drive their principles from the fundamental perspective of life. By and large this study shares a view of morality with Plato and Nietzsche; the personality behind any action and the style of conduct is as important as the action itself. Indeed, it is the person behind the action who becomes the action, as there is no distinction between the deed and the doer. This view is in sheer contrast to scientific culture, in which the leading principle is a matter of performing certain actions regardless of the sort of person one is and the spirit in which one performs those actions; actions are considered to be detached from personalities.[1] Generally, as will become clear, the ethical aspect of truth is important for this study.

Living philosophically, the individual is aware of his/her abilities and limits. Philosophical observation also redirects science's creative resources. In current circumstances, science has been very effective in the field of technological abilities. It also has been successful in inflicting an unconditional obedience on scientific man and made him an effective instrument in the service of scientific aims. However, when concentrating on problem-solving activities, science easily loses direction and falls prey to ideological interests. Thus, the man of science cannot play the role of intellectual leader or educator of our time and lay down norms for human knowledge. This task demands the perspective of philosophy. Generally speaking, our disposition toward knowledge, life and the world is a philosophical issue rather than a scientific one. Because of limits associated with science, art and philosophy taken each by itself, we need a fusion of these perspectives in order to transcend their limits and reach an inclusive understanding of the world. Besides, in such a perspective, the ground of each of these perspectives is made accessible by the means of the others. Having this inclusive perspective as a standpoint, we can inquire into the enigmatic character of being, without any violence against it. Aware of its interpretive character, this style of thought makes knowledge possible without resort to any transcendental source of legitimacy.

Philosophy, in its broadest sense, is a constructive cultural element. The same can be said of science and art. Working together they can build up an inclusive culture, a culture that possesses the vitality of uniting these perspectives artfully and in accordance with a single style. Such a culture is beneficial for the growth of human knowledge, human flourishing and enhancement of life. Characterised by a plurality of perspectives, it is transparent to itself; its basic presuppositions are accessible. The transparency of such a ground shows that it is changeable. Whatever the ground, it has to be changed and rebuilt anew time and again. Indeed, it was Kant who first grounded a new notion of philosophy, when he wrote:

> Here philosophy is seen in fact to be placed in a precarious position which is supposed to be stable—although neither in heaven nor on earth is there anything on which it depends or on which it is based. It is here that it has to prove its integrity as the keeper of its laws [*Selbsthaltrein ihre Gesetz*], not as mouthpiece of laws secretly communicated to it by some implanted sense or by who knows tutelary nature. (quoted in Heidegger 2005: 255)

This notion of philosophy places the sources of authority and legitimacy within philosophy itself. In so doing, it makes them immanent rather than transcendent. Thus, the context of the emergence and use of philosophical ideas becomes extremely important. Heidegger considers this interpretation of philosophy "the final turning of Western metaphysics" (Heidegger 2005: 255). Such a position takes philosophy beyond the confines of the ordinary definitions provided by the metaphysical tradition or science. It helps us to realise that the philosophical ground is self-created rather than based in some external source.

Philosophy as used here signifies the dialectical relationships between questioning and constructing, negations and affirmation. It does not surrender to science; rather, it questions the exclusive ground of science in order to pave the path to an inclusive one. This study is in agreement with Ricoeur and his view that philosophy "constitutes the problem of foundation". To his mind, the "philosophical subject . . . doubts and questions foundation" (Ricoeur 1965: 175). It is "a power, both corrosive and constructive" which concerns "the limitations and foundations of science" (175). This is indeed to consider philosophy as "the critical dimension" of thought. Seen in this light, philosophy is "questioning" par excellence. And such a questioning is to found "a new life, a new type of human relationship: the genre of philosophical life" (175). Thus, philosophy is not only the legislator and "the keeper of its laws", as Kant maintains, but also the legislator of philosophical life, a life signified by an anti-dogmatic and questioning style of thought. It is a critical perspective on science and issues related to the basis of science. It prevents science from becoming dogmatic by steadily questioning its ground.

Without a critical-philosophical perspective science becomes a blind drive to knowledge. There is an intrinsic contradiction in this drive that can get out of hand if we are not equipped with a philosophical outlook on life. On the one hand, the knowledge drive aspires ascetically to disinterested knowledge. On the other hand, it is paradigm-based and tends toward power, control and exclusion. Seen in the light of the latter tendency, as Fleck observes, there is no true and untrue science; rather, there is successful and unsuccessful science. Successful science is in a position to present itself as true. Indeed, the most persistent reason in favour of science being the only true picture of the world is the "Great Success of Modern Science Argument", the success of modern science in "predicting, controlling and explaining natural phenomena" (De Caro and Macarthur 2004: 5–6). Success is not to be confused with truth, however. To reveal the true nature of this success, we need philosophy, since science, as Kuhn (1970) observes, does not promote critical thought. Scientific explanations as well as disputes and consensus within the scientific community are mostly about successful application of the paradigm to the world rather than pursuit of truth.

Nonetheless, there is a naïve belief in science promoting truth. This belief leads inevitably to crises of value time and again. Nietzsche made some interesting observations in this regard. According to him, basic knowledge about the condition of knowledge is gained whenever the will to truth becomes aware of its problematic nature (GM, III, 27). As argued above, this insight is nihilistic because it reveals the true nature of reified thoughts and makes us aware of being alienated. To transfer this nihilistic insight into a culturally constructive force demands the critical outlook of the philosopher. Grown through bringing the foundation of science under philosophical scrutiny, this insight is an awareness that knowledge is interpretation. Improving our understanding of science, it reshapes the discourse of science. This new discourse derives its basic principles from the fundamental principle of inclusivity. It reveals the true nature of the Great Success of Science Argument as a will to exclude and dominate. These intentions are replaced by values based on insights into knowledge as will to interpretation. Based on an inclusive view of science, these values lead to self-mastery instead of domination of the other and the world, since the individual becomes aware of connections between knowledge and the individual qualities.

Nietzsche showed that a blind knowledge drive leads to asceticism, nihilism and despair. Fleck and Kuhn, in their turn, analysed the dogmatic and reified behavioural patterns of the scientific community. These observations reveal science's desperate need for philosophical critique. Functioning as the sole source of values, science becomes exclusive and leaves limited space for values other than efficacy. Such a knowledge system is a repressive one. It adopts the narrow and authoritarian perspective of weak objectivity. Philosophical engagement makes us able to oppose this repressive system. Through replacing the weak or exclusive notion of objectivity by an inclusive one, it widens human prospects. This process creates awareness of science's real conditions, its limits and possibilities.

ART, SEEN FROM THE PERSPECTIVE OF SCIENCE

In the previous section, I presented philosophy as the critical dimension of an inclusive view of the world. The relationship between science, the other component of this view, and philosophy was presented as connected with the critical appraisal of the foundation of science. This relationship, I argued, is based on critique and construction. In this section, I shall focus on the relations between art and science. To begin with, within the prevailing educational paradigm, art is considered to be a school subject and is evaluated from the perspective of science. It is not only seen from the perspective of science, it is also evaluated in terms of its usefulness for scientific culture. Traditionally, there is an unbridgeable abyss between art and scientific enquiry. Art is considered to be a matter of free fancies and a detour from gaining true knowledge. This perception of art is typical of the prevailing scientific paradigm and justifies the marginalisation of art and its being reduced to a school subject that should be taught scientifically. Refutation of art's cognitive value is based on a notion of truth proper as exclusively propositional on the one hand and an overestimation of theoretical knowledge on the other. I have already referred to Beardsley as an influential writer in this respect. He identifies knowledge proper with empirical science. On the other hand, he considers art to be a mimetic activity and reduces it to production of artworks or "aesthetic objects", as he himself puts it, rather than a perspective on the world. This issue receives more elaboration later in this chapter. Here, it is sufficient to mention that Beardsley considers philosophy as basically a linguistic activity and language as being representational. His notions of meaning and truth remain, hence, essentialistic. Truth is conceived as a matter of correspondence between thoughts and objects. Starting from these presuppositions, he concludes that artworks have no cognitive function. He espouses the view that non-literary art does not "give knowledge about reality, whether nature or supernature, whether in propositions, by revelation, or for intuition . . ." (1958: 391). Although with different intentions and in different nuances, these ideas have been repeated by other scientifically minded thinkers. This refers to an established style of thought rather than exceptional deviations from an otherwise acknowledged epistemic function of art. For instance, Ogden and Richards deny the cognitive value of poetry, since poetry, they argue, is not capable of "giving 'knowledge'" (1946: 158). Indeed, if we take Ogden and Richards seriously, a poem is cognitively empty, since it tells us "nothing" about the world (158). Whenever the cognitive function of the arts is recognised, it is done from the perspective of science. For instance, as Shusterman writes, the main concern of analytic aesthetic has been "scientific study of the different arts" (1989: 7). Seen from this perspective, the arts and aesthetics are reduced to the domain of subjective taste and feelings that have nothing to do with truth.

A common trait of these views of art is their distrust of non-scientific knowledge and overestimation of science as a self-sufficient perspective on the world as well as on other practices of knowledge production. Science becomes, then, the norm. The problem with such a norm is, however, that there is no eternal essence of science to be discerned. As has been mentioned on a couple of occasions in this study, scientific practices are signified by family resemblances among a variety of practices, methods of enquiry, problems, assumptions and fields of investigation. As mentioned earlier, within such a variety of practices, inclusion and exclusion occur in accordance with ideological and cultural values instead of being exclusively determined by epistemic norms. There are certainly grey zones and borderlands between scientific and unscientific investigative practices. Moreover, as argued in Chapter 4, the idea of correspondence between scientific facts and nature is outdated by Wittgenstein, Quine and post-Kuhnian science studies. The naïve belief that science is going to exhaust the truth about the world is also increasingly questioned. We have, thus, no basis to claim that being scientific means unequivocally true and being unscientific entirely untrue. Hence, the arts cannot be excluded from the domain of knowledge due to their not being scientific.

Another common trait of views discussed above is that they look at the role of art in the light of propositional knowledge. Cognitively speaking, this is a narrowing of the horizon of life and the scope of human knowledge. They not only contribute to marginalisation of an important element in human understanding of the world, but also diminish the possibilities of science itself. Contrary to this understanding of art, art is not a matter of merely propositional or abstract knowledge. Accordingly, it cannot be rejected by references to methods and demands of this type of knowledge. Not only do we shape our relationships to the world artistically, but the whole of human greatness in general is connected to art and human capacity as a creative artist. Or, as Aristotle puts it: "The magnificent man is like an artist" (*Nicomachean Ethics*, 1122 b). Seen in this light, all forms of knowledge acquire practical relevance to an active and creative style of life and conduct.

To use science as the only normative perspective is to disregard history. Indeed, history provides evidence against views that confine horizons of human knowledge to that of science. Seen in a historical perspective, it is quite recently that science has become the dominant form of collective knowledge. There have been forms of life like that of antiquity favourable to human flourishing and growth of human knowledge without being scientific. [2] Besides, science has not always been dominated by the current paradigm. Thus it is quite possible to produce a kind of science liberated from the current scientific paradigm. Such a science is allied with art and philosophy. The one makes it creative; the other examines the kind and quality of this creativity.

The importance of language in processes and end productions of cognition has been discussed. Considering every human being as an artist, I can now add that the whole of language is nothing more nor less than "an artistic process of metaphor formation", as Nietzsche puts it in "On Truth and Lies in a Nonmoral Sense" (TL). I will return to the metaphorical nature of language later. Here, I will emphasise that the relationship between the external world and the human world of language games is an aesthetic one. In this regard, I also draw on Nietzsche's writing: "between two absolutely different spheres, as between subject and object, there is no causality, no correctness, and no expression; there is, at most, an *aesthetic* relation. I mean, a suggestive transference, a stammering translation into a completely foreign language" (TL). This view of the relation between humanity and the world confirms the view that artistic activity is not limited to the creation of artworks in the conventional sense; rather, it is the main characteristic of human activities, including science. Seen in this light, not only is every human being an artist, but also every productive activity is an instance of aesthetical production. Thus, as will be explored later in this chapter, it is more fruitful to look at science from the perspective of art than the other way around.

In this study, art is considered a perspective on the world rather than a school subject. It is only through considering art a perspective on the world and a mode of understanding that we can do justice to it and its relation to science and philosophy. Seen in this light, art cannot be considered just a profession. Rather, it is synonymous with the creative activity of humanity in general. As human nature is based on man's labour or ability to work creatively, man is a creative artist by nature. In other words, any human being is an artistically creating being.

ART AS PERSPECTIVE

Connecting the issue of art to that of fulfilment, C. Koopman argues for art education in school and a "systematic training" in the arts by "general education" (Koopman 2005: 95). He rightly criticises the instrumental use of art and develops his own position on art as fulfilment. To relate art to general education is a crucial step in the right direction, but not sufficient. Koopman considers art as just a school subject among others and investigates it within the framework of scientific education. This means that art has to be taught scientifically. Considered as a basic characteristic of all human activities and a perspective on the world, art cannot be viewed as a subject to be scientifically taught, but more basically, it has to be seen as a perspective on science; science has to be done artistically. Moreover, in an educational context, the concept of fulfilment sounds essentialistic and teleological. It refers partly to an end that has to be reached and partly to an essence that should be fulfilled. These notions are closed and determined beforehand. Once we fulfil this essence we have reached the end of our development, a static state of affairs; we are consummated and do not desire any change or questioning of our state of being. Properly understood, there are no prefigured and constant essences to be fulfilled or final ends to be reached. There are endless processes of formation and transformation due to the unfolding of human creative resources. Our aspirations and goals outline the direction of our activities. They stimulate us to ever new kinds of activities and goals. Indeed, art signifies the changeable nature of humanity and the world; it signifies the endlessness of human creative resources and it's taking endless shapes. While these shapes are historical, human creativity as such is trans-historical. As human creativity is manifested in creative human labour, ever new heights of human development emerge as human labour brings into the light ever new horizons of human possibilities.

Another common flaw is to replace art as a perspective with art as works of art. Great works of art are of course a manifestation of art, but to limit art to them is to limit its scope and importance. To focus solely on works of art is also to limit art to certain artistic traditions, to certain styles and sets of aesthetical values and norms. Like paradigm-based science, this view of art brings members of a community together, but it also excludes all others that do not belong to the same tradition. Besides, as Lambert Zuidervaart observes, artworks can be used in political propaganda or turn into "hyper-commodities" (Zuidervaart 2004: 216). Indeed, this is the case in the contemporary socio-economical context; we easily make a fetish of works of art, whereby the artist and receiver are both alienated from the objectified work. By so doing, works of art become a part of reified human relations and block critical thought. Indeed, art would have to be freed from being a fetish so that it could become a key to human liberation.

One might well say that this is to reduce the importance of the work of art. What I suggest, however, assigns a much more important place to the work of art as a bearer of truth. At the same time, I suggest going beyond the work and focusing on the way a specific work conveys a truth; we have to focus on how a certain artist looks at the world and how she/he answers a specific question. By so doing, we are not passive consumers or owners of a precious commodity. We are, rather, engaged in a participatory mode of thought and involved in an interaction between freedom of interpretation and determinacy vis-á-vis the work. Indeed, the interpreter becomes an artist/creator not only through interpreting the work in an innovative way, but also through reorienting his/her own experience of the world in the light of this interpretation. The work, then, provokes the interpreter's own creative resources through opening a new perspective on the world rather than imposing the authority of its originator. It does not demand that our experiences of the work be fixed or identical with those of the artist. The work is then not a finished product ready to be consumed, but an ongoing process which constantly receives new meaning and significance; it is created time and again through new interpretations. Its very existence as a work of art is dependent on an open-ended interaction between the work and the interpreter. [3]

Art as a perspective goes far beyond different artistic traditions. Indeed, art as a perspective is indispensable, while no tradition or work of art is indispensable. As mentioned earlier, art as a perspective on the world is trans-historical, while works of art are historical "works that were not produced as art . . . [but] are able to become art . . . Equally, what once was art may cease to be art" (Adorno 1997: 300). Art as a perspective is related to the acute need of any age to become conscious of its central issues and problems. Any age has basic problems that can hardly be understood through philosophical or scientific discourses. Even if we capture them in words, they become trivial or reduced to dead words and conceptions. But to let them become manifest in art is to understand them in their totality. Indeed, good art is signified by the ability to discern the vital problems of the age. An art that fails to do so is not true to its time. This is the meaning of artistic truth. Through revealing the essential problems of their age in an artistic manner, works of art get an afterlife and become universal. As will be argued later, to claim this is to oppose the thesis of incommensurability. Perceived as the human ability to create, art makes different life-worlds as well as different spheres of experience translatable into each other. In this regard I am in agreement with Dewey when he claims that through art we can "install ourselves in modes of apprehending nature that at the first are strange to us" (Dewey 1934: 334). And this leads us to art as a perspective on the world.

SEEING SCIENCE FROM THE PERSPECTIVE OF ART

To look at art as a perspective, I have argued, is much more fruitful than looking at it as a school subject or limiting it to works of art. The importance of this view of art lies in its being a revealing perspective on the most basic issues of any age.[4] The most central problem of our age is science. Following Nietzsche, I have argued that the problem of science depends on science being seen from the perspective of science itself. To resolve this problem, an art true to our age provides a perspective on science; it lets science be manifested as it is. In this regard, I have drawn on Nietzsche's suggestion "*to look at science in the perspective of the artists, but at art in that of life*" (BT, Pref. 2). To establish this kind of relationship between art and science is a productive way of judging science and gives art its due place.

This study suggests art as the other of science, meaning that art provides a perspective outside science in which science can be evaluated and judged. To look at science through the prism of art reveals truths about science that would remain masked if we looked at science from the perspective of science itself. Through this shift in perspective, science becomes aware of its limitations and possibilities. An artistically informed science is aware of being based on changing presuppositions created by human imagination. Through coming into interplay with art, science becomes inclusive and covers a wider range of human experiences; it affirms the multiplicity of interpretation. Through these processes, the exclusive character of scientific truths comes into the day light. To see science from the perspective of art also reveals its ascetic tendencies, its being aimed at general conceptions and definitions.

While art is the other of science, life provides science and art with a perspective outside both of them. This enables art to look at itself from a perspective outside art itself on the one hand and function as the link between life and science on the other. This enables art to protect life against science's ascetic tendencies toward general forms and abstract knowledge by revealing the totalitarian character of this genre of knowledge. Such a knowledge becomes oppressive and authoritarian in that it demolishes the uniqueness, vitality and contingency of phenomena, detaches them from their contexts and subdues them to authorities outside history and culture who compel universal submission and acceptance. The scientific world view is then introduced as the only true account of the natural phenomena and science's depersonalised method of enquiry is upheld as the only way to true knowledge. Indeed, life is the utmost perspective in which all human knowledge and deeds should be judged. To look at art from the prism of life reveals the necessity of artistic creativity, art's ability to create life-enhancing illusions on the one hand and its ability to unmask the authoritarian and exclusive nature of metaphysical truths on the other. This issue will receive more elaboration in Chapter 7.

Because of its importance in the context of this study, the exclusive feature of scientific truth deserves more attention. One main reason why scientific truth is exclusive lies in the interconnectedness between this kind of truth and an imperialistic will to conquer and to dominate. Indeed, scientific acts and methods have been used not only in the rational systematization of life in the West, but also in the colonial and neo-colonial expansion of the Western powers. Post-colonial science studies show that science and the European colonial powers grew together and one was not possible without the aid of the other (Gilmartin 1994 and Harding 1993). The current asymmetry in power relations between the West and the rest of the world is also unthinkable without the aid of the sciences. Science and the related technologies are not only enhanced and sustained by the current dominant politico-economical powers but are also provided the basis upon which their future development is founded. Importantly, this is not to defend the provincialism of local cultures and disfavour scientific universalism. In my view, scientific universalism is liberating in comparison with limitations that localism imposes on thought, but universalism becomes totalitarian if it shows a will to totalise. The diversity of perspectives will disappear if universalism comprehends its task as the reduction of everything to general scientific definitions and conceptions. What are at issue are the instrumental use of science, the imperial will to dominate and violent attempts to dissolve the plurality of perspectives into a single one which is considered exhaustive and self-sufficient. From the point of view of the present study, the idea of understanding the world from a single perspective is a sophisticated form of epistemic violence. Indeed, this form of violence has been based on the notion of scientific truth as correspondence between propositions and reality or thing-conception correspondence. Commands from above as well as scientific facts have been driven by the apparently innocent will to "unity of truth".

SCIENTIFIC TRUTH AND AESTHETIC TRUTH

My critique of the exclusive notion of truth is not to be understood as a rejection of truth. Indeed, to come to terms with the totalitarian view of truth, we do not need to reject truth as such, since truth is not culpable in itself. We need, rather, to nuance our view of truth by establishing an inclusive notion of it. Heidegger's distinction between the Latin expression *veritas* and the Greek expression *aletheia* is helpful in this context. Though signifying truth, these two notions, as Heidegger says, "arise from quite different fundamental experiences" (Heidegger 2002: 9). While *aletheia* signifies a notion of truth based on the freedom of letting beings be as they are, the notion of *veritas* marks a militarised or "Romanized" notion of truth based on a will to defeat adversaries in the name of truth. There are parallels to be drawn between the *veritas/aletheia* distinction and the notions of scientific truth and artistic truth presented here. Indeed, *veritas* is Heidegger's word for truths as "correct and valid propositions" (9). It marks truth as concept-thing correspondence (Heidegger 1992: 53). In his view, as Herman Rapaport points out, *veritas* is based on "domination over an other". It expresses "an imperial will to power that requires decisiveness or victory that not only brings about a fall, but also justifies this toppling in the name of truth" (Rapaport 1997: 20). Consequently, *veritas* not only encompasses exclusion of the other, commands from above, but is also marked by violence, since it marks marginalisation and domination of the other. It is a truth legitimated through references to external authorities like God or Reason (Heidegger 1992: 53). This way of understanding the world brings to mind what Adorno terms "administrative research" (1998: 219) that dominates the academic world of today. Most school work and academic research is done in the spirit of *veritas*. It is based on collecting "data", registering and classifying "facts" and making them available as useful information. And this is the elegant ground of academic objectivity, the supposedly firm basis of propositional and formalised truth-claims. As a result, truth is considered an external source of authority and legitimacy. Such a notion of truth has nothing to offer when it comes to the flourishing of inclusive notions of life, knowledge and culture.

Truth has, as hinted, different dimensions. The aesthetic dimension of truth is signified by the notion of *aletheia,* truth as "disclosedness" and the "unhiddenness" of being. The question may arise whether art has anything to do with truth. Further, we can ask what has artistic truth to do with the social organisation of science and life? As mentioned above, art is not just free fancy. I also mentioned that art is not limited to the ornamental margins of life, but is a perspective on the world and a mode of experiencing and understanding. Accordingly, there is no art without respect for the properties of the material it works with as well as knowledge of the characteristics of artistic means of expression. It may be objected that this is obvious in the case of, say, architecture, sculpture and painting, but what about an art like music? As a mode of understanding and a perspective on the world, music shares much with other kinds of art. Although it may seem introverted, musical imagination has it own constraints. On the one hand, any musician has to have some knowledge of craft, albeit "tacit knowledge" (silent or implicit knowledge). The concordant intervals of the musical scales, for instance, are determined by numerical ratio. There are also principles guiding harmony and proportion. Even those who break the rules of harmony have to respect these rules in order to be able to do so. This aspect of music can be rendered by the notion of *veritas*. At this level music and art have nothing more to add to our understanding of the world than what science offers. However, contrary to science, music and art are not limited to this aspect of truth; they reach beyond this type of knowledge by penetrating behind dichotomies between feeling and thought, between order and chaos, to a pre-verbal sphere of experience, where the world is not ordered by conceptions and definitions. This primordial world cannot be revealed by scientific enquiry or administrative research. It is free from rational commands from above. Only art is able to dig down to the level of the "naïve evidence of things" (Merleau-Ponty 2005: 197). At this level, the aim is not to conquer or possess things, but to experience them. Consequently, art lets things show themselves as the beings they are. It is in this sense that an artist like Cézanne wanted to "show nature pure" (Merleau-Ponty 2005: 204). Such a view questions the correspondence between propositions and things and "seeks beings in their unhiddenness as being" (Heidegger 2002: 9). The Heideggerian notions of unhiddenness and disclosedness refer to the way in which the world shows itself to humanity. These notions mark a region where being is open and available to humanity. They bear witness to the self-manifestation moment of being. Such a self-manifestation happens in the work of art and art bears witness to such a moment. As such, truth is neither a thing that can be put into art nor a general conception that can be formalised. Nor is it an external source of legitimacy. It happens in and through art. *Aletheia* marks this happening of truth in art. It marks art's ability to let the central issues of each age become manifested.

Instead of dominating being, *aletheia* is connected with freedom or "disclosive letting beings be" (Heidegger 2005: 251). This logic of letting beings be the beings they are is liberating in relationships between humanity and nature as well as in relation to science. Humanity is liberated from what Ricoeur calls "the dehumanization of man by scientific objectivity", since we do not reduce human beings to creatures in the service of the market. It is also a rejection of the "objectification of nature" (Ricoeur 1965: 190) by the sciences, since we do not aim at conquering nature. Consequently, letting beings be is not only freedom from the commands of a hierarchical will to power, but also freedom from alienation and nihilism.

In summary and seen in the light of art, since science is dominated by a notion of truth as an authoritarian will to command from above, art becomes the place where science manifests itself and becomes available to us. Through becoming an artistic truth, science liberates itself from external authorities since the truth of art is an immanent truth; art does not yield to external or metaphysical authorities. Following Heidegger, Gadamer presents poetic truth as the paradigm of artistic truth. According to Gadamer, poetic truth becomes autonomous since not only is the correspondence between a poem and "what lies outside it" suspended, but also poetry questions "anything that might verify it" from outside (Gadamer 1986: 110). "We construct", Gadamer maintains, "the world of the poem from within the poem itself" (112). Hence, poetic truth becomes immanent in its own world; poetry is accountable only to itself. The autonomy of aesthetic truth was also argued by Ricoeur. To his mind, "The true artist only experiences the motivation which is proper to his art and does not yield to any commands exterior to his art" (Ricoeur 1965: 174). Indeed, in an age like ours, with its enormous resources for conformity and the manipulation of the masses, this trait of artistic truth is needed more than at any other time.

A further aspect of aesthetic truth has to do with the notion of communication. As I will discuss later, verbal forms of communication are of limited value when it comes to inner states. Through the process of familiarisation, verbal communication makes the original common. Language then becomes a language of reified conceptions.[5] Art, by contrast, defamiliarises the familiar, to use a couple of notions borrowed from Russian Formalism. Art does this through using innovative means of expression and letting beings manifest themselves as they are. It puts aside the sedimentations of the old established knowledge and casts new light on the world. By so doing, art refreshes our perception of the world; we see the world anew. Habermas refers to this characteristic of art as its "illuminating power". He confirms the view explained above by writing that art discloses "anew an apparently familiar reality" (Habermas 1985: 203). Seen in this light, like great philosophers, great artists are the innovators of their time.

ART AND PHILOSOPHY

I have looked at relationships between philosophy and science as well as those between art and science. While philosophy engages in a critical examination of the ground of science, art lets the truth of science be manifested. Put together, they can contribute to the improvement of science and to the emergence of an inclusive notion of science. The focal point of this section is the conditions of this contribution and how these two perspectives go together.

For the purpose of this study, the relationship between philosophy and art is seen in the light of their contribution to an educational renewal. They can become engaged with such a renewal not only by contributing to a cognitive pluralism based on art, science and philosophy, but also by unmasking the basis of alienation and nihilism in scientific culture and suggesting ways of overcoming them. Philosophical critique takes the first step toward a genuine educational renewal by questioning the weak notion of objectivity and the notion of science based on it. Insofar as philosophy questions the ground of science, it is destructive and nihilistic; it negates the old basis of science without creating a new one. At this stage, philosophy is engaged in discursive disputes with the established view of science. Since it uses the same discursive language as science, philosophy can be reduced to a science of science or a special kind of philosophical knowledge rather than being the basis of a philosophical life and a mode of understanding. At this stage, philosophy can at most, as Nietzsche puts it in "The Philosopher" (P, 27), "*recognize what is needed*". In order to become a constructive educational force, philosophy has to take a further step. At this stage, philosophy needs the assistance of art. This is because art is able to let the problem of education be revealed in its totality beyond discursive philosophical critique. On the other hand, artistic creativity contributes to the creation of new notions of objectivity and science and releases philosophy from negative nihilism. This means that philosophy cannot easily release itself from the burden of old educational values through simply negating them. It has to reach a new beginning by affirming the necessity of artistic creativity. It is in overcoming negative nihilism that philosophy becomes an active legislator of new educational values. This means taking a step further beyond knowledge into creativity and into the realm of art; philosophy becomes then an artful philosophy. This philosophy transcends the dichotomy between art and philosophy and is art and philosophy at the same time. The same can be said of science. This is an educational process whereby science, art and philosophy learn from each other.

It is worth mentioning that the thought style defended here is not a simple conglomeration of different forms of knowledge and perspective. There are tensions as well as cooperation between these perspectives. Art, philosophy and science receive new signification and meaning through coming into interplay within an inclusive perspective on the world. This perspective educates humanity against despair because it enjoys a multiplicity of perspectives, each criticised and protected by the others. If one of them fails in some respect, it is just the failure of that single perspective. There is still the possibility of using other perspectives.

TRUTH AS A NORM THAT GUIDES OUR ACTIONS

The question of truth can be discussed from different points of view. The focus of this study is epistemological. However, since I am not only concerned with theoretical knowledge, connections between truth and human action become important. This means that the epistemological aspect of truth comes into interplay with its ethical dimension. Regarding connections between ethical and epistemological orders of truth, it is particularly revealing that, as Medina and Wood believe, discussions on truth have taken "*a normative turn*" (Medina and Wood 2005: 2). Truth as a norm refers to its being the guiding principle of our practices as well as our experiences of life and the world. In the context of this study, truth is the guiding principle of our educational practices.

It is worth mentioning that from the perspective of this study, truth, as in the case of knowledge and art, is not a transcendental ground that exists outside human practices and experiences. Neither is it imposed on them; rather, truth is inseparable from these actions and experiences; it is embedded in our practices, in their contents and ends. Hence, instead of focusing on truth as a transcendental source of legitimacy, emphasis has to be put on the relationships between human actions, truth and the framework within which truth emerges. And this brings to the fore the performative aspect of truth, truth related to human discursive practices or "language games", to use Wittgensteinian terminology. Such a connection shows that truths emerge in our discursive practices. This is to say that, contrary to the representational notion of language, instead of being a closed picture of reality, truth is an open process based on "our acting" (Wittgenstein, 1969: § 204). This means that truth is actively created through activities we perform. These activities cover a wide range of actions like confessing, saying, accepting or rejecting truth in different situations. Here, I am trying to call attention to the important point that thoughts are not true intrinsically; rather, as William James says, they are "*made* true" (James 2005: 27) through active engagement of the human agency.

As we have seen, creativity is the basic human characteristic; man is a creative artist by definition. I have also emphasised the dialogical nature of life. Together, these two notions lay the foundation of human practices. On the other hand, all human activities take place in the framework of forms of life. Within these frameworks, perception, knowledge and action are related entities, as are aesthetics, epistemology and ethics. Indeed, a mutual encompassment of knowledge and ethics can be based on Aristotle, when he writes: "All art is concerned with coming into being, i.e., with contriving and considering how something may come into being which is capable of either being or not being, and whose origin is in the maker and not in the thing made" (*Nicomachean Ethics*, 1140a). Besides their ontological, epistemological and aesthetic aspects, these claims have also an ethical dimension, since the emphasis is placed on human agency or "the maker" and its productive actions. The sphere of human action, in its turn, is the framework of our ethical considerations. The ethical implications of any action lie not only in our ability to act or produce, but also in the fact that we can act in different ways, some of which can bring forth destructive forces. In other words, not all human discursive actions are desirable by definition. This brings into play an ethical consciousness and a sense of moral responsibility. At the level of our discourse, this responsibility is both epistemological and ethical. In saying this, I mean that we are not only ethically responsible to behave in a proper way, but also, as Husserl considers, we are epistemologically responsible to make the ground of our truth-claims available to others. In other words and seen from a normative perspective, to make available the foundation of one's truth claims to others is both an epistemological and an ethical concern; truth functions as both an ethical and an epistemological norm. Considering truth as testimony, Catherine C. Elgin emphasises the interconnectedness of moral and epistemological norms by writing: "False testimony is morally wrong because it is epistemically wrong" (2005: 275). As she observes, testimony brings about an ethical responsibility, since it "serves as a conduit of epistemic entitlement" (275), which is to be administered properly.

To highlight the interconnectedness of epistemological and ethical aspects of truth is in line with the position of this study. I discuss the notion of truth in the wider context of overcoming alienation and nihilism through unmasking the ground of knowledge and validation procedures. This approach highlights the ethical aspects of truth claims through suggesting solutions based on recognising the active role of the knower in the process of making things true. This means that the individual acts properly inasmuch as he/she is aware of his/her own active part in the production of truth and knowledge, on the one hand, and is ready to make the grounds of her/his truth claims available to others, on the other. In a scientific context, this means reliability of scientific research in terms of individual agent's being aware of their cultural and individual presuppositions, as well as the reliability and transparency of research reports. The agent of experimentation and observation is in a position that brings him/her not only epistemic entitlement, but also ethical responsibility.

A further area where the interconnectedness of ethical and epistemological norms becomes important is the social organisation of knowledge. As discussed above, the social organisation of science is constitutive of science. The management of scientific affairs involves not only issues of the kind of knowledge, but also the issue of who we are, both culturally and individually. This sheds light on the position of this study about the intrinsic connections between personal characteristics and the kind of knowledge one produces. This brings to the fore reflections not only on what is done, but also on how things are done. While the former is based on the traditional notion of objectivity (a notion of truth as *veritas*), where deeds are detached from the doer, the latter engages the question of the doer's presence in his/her deeds. Kierkegaard calls the latter style of thought "subjective thinking" and the former "objective thinking" (Kierkegaard 2005: 48). However, these two modes of action do not exclude each other. This point deserves some clarification. No doubt, in any discursive act, the most important thing is whose knowledge is the norm. This can be said especially of educational practices. In the absence of transcendental sources of legitimacy and a representational notion of language, cognitive entitlement is immanent in the context of knowledge. The question of how this entitlement is administered (how things are done) can be properly understood by reference the notion of style. As we will see, as an organisational principle style has two interconnected aspects, a cultural one and an individual one. The cultural aspect signifies constitutive elements of knowledge like the "standards of the community of inquiry"

(Elgin 2005: 285). These standards and values are either inclusive and facilitate an inclusive organisation of knowledge, or exclusive and block it. Individually, the focus is on individual characteristics like self-discipline, stringency of argumentation and reliability in communication with others who can also facilitate or block an inclusive organisation of knowledge. The demand for an inclusive notion of objectivity and a strong notion of the individual, defended in this study, makes sense in this connection. Seen in this light, an inclusive notion of knowledge lives up to the demand of objectivity on the one hand and to an inclusive style of organisation on the other. Thanks to such an organisation of science, truth-talk is not limited to each thought collective's answers to its own problems, but to engagement with others in mutual inclusion and cooperation.

In summary, my focus is not only on what science enables us to do (or better, what we generally can do, since our current ability to do things is basically based on science), but also on what we should do (what is ethically and scientifically true). In modern times, science and its related technology have enlarged the human capacity to produce. Human access to atomic energy and our ability to modify genes are among scientific achievements. These achievements cannot, however, be defined just in terms of the possibilities they offer. They also give birth to dangers that threaten life on the earth. They create anxiety, threats and fears which are not of a theoretical character or restricted to the theoretical world of physicists and biologists; rather, they concern our shared world of everyday life. Such concerns are not just a matter of epistemological concern, of specific theories being true or false. Rather, they concern our human responsibility to properly manage scientific achievements. In other words, scientific progress does not just produce fear. It also brings about ethical reflection. We cannot avoid questions like: What shall we do with the sciences? To my mind, this refers to the mutual encompassment of knowledge and ethics. In this way, the ethical and the epistemological come into interplay, since the question of truth becomes related to a complex whole of issues like what we can actually do, what we can know and on what ground. For instance, science enables us to modify genes. This raises the question of how we should use this possibility to create a better world to live in and to strengthen solidarity with the environment and other people. Simply expressed, it can be used in a way that protects life and the environment or endangers them for the sake of political and economic gains.

6 Plurality of Perspectives and Unity of Style

In the preceding chapter, truth was presented as a normative principle that guides our educational actions. Truth, science and education were based on the notion of inclusiveness. I also argued that the social organisation of science is constitutive of knowledge. The question now is how can we organise the plurality of outlooks without being torn apart in different directions by all too many perspectives on the world? There is certainly a risk of the individual becoming dispersed into different ways of thinking, without being able to organise the diversity of orders of truth and domains of thought. Since there is no natural organisation of thought, we have to find ways of organising our cognitive activities. This is to say that the world manifests itself to us in a variety of ways. Rather than exclusively verifying and organising a set of ideas, nature constrains our thoughts and ideas. Organising as well as confirming thought is a human task. It demands basic organisational principles which are transparent to us. To my mind, the notion of style can function as a regulative concept in this regard. Through this notion we can organise the plurality of perspectives, modes of understanding and levels of truth, socially and individually. From the point of view of this study, the notion of style is a proper organisational principle; it constrains as well as stimulates creative resources within the individual and the community. In traditional ways of organising knowledge, commands from above, either political or theological, impose unity on ideas through denying the diversity of perspectives. The notion of style, on the contrary, is an aesthetic organisational principle. It is immanent in the very process of knowledge and discursive actions instead of being external to them. Indeed, it signifies the denunciation of external authorities. As a result, it demands individual freedom and self-determinacy as well as inclusive cultural climates. This is to say that style is both of a cultural and an individual character.

THE COLLECTIVE ASPECTS OF STYLE

Style, I argued, has a collective and an individual aspect. Fleck and Nietzsche are among the thinkers who discuss these two aspects of style. Fleck does not offer much help. He uses the notion of style in order to eliminate the individual as a cognitive being. His notion of style becomes one-dimensional and authoritative. He studied the collective nature of style by focusing on the relationships between the individual, the object of knowledge and styles of thought. His main concern was the ways in which communities of thought organise perceptions in recognisable and communicable forms and categories of consciousness. Fleck observed that although thought styles originate in communities of thought, they become thought constraints once they take shape and get a hold on individuals' minds. They are the organisational principles of cognition and impose unity on collective knowledge.

Fleck rightly emphasises that thoughts necessarily occur within the boundaries of a style of thought. But he goes to the extreme in claiming that "thinking [is] a supremely social activity which cannot by any means be completely located within the confines of the individual" (Fleck 1979: 98). In this view, the individual subject collapses into a collective psyche that thinks and acts independently of individuals. To Fleck's mind one can eliminate both individual and reality and still be able to explain cognition. This is because, he claims, reality is materialised ideas belonging to the collective and the individual is nothing more than a representative of the collective (40–41). The notion of thought style signifies just this elimination of the individual.

Fleck discusses the thought style of modern science and its connectedness with the hierarchical structure of scientific community. Being initiated into this thought style, the individual is rarely aware of the cultural grounds of science's social organisation. Scientists take their thought style as natural and function as representatives of the community. Repeatability is the basic feature of scientific method; in the scientific community any individual can repeat any experiment and reach the same result (Fleck 1979: 98). This scientific trait strengthens the illusion of science being independent of scientists' background beliefs and their contexts of activity. This de-personalised research method signifies an alienated situation in which reified ideas dominate humanity, though Fleck does not discuss these issues.

Fleck's description of the notion of style gives us hints of current scientific praxis, where individuals are formed in the image of the scientific thought style. However, it offers no help when it comes to inventing new images of knowledge or finding solutions to problems associated with the current exclusive social organisation of science. As an unintended result of his theory, we become aware of how humanity is instrumentally used in the service of science and how truth is reduced to stylised inquiries performed by depersonalised scientists. This signifies alienated labour and a sublime type of enslavement without any sense of giving truth and life their due. As a sociologist of knowledge, Fleck thinks that this is the way human beings operate. He does not pay due attention to the possibility of critique and presenting alternative ways of organising knowledge. Since he reduces philosophy to sociology of science, the possibility of critical thought becomes minimal. For Fleck, individuals share the characteristic of being formed by the thought style and subjugated to it. It is as if this is intrinsic to cognition. Such individuals are scarcely capable of participating in a creative transformation of the thought style: neither are they able to shift perspective or resist cultural values inimical to an inclusive social organisation of science; they are weak individuals. They just implement collectively recognised standards of organisation knowledge and experience. As discussed in Chapter 5, we in any case need a set of cultural standards of organisation. Hence, the main issue is the kind of standard. It is to be inclusive instead of exclusive. This criterion is necessary but not sufficient; standards of organisation must also not be reified general conceptions and function as a source of alienation and conformity. In this case, they destroy individual differences and mask the active part of the individual in cognition and the organisation of thought.

THE INDIVIDUAL ASPECTS OF STYLE

We can come to terms with this problem through highlighting the individual aspect of style. In so doing, we equip the individual with an organisational tool that can be used actively and creatively. Nietzsche, contrary to Fleck, relates style to the individual and considers it something actively acquired by rather than imposed on the individual. Style is seen in a wider context of life than just that of knowledge. The individual chooses not only to organise his/her knowledge in accordance with a style, but also to live in accordance with the constraints of a style, since such constraints are necessary conditions of thought. This mode of understanding is a pre-condition of a life lived artistically. This is also a non-alienated state of mind, since the individual is an active organiser of his/her life and knowledge. Considering education as mostly self-education, Nietzsche believes that the most important aim of the "great and rare art" of education is, "to 'give style' to one's character" (GS 290). Properly understood, this position confers on the individual the crucial role of forming and transforming his/her knowledge, character and style. These changes take place in accordance with a style. There are, however, differences between different individuals, since this characteristic is not naturally given. It is in this connection that Nietzsche talks of rank and order between strong and weak natures; some people take responsibility for their lives and become active organisers of their greatness; they are able to see things from different perspectives. At the same time, they are able to create a style of their own and organise their life and knowledge in accordance with a single style. There are also individuals who lack this ability. They prefer a comfortable state of being and let themselves be mastered by the collective standards; some become masters and others slaves. It goes without saying that the former type of individual assists the improvement of our understanding of the world, while the latter worsens it. As already stated, strong individuals have the ability to control their arguments. They are sovereign individuals and enjoy self-autonomy and self-control and let their beliefs become action according to a single style; they are at one with their style and actions. This style is, in its turn, an inclusive one.

There is a difference not only between different individual styles of organising thought and conduct, but also between different cultural styles. The distinction between inclusive and exclusive styles has been mentioned already. Here, I emphasise the aesthetic aspect of the notion of style. As in the case of individual greatness, cultural greatness also has an artistic or active aspect. In Nietzsche's *David Strauss, the Confessor and the Writer*, a genuine "culture is a unity of artistic style" (DS, 1). To make this clear, unity of style gives cultures and individuals the strength to organise their inner world as well as their relation to the external world according to a plan of their own. While inclusiveness of style enables cultures and individuals to live in solidarity and harmony with others, the artistic trait of style enables them to have their distinctive character and take control of circumstances. Nietzsche and Fleck are aware of style being a thought constraint. But Fleck has the collective as the starting point. Contrary to this, Nietzsche focuses on the sovereignty of the individual. While in the first case style is conceived as a means of conformity, in the latter it is a means of individual distinction and self-discipline. As Nietzsche puts it in *The Antichrist*, "the great style" is "keeping our strength, our *enthusiasm* in harness. Reverence for oneself; love for oneself; unconditional freedom before oneself" (A, Preface).

Thus, besides organising our knowledge of the external world, the notion of style enables us to organise our inner life through aesthetic self-mastery; we do not do this in accordance with commands from above, but as an inner source of vitality. Having love and reverence for oneself as a starting point, one can claim that despite constraints of social circumstance, there is always space for individual freedom. There is an ongoing struggle between the demands of collectives and individual freedom, within the individual and within community. A creative and active individual is able to get the individual and collective aspects of style to go together artistically. This brings his/her freedom. There are exclusive collective styles which repress individual freedom as well as slave individual styles incapable of using this freedom. There are also inclusive cultural styles because there are master individual styles. These types of style and individual correspond to each other.

TRAGEDY AS AN ORGANISATIONAL MODE

A desirable style is thus inclusive and artistic. It brings freedom and constrains at the same time. It not only goes well with the inclusive notion of objectivity, but also paves the way for a creative individual life with others. A further aspect is its being tragic. This means that it is aware of its communal and individual possibilities and limitations. In order to illustrate these points, we can use the art of tragedy as an organisational model applicable to knowledge and life. As the structure of tragedy covers all these aspects, it can be used as an artistic, inclusive and tragic model structure for the organisation of thought.

For the purpose of this section, Nietzsche's analysis of the art of tragedy is helpful. He sees tragedy as "*the union*, indeed the *identity*, of the *lyrist with the musician*" (BT, 5). Besides being tragic and artistic, this organisational principle is inclusive; while the musical dimension of tragedy refers to the non-verbal aspect of our relationship to the world, its lyrical aspect refers to the verbal one. Obviously, tragedy shares the feature of discursiveness with science and philosophy. It is the level of ordinary language use and refers to truth as *veritas*, to verbally communicable forms of knowledge. Importantly, in tragedy lyrics and music meet and reach an aesthetical balance. In this way, truth not only becomes articulated but also manifests itself. In other words, tragedy covers both aspects of truth, *veritas* and *aletheia*. This way of organising knowledge not only translates the world of objects into words, but also lets it manifest itself as it is, without being moulded in words. Through music, tragedy penetrates to the pre-linguistic sphere of the world, where beings are not reduced to systematized general conceptions. At the same time, it does not dwell at that level for ever. It brings us insights that are verbally communicable. It is a perpetual movement between the pre-verbal and the verbal. It brings us insights based on this multiple perspective. Through showing the chaotic pre-verbal sphere of being, it not only threatens our comfortable existence in the discursive order of things, but also entices our organisational and order-creating ability; it encourages us to actively use our artistic as well as discursive ability to organise the chaos. Seeing that deep into the nature of being, humanity refrains from conquering nature and acquires the insight to live in harmony with it. The tragic style then becomes the main organisational principle; it brings forth awareness of human limits and possibilities. By letting humanity appear as both lyrist and musician, tragedy organises verbal and non-verbal experiences in a single work of art and according to a single style. It includes ways of understanding beyond philosophy and science, which are limited to verbal means of expression.

Tragedy as an organisational principle is applicable to educational practices. Indeed, education needs to be guided by an artistic, tragic and inclusive organisational principle. Artistic organisation, philosophical contemplation and scientific stringency together make education a non-violent process, where the uniqueness of each individual and each perspective is recognised and respected. At the same time, the individual and the collective are reconciled and come into interplay in the same process. As a result, the individual connects his/her life to that of the collective and his/her interest becomes that of society. In this way, egoistic individualism and collectivistic conformity are avoided. The aesthetic principle of organisation relates the general to the particular without negating the one or the other; it is anti-authoritarian and opposes alienation.

7 The Question of the Ground of Understanding

As argued in the preceding chapter, style creates unity among the diversity of cultural and cognitive perspectives. To have a multiplicity of perspectives as the ground of objectivity means also a multiplicity of cognitive devices such as observation, reading, reflection, translation and interpretation. The question to be discussed here is on what basis styles organise these different means.

Primarily, the problem of the ground of understanding has to be considered in the wider context of culture rather than in isolation or in the context of understanding itself. Bearing this in mind, our concern should not be limited to theoretical knowledge. Human behaviour and practice are also of concern. The other aspect of the issue is the awareness that whatever ground we choose is constructed and temporary rather than natural and eternal. Nietzsche and Wittgenstein observed the illusory nature of these grounds, or their being groundless. I have already referred to the Wittgensteinian view of the abyssal character of the world. Here, I use Nietzsche to underpin claims about the nature of the foundation of our knowledge and understanding of the world.

I have already emphasised the importance of art as a perspective. Art also was considered as general human ability to create. To connect these aspects of art to the question of the ground of knowledge, we must now focus on art's ability to create illusions. As we shall see, artistic illusions are of paramount importance for the ground of action and knowledge. This means that these grounds, whatever they may be, are human-made and embedded in the contexts of knowledge and action instead of being transcendental. On the other hand, life was presented as the utmost perspective in which art, action and science should be judged. As such, life, in its cultural and biological senses, goes far beyond our individual mortality and contexts of actions. In this sense, life is eternal or trans-historical. Accordingly, it can function as a universal basis regarding our judgements about knowledge and its ground. This means that, as the basis of knowledge, artistic illusions are to be judged in the perspective of life; they can be rejected or confirmed by references to their being life-enhancing or life- decreasing. This can be said of the ground of knowledge as well as those of cultures.

Reference to Nietzsche enables us to shed light on these subjects. Through genealogical studies of ancient cultures, Nietzsche came to believe that any culture is based on certain intuitive and unexamined presuppositions. Regarding the ground of knowledge, it was indeed Aristotle who observed the necessity of self-evident and unexamined axioms for any type of knowledge (*Metaphysics*, 1005b–1006a). Inspired by Nietzsche, we can extend the domain of axioms to all spheres of life and culture and call them axioms of culture. To Nietzsche's mind, these intuitive sources of cultural vitality are based on a specific form of illusion.[1] He writes: "every people, indeed, every human being who wants to become mature needs . . . an enveloping illusion, . . . a protecting and enveloping cloud" (ULH, 7). Nietzsche sees these illusions as the necessary ground of life so that "if this cloud is removed, if a religion, an art, a genius, is condemned to be a planet without an atmosphere, then we should cease to be surprised that they quickly wither" (7). The needs of life are here prior to ascetic search for metaphysical truths. Stemming from human imaginative creativity and immanent in the context of their emergence, these illusions are not a matter of theoretical speculation; rather, they emerge because of life's practical needs. They are necessary for our laying down a horizon of thought and action, without which we would not be able to act or acquire knowledge of the world. A main problem in this connection has been human forgetfulness; we forget the man-made nature of these horizons of action and understanding. As a result, they become reified.

The problem dealt with here is one of the oldest of philosophy, the problem of the changing nature of our empirical reality and our aspiration to catch it in stable conceptual schemes, the problem of having a stable point amid a changing world. To catch ever-changing reality in universal and objectively true knowledge has been the everlasting dream of philosophies that ground human actions in knowledge, since actions grounded in knowledge are considered good. Since Plato, philosophers have tried to give us a stable ground for our knowledge and actions; famously, Plato invented the eternal Forms. Kant invented the universal forms of intuition in order to establish an objective basis for knowledge. The main concern has been to transcend the stream of empirical impressions and the diversity of conflicting contexts and attain universally valid knowledge. Nietzsche shifted the focus away from the constancy of the ground of knowledge to truthfulness to an ever changing reality. He questioned both constant poles of eternal knowledge; categories of understanding and a constant world of objects. This is a move away from alienation and nihilism. By basing the foundation of the organisation of thought and knowledge on art or human creative resources, we avoid their becoming metaphysical categories of thought; they are placed within human reach and are subjected to perpetual change and revision. This makes the meaning of an artful science clearer; properly understood, science is based on art. Indeed, this notion of science can be traced to both Aristotle and Nietzsche, when they indicate that science is not based on eternal metaphysical grounds but on illusory or intuitive foundations. Unaware of its artistic basis, the current notion of science has become ascetic. It functions as the basis of alienation. Seen in this light, awareness of artistic illusions constituting the basis of our actions becomes necessary not only for science and education, but also for whole cultures.

I have already presented tragedy as the organisational principle of knowledge. Now I should add that the same principle can be used in the wider context of culture. The intuitive basis of culture or axioms is then related to the musical or pre-verbal aspect of tragedy, while science and different forms of knowledge are analogous with its verbal aspect.

ACTIVE AND PASSIVE ELEMENTS OF THOUGHT

As argued above, besides having an organisational principle, we need a foundation on which this organisation can rest. We have also argued that this basis is artistic. This means that it is provisional and contextual. This view of the issue is the opposite of the traditional one, since it considers the Platonic eternal ideas and the Kantian a priori forms of intuition, time and space as historical notions connected to particular forms of life. Important as it is, this point deserves more attention.

The Fleckian model of active and passive elements of thought offers the analytical tool we need. In fact, Fleck's theory confirms the Nietzschean view about the aesthetic nature of the ground of knowledge by characterising a thought style as a "harmony of illusions" (Fleck 1979: 38 and passim). Indeed, the Aristotelian notion of axiom, the Nietzschean notion of illusion and the Fleckian notion of active elements of cognition refer to the same thing; together they reveal the intuitive, aesthetic and human-made nature of the basis of our knowledge. In the context of this study, I prefer, however, to use the Fleckian notion of the active element of cognition. While the old notion of axiom may remind us of the metaphysical notion of knowledge and the notion of illusion may confuse artistic illusions with free fancy, the notion of active elements of thought implies the creative part of the cogniser in constructing starting points of knowledge more clearly. In Fleck's model, active elements of knowledge are our presupposed starting points of cognition and passive elements are resulting consequences given the constraints of these starting points. They correspond to the traditional notions of subjective and objective elements of knowledge, respectively. Active elements are created and presupposed actively by us and cognition cannot work without their being presupposed (Fleck 1979: 40). They are illusory in the sense that they give an impression of being stable and natural, while in reality they are human-made, temporal and products of our imaginative creativity. The inter-connectedness and inter-changeability of active and passive elements affirm the changeable nature of the ground of knowledge. Active and passive elements of thought can interact within the framework of a thought style. Fleck's favourite example of the imaginative nature of active elements and the inevitability of their constrained results is the ratio between the atomic weights of oxygen and hydrogen:

> The origin of the number 16 for the atomic weight of oxygen is almost consciously conventional and arbitrary. But if 16 is assumed as the atomic weight for O, oxygen, of necessity the atomic weight of H, hydrogen, will inevitably be 1.008. This means that the ratio of the two weights is a passive element of knowledge. (Fleck 1979: 83)

Here, forms of thought are parts of cognition itself rather than existing in the external world, as the case is with Platonic or Kantian forms; they emerge as a result of interplay between active and passive parts of knowledge. As social reality is constitutive of these forms, on the one hand, and changeable, on the other, these forms cannot be fixed or stable. If we change the atomic weight of oxygen, the ratio of the atomic weights of oxygen and hydrogen will also change. However, as a result of history, education and tradition these stylised relations become accepted as everyday facts and seem natural. In reality, however, knowledge is a result of the inter-play between two unstable poles, the active and the passive. We actively presuppose certain starting points at the first stage. At the next stage, we accept results that necessarily follow given these presuppositions. Knowledge embraces, then, active as well as passive elements of thought. To prevent misunderstanding, we cannot presuppose as active elements of knowledge whatever we wish. Thought style constrains these presuppositions.

To see knowledge in this light is to affirm the changeable character of the world and let it manifest itself in all its ambiguity. It is not only to agree with the multiple characters of interpretation, but also to concentrate on cultural conditions constitutive of human understanding. Consequently, the ascetic will to truth or abstract knowledge become secondary in relation to the artistic will to interpretation. One implication of this view is the primacy of action in relation to theoretical knowledge. Since "action requires the veil of illusion" (BT, 7), the notion of illusion becomes central to philosophical enquiry. Consequently, the shift of focus is away from the general and the formal to the actual. It not only moves away from pure knowledge to action but also to a kind of action and its presuppositions. The most important thing is, then, the style according to which the active elements of cognition, or ground of understanding, are put together.

It is worth mentioning that the framing limit of a thought style against which the world and life are made understandable is necessary, otherwise the form-giving capacity of humanity would be dissolved in the chaotic and perplexed stream of empirical impressions. As a result the world would appear as inconceivable. The strength or weakness of cultures is demonstrated in their being or not being able to create inclusive styles by which life flourishes. If the form-giving resources of humanity are not capable of establishing the frame of reference of a style then knowledge as well as culture become impossible. To have a style of thought is thus a precondition of any form of knowledge, life and culture. At the basis of each style of thought the creative or artistic resources of humanity are at work.

As discussed in Chapter 4, some cultural values and conceptual frameworks are more beneficial to the enhancement of life than others. Accordingly, some active elements of cognition promote the growth of knowledge while others damage it. Thus, illusions or active presuppositions of thought are neither to be unconditionally affirmed nor unconditionally negated. A distinction has to be made between different kinds of active elements of knowledge. Generally speaking, genealogical analysis is based on retrospective studies and traces the genesis of any presupposition back to its motives. Such studies reveal two important points about active elements of cognition: First, the style and motives behind them are as important as active elements themselves. Secondly, there is an intrinsic connection between the kind of active presuppositions of thought and the human type behind it. Thus, critique of active elements happens together with critique of their originators. The question of what kind of needs motivate humanity to adopt certain kinds of presuppositions then becomes the most basic issue. Genealogical analyses are also educational and offer good examples of how certain cultures with a horizon of life based on life-affirming active elements as their axioms have organised sustainable forms of life. They show that illusions based on an ascetic will to truth are inimical to life since they subdue life to general and abstract truths. Fully aware of the active part of the subject in the creation of the basis of knowledge, active styles are, by contrast, in the service of conducting an active life. They signify human self-mastery. Contradictory as it may seem, this is a state of mind characterised by disillusionment, as active elements of thought are transparent and are consciously used to enhance a healthy culture; we are aware of their being our own creations. Emphasis on the artistic nature of the basis of knowledge is therefore necessary.[2] Being healthy and strong, such a basis contests the weak or ascetic basis of knowledge. It reveals the exclusive nature of the ascetic will to truth on the one hand and its tendency to conquer and dominate in the name of truth on the other.

Indeed, metaphysical truths are opaque illusions; they are illusions masked as universal truths or pure knowledge. Platonic eternal ideas, the Cartesian notion of the subject, Kantian *a priori* forms of intuition, for instance, are such illusions. They function as predetermined determinants of knowledge, beyond human reach. The individual is, rather, subordinated to them. Schooled in such a knowledge paradigm, people are rarely aware of these illusions being human-made. As a result, these illusions are neither transparent nor do they have a constructive use in the service of proper understanding of the world. Ascetic disinterestedness is properly understood if we interpret it against a background of the emergence and development of scientific education discussed in Chapter 2. It has also to be seen in the light of the fact that in reality it is absolutes like "national security", "good career choices", "economic competitiveness" of nations and the "needs of the labour market" that decide the aims and contents of scientific enquiries and science-based education.[3] Seen in the light of what has been said so far, this signifies a state of mind characterised by alienation. Initiated into such knowledge systems, people inevitably run the risk of nihilism as soon as they become aware of their truths being either metaphysical illusions or interests of empowered social groups masked as truths.

A healthy culture is signified by the ability to overcome alienation and nihilism. This is done through its use of education as a therapeutic tool to reveal the true nature of the ascetic will to truth and its aspiration to pure knowledge. It also presents life and its needs to flourish as the utmost perspective in which art, science, truth and education should be evaluated. To have life as the utmost perspective means to reconcile truth with human interests rather than interests of a specific social group. This means inclusiveness of the basic presuppositions of knowledge, on the one hand, and the awareness that whatever truths are, they are based on these active presuppositions, on the other. Being constitutive of knowledge, these presuppositions should be life-enhancing instead of life-negating. Seen in this light, we recognise the heterogeneity of truths and try to make them inclusive rather than pure. In such a cultural climate, communal and individual lives thrive, since the interests of the individual coincide with those of the community. Communities, in their turn, do not confine themselves to just their own interests; rather, they connect these interests with those of humanity. Indeed, this inclusive attitude toward the other is necessary in a world of increasing global interdependencies. It includes all qualified perspectives in the production and dissemination of knowledge and protects them against cultural values that distort our understanding of the world. Democratic values are among the former category of values and racism and sexism among the latter.

To make it clear, an inclusive notion of knowledge has to be based on a plurality of cognitive perspectives, art, philosophy, science and history. Art determines the active elements of knowledge production practices; it is the ever-changing foundation of knowledge. Science can then be related to the results that necessarily follow given these presuppositions—the passive elements of cognition that are to be accepted unreservedly. These results enter the domain of public knowledge. As such, they are to be justified by reference to a publicly agreed and communicable style of thought. In this sense, "characterizing an episode or a state as that of *knowing*, we are not giving an empirical description of that episode or state; we are placing it in the logical space of reasons, of justifying and being able to justify what we say" (Sellars 1997: 76). In my account, this justifying occurs in the light of the active elements or starting point of knowledge. Any passive element of knowledge has to be consistent with its starting presuppositions. These starting elements, I argued, are artistically invented and actively presupposed. As the passive component of knowledge, science is then to be seen from the perspective of these artistic illusions. This means that science is seen perpetually in the light of art. Philosophy, in its turn, was presented as our critical horizon regarding the foundation of science. Being a perspective outside this foundation, philosophy contributes to a critical appraisal of science's foundation. It investigates consistency of the active and passive elements of cognition as well as stringency of thought. Through constructive affirmation and reconstructive questioning, it contributes to the renewal of starting presuppositions of knowledge and reshaping of their end results; it prevents their becoming rigid and reified. History, on the other hand, brings to light the past as the educator of the present; it shows how past generations established styles of thought beneficial to growth of knowledge and enhancement of life. And what lessons we can learn from their successes and failures. Linking of knowledge from the multiplicity of perspectives creates a synthesis or unity from inherent difference, which does not suffer shortcomings such as science being its own foundation or a perspective on itself.

On the other hand, an inclusive notion of knowledge has to be based on a plurality of cultural and social perspectives like those of men and women, different cultural and ethnic groups. Critique will be impossible if active elements of cognition are based on the single perspective of science and if science is based on the perspective of a single social group. We cannot then look at our own perspective from those of others or look at the perspective of science from those of art and philosophy. Having an inclusive style of thought enables us to be both committed to and critical of our frames of thought, to be within and outside knowledge systems at the same time. As physiologically and culturally embodied beings, we cannot leave our Platonic cave of culture and embodiment in order to bring the light of absolute truth into it. However, we can use different perspectives to shed light on the same subject. Educated in an inclusive style of thought, we would be able to shift perspective whenever it is needed.

The social and cognitive worth of such a multidimensional notion of knowledge dwells in its receiving its purpose and orientation from life itself; it is motivated by human needs to act rather than by a blind drive to pure knowledge. Science makes sense within our complicated world of interests, language games, cultures and traditions, with their hierarchies of power and disempowerment as well as regimes of inclusion and exclusion. It cannot remain neutral or pure. The same can be said of nature; it is mediated through the prisms of tradition and language. Pure nature is thus out of human reach. Cognitively speaking, we encounter nature as an object of knowledge. This means that it comes to depend upon our constitution of it as an object of knowledge, as Kant has taught us. Nature becomes, then, known within the framework of culture. In other words, "In science, just as in art and in life, only that which is true to culture is true to nature" (Fleck 1979: 35). Informed by this insight, the notion of science used here does not mask established interests behind claims about neutrality of scientific research methods and practices. It asks, rather, questions about the kind of interests that inform science. As argued earlier, any art true to its time has the ability to recognise the basic problems of that age. Having this ability, it becomes the site of disclosure of truth about the nature of these problems, on the one hand. On the other hand, it contributes to these problems being properly addressed. This is done through shaping the active elements of thought in such a way that prefigures solutions proper to these problems. Through making these presuppositions inclusive, art not only brings to the fore our time's demand of cognitive justice, but also prefigures the basis on which such a justice can be achieved. This inclusive basis maximises objectivity of science by activating democracy-increasing values. Interests to be perused, problems to be solved and questions to be answered are selected on the basis of perspectives of men, women, children and marginalised people. Philosophy contributes to this inclusive notion of knowledge by bringing about consciousness regarding unexamined cultural values like sexism, racism and Eurocentrism, and it makes the sciences free of them. Thus, active elements of cognition are invented and the consistency of its passive elements are maintained in close connection with the cardinal problems of each age. In my account, these endeavours all occur within the same context of interrelationships, overlapping, differences, conflicts, border-crossing and cooperation between science, art and philosophy. Rather than reducing the issue to dividing lines between the "context of discovery" and the "context of justification" or the division of labour between science, art and philosophy, we must use them adequately in order to pave the way for changes in reified systems of knowledge and alienating patterns of behaviour.

In accord with the line of argument sketched above, knowledge becomes an open system in perpetual interplay with its environment. Instead of being initiation into closed and homogenous systems of knowledge, where all details are predetermined, education becomes an introduction into an open cognitive space where a variety of cognitive means, like those of art, philosophy and science are available. It equips the individual with actual abilities to creatively use these means in order to construct and reconstruct knowledge. This notion of education does not suffer the problem of the scientific education outlined in the Introduction. Indeed, new information technologies and conditions of thought make such systems of knowledge and educational practices necessary and possible.

8   Education and Educators

In the preceding chapters, I have criticised established notions of science, epistemology, truth, and objectivity. I have also tried to spell out the characteristics of alternative notions. In the coming chapters, I shall try to relate these new notions to education. In order to do this, we need a new notion of education, since changes suggested here are not achievable within the framework of the current educational paradigm. Thus, I suggest radical changes in this notion of education. Traditional education is based on abstract knowledge and also on the needs of states and the market, like "national security and economic competitiveness". Since the focus is on the latter aims, educational goals like personal development and social engagement become abstract notions without any or few practical implications; they comprise the rhetorical aspect of education. Focused on the short-term interests of states and the market, such an education neglects long term interests of humanity as such. As Mitzes and Wandersee write, shifts in curricular emphases and instructional practices at elementary and secondary school levels in the United States "reflect a response to some real or imagined threat posed by domestic or international circumstances in the political, social, economic, or military areas" (1997: 29). At the root of this problem they see "the acknowledged role of science and technology in service to the national defence and welfare" (29). I mention the United States because of its leading position in scientific education. This situation is not unique to the States; rather, it is the general situation of scientific education.

Due to the enormous influences of forces external to science and education, scientific education gives birth to values, skills and habits of mind that damage the growth of knowledge and prevent the establishment of a sustainable and inclusive organisation of science and society. In order to overcome these narrow-minded emphases, we need a notion of education that encompasses the positive aspects of the current education and goes far beyond it. By going beyond science teaching and focusing on the major principles of scientific education as such, I wish to emphasise our huge need of radical educational changes. I hope to spell out the kind of changes and open new horizons of educational discourse and practice.

Besides being based on elements like cognitive democracy, the inclusive notion of objectivity and individual rigour, the notion of education suggested here is based on the idea of educational exemplars. These reveal to us new cognitive, educational and cultural values beneficial to the growth of human knowledge and long term social and environmental interests. In the following sections several exemplars will be discussed and criticised in order to finally establish an inclusive notion of educator. Once this is done, we will be able to highlight links between the notion of education and new notions of truth, knowledge and objectivity.

SCIENTIFIC OR WEAK EXEMPLARS

The use of scientific exemplars is nothing new. They are widely used in prevailing practices of scientific education. Scientific exemplars are "the shared examples among scientists" (Duschl 1994: 445). Indeed, the notion of scientific exemplars emerged in Kuhn's postscript to *The Structure of Scientific Revolutions*. In this postscript Kuhn tries to explicate the notion of paradigm in order to meet criticisms of ambiguities. As a part of these endeavours, he replaces paradigm by notions of theoretical generalisations and exemplars (exemplary matrixes). I choose to concentrate on the notion of "exemplar" as it refers to the relationship between a paradigm and education. By exemplars Kuhn means the solutions to problems and questions used in educational purposes. They are problems and questions that are placed at the end of each chapter of a science text, in laboratory exercises and examinations or designed as homework and training. If we take Kuhn seriously, these exemplars outline the future direction of scientific inquiry. Indeed, this view is based on actual educational practice. Exemplars signify consensus among scientists and are based on undisputable "facts, principles and lawlike statements that are molded together by accepted methodological and axiological practices" (Duschl 1994: 461). Thus, they comprise the core of science education and are supported by the scientific community.

In short, Kuhn claims that the cornerstone of science education is initiation through exemplars. He underpins this claim with the Wittgensteinian notion of "family resemblance". Instead of defining activities in a traditional sense, Wittgenstein considers each activity as a natural family. In his view, we can never exhaustively give all the necessary and sufficient conditions for an activity to be, for instance, an educational activity. But we can, by contrast, successfully identify an activity as educational. This can be done by identifying the overlapping resemblances and networks of characteristics that signify an educational activity. During the process of education students of science solve numerous exemplary problems, perform standard experiments and acquire the ability to recognise group- and paradigm-permeated resemblance. They learn to see the resemblance between exemplars and different situations in real life and act accordingly. Once this ability is required, "the science student, confronted with a problem, seeks to see it as like one or more of the exemplary problems he has encountered before" (Kuhn 1977: 308). Paradigmatic creativity means that one must find ways in which these similarities can come to the fore clearly.

Contrary to the traditional realist belief that words and linguistic signs refer to real things, this view rests on a non-essentialist language of science; it also uses scientific theories as instruments rather than considering them as true of external reality. After long periods of experiencing and doing exemplars, students learn a language, or conceptual scheme. They learn the meaning of each concept by performing certain actions, standard laboratory exercises, examinations, and homework. This means that scientific education is, as Kuhn sees the matter, a "process of learning by finger exercise" (Kuhn 1970: 247). In other words, theories are learned performatively, through their concrete applications.

One can ask what is wrong with learning theories through application rather than through abstract definitions. It must be considered as its strength rather than its weakness. Kuhn has two points in mind when he criticises this pedagogical approach. First, the industrial dehumanisation of students; going through this type of education, scientists just do their work in accordance with paradigmatic models and procedures in which they have been educated without any further reflection on the basis of their field. Kuhn does not explore this point fully. But the critique must be directed against the autoimmunisation of scientific praxis that masks the man-made ground of science and the active part of the individual in any scientific activity. Due to the dominance of this unconscious pattern of behaviour, the scientific community succumbs to crisis when habitual behavioural patterns show their inefficiency. And this functions as a perpetual source of nihilism. The other and more important point is the misrepresentation of actual scientific praxis and its pedagogical practice; the exemplary solutions of problems create the illusion that the truth and falsity of scientific theories are unequivocally determined by the confrontation of statements with facts and observations. Through believing in correspondence between theories on the one side and reality on the other, this educational model creates the illusion that scientific facts are independent of the human world. Kuhn thinks that application should not be taken as evidence for theories. Neither has scientific education to do with the truth or falsity of theories: "Science students accept theories on the authority of teachers and text, not because of evidence" (Kuhn 1979: 80). Indeed, the target is the positivistic assertion that science is constructed upon sense data.

Normal scientists strive constantly to bring theory and observation into closer agreement. But this should not be taken as falsification or confirmation. It is, rather, the most commonplace, normal scientific activity, puzzle solving. According to Kuhn, the individual scientist does not confront his research directly with observation. She/he learns, instead, how to connect his problem of research with existing and paradigmatically accepted knowledge.

By functioning as educational exemplars, paradigms influence education in two ways. On the one hand, the paradigm functions as the general intellectual climate within a certain scientific community, as the practical and theoretical presuppositions of education. On the other hand, it functions as the educational exemplary model that has to be imitated. Scientific exemplars satisfy our time's need for the mass production of labour power for laboratories and factories. Due to the dehumanisation of human relationships by the education industry, interpersonal contact between human beings, between teachers and students, becomes impersonal and paradigms take the place of living human beings as educators. Such an educational model functions at an impersonal level and veils the active part of the individual in cognition.

The question is not simply whether to accept or reject Kuhn's view of the connections between education and examples. Such an approach would carry us away from the issue. Indeed, Kuhn provides us with valuable insights regarding local aspects of science and education. He is right in his claims about the contextuality of educational practice and the locality of educational examples. However, this is not the whole story. He becomes fixated on his knowledge about the local aspect of education and does not take into consideration the universal aspect of the logic of exemplarity. He is unable to comprehend that universality and locality, objectivity and subjectivity do not exclude each other. Rather they presuppose each other, and each is as necessary as the other, and this mutual necessity constitutes the core of the problem of education and knowledge as such. Problems associated with Kuhn's educational theory depend on its being limited to scientific or paradigmatic exemplars. To come to terms with these problems we need other types of exemplars.

CULTURES AS EDUCATORS

Not only paradigms, but also history and cultures can function as educators. Examples of past cultures show, by the example of their achievements rather than theoretical argumentation, how and by which means we can organise our relationships with the world and with each other. Past cultures show how they created material and intellectual climates favourable for individual and cultural flourishing as well as for the improvement of knowledge. Regarding the ecological threats of modern science and technology, we can add a new dimension to the subject. The question is how can we combine individual flourishing with cultural excellence and the preservation of a healthy environment?

A sustainable form of life is a healthy order based on a balance between different aspects of life. A main source of health is the ability to distinguish between genuine needs and needs alien to the cultivation of individuals.

Using this logic we can easily comprehend that it is not just the needs of the labour market that we have to concentrate on, as current education does. Adapting the individual to the demands of the market, science and national security are alien to a true education of mankind. These demands corrupt human relations and lead us into disorientation and reified social relations. On the other hand, there are progressive values like solidarity, justice and inclusiveness. The challenging task of educators is to shift the focus from the former set of values to the latter which are based on genuine humans needs. As already discussed, genuine needs are connected to human nature, to love and creativity based on love.

A genealogical apprehension of past cultures not only enables us to shift perspective and see our own culture in historical terms, but such understanding also shows the possibility of cultures flourishing without being exclusively based on the single perspective of science. Rather than being a model for imitation, these cultures show different possibilities of cultural development. They also show that the current social order is neither the only possible one nor the best possible one; neither is it the last one; history is open-ended. Past cultures show us already tested manners of life and styles of thought. This is not to try to bring back the past cultures; that is impossible. To have in view past cultures, their emergence, development and fall helps us to orientate ourselves in the present and shape our future. The point is to discern the recurrent and the monumental in the past, to revere what deserves reverence as well to criticise it.

Nietzsche observed that the high culture of the ancient Greeks demonstrated a deep understanding of the nature of life. In his view, their strength did not reside in their authenticity or singularity of perspective; rather, they were open to other cultures. They had the tragic as the principle of organisation, by means of which they succeeded in organising different elements of life and creating a culture signified by unity of style. To have a tragic individual and cultural disposition means having an awareness of one's limits and possibilities.

The notion of high culture is openly political and based on certain perspectives. Such a culture can work exclusively and marginalise non-Western cultures. No doubt ancient Greece reached unprecedented heights of cultural excellence and is worthy of imitation. But, a one-sided emphasis on the Greek culture marginalises and excludes other great cultures of the past. Greek culture has gained fame for factors other than its own achievements. For several centuries, this culture has been studied in detail and referred to repeatedly by thinkers like Winckelmann and Nietzsche, while other cultures are not given as much attention. In fact, through his high esteem of Greek culture, Nietzsche contributes to Eurocentrism, since he admires this culture as the single culture worth imitating. There are certainly other examples of cultural excellence worthy of being studied and used as educative exemplars. Indeed, in a world of global interconnectedness and interdependencies this is highly necessary. It is quite possible to put together a model culture out of different elements borrowed from different cultures. Such a culture can be a genealogical device, which delineates the contours of a desired culture. It is a thought experiment, first imagined and then connected to the factual at the next stage.

Another problem associated with this model is the arbitrariness of interpretations of the past. History can be misrepresented and misused for ideological gains. There is an important point to be learned regarding the use of history as an educational tool. The Nietzschean distinction between the past reduced to a science of history and history as the insight of life being eternal despite our individual mortality is fruitful. Contrary to the thesis of incommensurability, genealogy renders communication over generations and epochs possible. In this sense, history itself can function as an educator and becomes a distinctive part of an inclusive perspective on the world. Nietzsche distinguishes three different modes of historiography, a monumental, an antiquarian, and a critical one (ULH, 2). The monumental approach can demonstrate the exemplary achievements of the past, both individual and cultural. The antiquarian can collect, revere, preserve and transfer these to the next generation. Through these two aspects of historical consciousness we can come in contact with the past. However, we need the critical approach in order to learn from the past and at the same time be liberated from its burden. It is not each of these approaches in isolation that is the desirable historical approach; rather, a desirable approach combines all the three—past, present and future come together. This is the supra-historical aspect of history. It refers to the question of how past cultures become educators of the present and the future. There are aspects of life and issues common to all ages which function as the basis of communication and learning between different ages. In some sense, philosophy is awareness of and reflection on these problems.

Since the current culture, due to its high concentration on the "greed of the moment" and on the benefits of a very limited part of humanity, cannot be used as an educator, we need alternative behaviour and ways of thinking. The main target of such opposition is not only states but also cultures. And this refers to another aspect of education through exemplars, individuals as educators. Such individuals not only challenge established values and attitudes but also do this in a constructive way by working for a new culture. In fact, the cultural educator shows the kind of society that can be built up using the example of the individual educator. Before entering into discussion on this topic, some words about great works and their role in education have to be said.

GREAT WORKS AS EDUCATORS

In addition to paradigms and cultures, great works of art, different religious, and philosophical, literary and political works function as educators.

They are standard works that are the theoretical basis of paradigms and justify their dominance. Harold Bloom (1994) uses the notion of canon to signify standard works in a literary context. This notion has, however, an educational aspect. Raised to the status of canon, different works become sources of authority. A reference to Bakhtin can shed light on the issue. He writes: "In each epoch . . . there are always authoritative utterances that set the tone—artistic, scientific, and journalistic works on which one relies, to which one refers, which are cited, imitated, and followed" (1986: 88).

Besides classical or canonical works, each canonical tradition introduces canonical names and categories to interpret the canon. Based on these elements, they introduce normative notions of "we" and "us" used in different discourses and exemplary problems and their solutions. These notions include certain groups and exclude others. As a result, each canonical tradition champions some works and names and challenges others. The current educational canon comprises solely Western, white and often dead men and their works. It excludes women and non-Western thinkers and works. Generally speaking, the Cartesian or canonical notion of reason is male and Western. Feminist and post-colonial philosophers are trying to enlarge the notion of canon by including women and non-Westerners in it. They suggest new readings of old canons and reinterpret and redefine the notion of canon. By revealing the misogynistic aspects and gender biases of apparently universal theories based on the current educational canon, feminist philosophers show that gender is intrinsic to knowledge. The same can be said of cultural belonging. Universality of knowledge thus demands an inclusive notion of canon. Such a notion represents a variety of works based on different traditions. It widens the basis of human knowledge. Having such a wide basis, we can legitimately claim universality for the notion of canon. In any case, canonical works transcend their context of production. The only thing needed here is to accept the plurality and polyphony of canons.

GREAT INDIVIDUALS AS EDUCATORS

This new educational model is based on individual life and conduct. Paradigms, cultures and great works signify the collective aspect of education. These notions and their educational ideals need to be exemplified by some extraordinary or great individual. Indeed, great thinkers always function as educators of humanity. They are founders of new value systems and styles of thought. As such, their influence transcends their locality and reaches beyond the context of their individual lives. Consequently, their personalities and ideas endure for centuries. They contribute to the continuity of thoughts and ideas. At the same time, they cause discontinuity of thoughts due to their questioning of established traditions. This means that they both establish new values and question old ones. Hence, their emergence signifies turning points in the history of thought; they determine the future of thought. They set their imprint on whole cultures.

The notion of greatness as used here is based on Aristotle and Nietzsche. As already mentioned, they connect this notion to artfulness and the individual's ability to shape his/her life by using his/her creative resources in accordance with a personal style. Besides the ability to use a plurality of perspectives, such an individual is characterised by a healthy style of thought, sovereignty, intellectual integrity, self-discipline, the courage of truth-telling and going her/his own way. Generally speaking, such an individual conducts an "examined life", as Martha Nussbaum (1997), following Socrates, puts it. In the context of this study, this notion highlights a couple of interrelated points. First, an examined life is a life characterised by critical thinking and perpetual "examining both myself and others" (*Apology*, 38A), as the Platonic Socrates puts it. To this we can add a second point: An examined life is a life being proved in practice, a life being examined through being lived in a way that qualifies it for being worth imitation by everybody; it is an exemplary life. To my mind, these two aspects of life can be brought together by the notion of truth-telling. Following Foucault, I use the notion of *parrhesia* to signify this feature of an exemplary life. In Foucault's wording, *parrhesia* "is a verbal activity in which a speaker expresses his personal relationship to truth, and risks his life because he recognizes truth-telling as a duty to improve or help other people (as wells as himself)" (Foucault 2001: 19). An educator is not only an individual who recognises and tells the truth about the most central problems of his/her time without being afraid of the dangers, but also one who lives this truth.

History can be presented as the struggle between different value systems and their founders. Socrates and Descartes are, for example, such educators. They are examples of examples. In other words, they are their own example. Since such examples did not exist before them, they were themselves the truth of their teachings. They had the exemplary task of establishing their own truths through questioning an established thought system. Such individuals are destroyers and constructors at the same time.

In recent decades, philosophers like Sartre, Russell, Derrida, Habermas and Harding have been engaged in local and global issues. Through undertaking certain actions, they demonstrate examples of their truth. As such, they call people to follow their example. In this sense their behaviour becomes universal; they act in a way they wish all people to follow. It is the active mode of their life that is valuable. One does not need to subscribe to their political or philosophical views in order to use them as educators. As human beings they certainly have their own weaknesses and strengths. Through using their strength one can overcome the weakness in oneself as well as in one's time. This is the dialectical relationship between educators and learners. These roles are not rigid and fixed, they are interchangeable. An educator cannot be positive and imitable through and through. Such an individual would be an abstraction rather than a living being. Besides, desirable characteristics change over time; different times expect different characteristics of educators. Generally, any educator is too multifaceted a person to be rejected or affirmed unambiguously. In any educator, we can attack the socio-cognitive conditions which block the enhancement of life and the enlargement of knowledge. At the same time we can admire those conditions that are life-enhancing.

As discussed, current situations demand radical changes in our notion of education. Thus, a true educator is an oppositional individual, a truth-teller. Primarily, an educator presents a new notion of education by presenting her/his own life and conduct pedagogically. She/he does not do this just by providing theoretical instructions about how people should live; rather, she/he is a pioneer in following the path she/he recommends to others and trying to live up to her/his own philosophical standards. Being an oppositional educator means being liberated from dogmatism and the tyranny of the prevailing paradigm. Such an educator reveals elements that block our understanding of the nature of knowledge. Through possession of an inclusive perspective, educators extend the horizon of interpretation beyond science. Indeed, paradigmatic examples are included in this extensive notion of education. But they are no longer considered to be absolute truths or universal facts. Through our becoming aware of the nature of scientific facts and our own active part in creating and establishing them, problems associated with objectivism are solved. Indeed, embedded in the notion of being oppositional is also the notion of being an agent of change. Hence, changes are not imposed on a thought community and individuals but are actively posed and accepted. Education is an open-ended and dynamic process of overcoming stimulated by the individual's inner drive to higher levels of self-consciousness and self-determination. Properly understood, any educator shows the possibility of a certain human type rather than a final state of being; she/he does not create learners in her/his own image. Instead of assimilating the learners' perspectives, a true educator makes room for their distinct existence.

The individual has to have the ability to use educators properly in his/her education and self-education; in the long run any true learner goes beyond her/his educator. While scientific exemplars are based on technical-scientific knowledge and skills, the notion of educator defended here adds a philosophical-artistic dimension. Such an education is not authoritarian because there is no need to marginalise the perspective of the other. The very fact that the other is different from me and sees the world from a perspective other than mine constitutes the enhancing condition of productivity and the growth of knowledge. While the scientific paradigm claims an exclusive right to truth, the philosophical educator confirms differences. There is a manner of life to be followed, but each individual does it in her/his own way as there is no universally valid style of life. Educators go through the same process of self-overcoming that they enjoin on learners.

There is a risk of two extremes. A one-sided emphasis on individual interests and needs leads to lack of solidarity and egoism. A one-sided focus on the collective, on the other hand, can lead to conformity. Educators show, by the example of their own lives and the culture they embody, how and by what means we can, through establishing a balance between these aspects, avoid these risks. Chapter 11 will deal with this issue.

9 Relations between Educators and Learners

The notion of education presented in the previous chapter demands a new kind of relationship between educators and learners. In traditional education these relations are based on the transmission of ready-made knowledge. Learners are considered to be empty vessels and passive receivers of knowledge. Teachers, on the other hand, are considered to be transmitters of knowledge. There is a power imbalance between learners and teachers.

The notion of the superaddressee as a source of authority was introduced in Chapter 3. It refers to an invisible third person implicit in any and each discourse; it functions as a source of authority. Within scientific communities, science has taken the position of superaddressee. In Chapter 5, the notion of polyphony was introduced as plurality of voices and perspectives. Traditional education was described as monophonic, since in this education the first voice, the voice of the teacher, is dominant. It bases its authority on the third voice, the voice of the superaddressee, which is characterised by perfection. The word of God, for instance, is the third voice in religious contexts. Within the framework of scientific education this third voice is science. The first voice (the voice of teachers), it is presupposed, interprets and is in contact with the third voice (science) and draws upon it. The third voice talks through the first; science, for instance, talks through the voice of the teacher; the first voice is a ventriloquistic instance of the third (Bakhtin 1981). The first voice can also draw upon the notion of educational canon, the locus of the third voice. The second voice is that of learners and is characterised by deficit and ignorance. This voice is guided by the first and the third voices toward pre-determined educational goals. These goals are given by the third voice, curriculum, national security, economic competitiveness and the like. The point here is that the first and the third voices know beforehand where education is heading. The source of authority is external to teachers and learners; they both are subordinated to the third voice's omnipresence and omniscience. In the coming sections I shall try to discern some authoritative voices in educational contexts, in order to finally spell out the kind of relationships between educators and learners as they are suggested here.

RATIONAL COMMUNICATION

In Chapter 2, following Weber, we argued that the use of rationality for the sake of economic interests is the core of social life in contemporary societies. This means that this type of rationality is the basis of scientific education as well as relations between educators and learners. In this section, rationality is discussed in connection with the relationship between educators and learners. This relationship is, in its turn, considered in the light of the nature of human communication, its individual and collective aspects. Regarding human communication, traditional ways of thinking are based on either incommensurability and relativism or rationalism and absolutism; they lead either to an unengaged relativism or fundamentalism and absolute univocity. This means that, according to these views, there is either no understanding whatsoever between different styles of thought or they are transparent to each other and a total understanding is the case; either different styles talk untranslatable languages or their words are identical. These positions, paradoxical as it may seem, presuppose each other. The incommensurability thesis presupposes metaphysical realism, which in its turn is based on an essentialist view of meaning. Indeed, the problem of incommensurability arises whenever, starting from essentialism, one demands total understanding and transferability of *the* meaning. Since meaning is considered to be constant, its authenticity and uniqueness has to be preserved and transferred in any act of communication. Meaning is the voice of reason, God or eternal ideas. Since such a total transference of meaning is impossible, the incommensurability thesis concludes, there is no communication and understanding between different communities of thought. The authority of the canon or the third voice is questioned, without being substituted by a new authority; all authorities are considered equally good or equally bad. Nihilism is then a fact.

Genealogically considered, monophony of thought goes back to the Platonic Socrates and his emphasis on univocity of rationalistic dialectic. Since scientific rationality is based exclusively on European male reason and its economic interests, the opposition to rationalism is thus an opposition to just this particular way of using reason and associated authoritative attitudes toward others rather than opposition to reason as such or opposition to being reasonable. It resists the authoritative imposition of a single meaning and exclusion of plurality of meaning. Analogous to its belief in correspondence between theory and reality, rationalism demands a correspondence between its own words and words in other thought styles; there has to be a total identification based on the authority of the reason, the third voice. And on this basis it demands agreement, consensus and transparency. Its being exclusive and authoritative blocks our understanding of how language, meaning and communication work. We have, then, to find new ways of explaining communication across communities of thought without reducing their differences. Such explanations cannot be based on incommensurability or absolute identity of meaning based on rationality, since they are themselves parts of the problem. This point deserves more elaboration.

Weber taught us a lot about the use and abuse of rationally in social and economical contexts. He also taught us that rationality is context-dependent. This means that rational thought has an ideological aspect related to power struggles between different interests; it is a will to power. In order to show the epistemic significance of these ideas, I shall refer to Nietzsche and Fleck. They, each in his own way, have discussed mechanisms at work behind the traditional notion of rationality and questioned its claims to universality. Using Nietzsche and Fleck, we can reject the idea of pure rationality. This study is in agreement with Fleck when he rejects the idea of rational thinking, emotions and feelings working independently of each other. He tries to explain rational thinking in terms of difference and agreement between collective emotions and feelings. He insists that there is no "emotionless state" (Fleck 1979: 49). As a result, "pure rationality" is totally out of the picture. Like Nietzsche, he distinguishes a tendency to schematisation and formalisation at work at the heart of rationalism. Having this starting point, Fleck espouses the view that some types of thinking can easily be schematised and formalised. They are consequently easily communicable. Any member of a thought community can easily recognise them and agree with them as soon as she/he encounters them. They signify the agreement in feelings of a given society. Since they are schematised, abstract and easily recognisable, they are called rational or objective. As such, they are conditioned by a given thought style, active and passive elements of thought. Thus, a uniform national rational thinking for the whole of humanity is impossible.

Fleck refers to mystics, agnostics and people with "primitive" thinking as having different types of logic than the rational scientific one. He questions, thereby, the universality of formal logic. In Fleck's world, there has to exist a thought collective for all Homo sapiens in order for a universal logic to make sense. Only under such circumstances can a uniformity of feeling among the whole of humanity take shape. He considers the possibility of such a thought collective too weak: "the intellectual interactions between different types of human society are too weak" (174, note 41). In other words, they are incommensurable. This theory suffers from a serious flaw. Fleck demands total understanding and since such an understanding is not possible by verbal means, he questions the possibility of understanding. One can cast doubt on this assertion by arguing that in a globalised world, with its huge capacity of communication, the emergence of some sort of uniformity of emotions and feelings is quite possible. Indeed, Fleck himself refers to many thought collectives across racial, cultural, political and geographical borders. The thought collective of fashion is, in Fleck's view, one example. This critique notwithstanding, Fleck's theory of thought style explains the form of thought we call rational thinking in a satisfactory way. He writes:

> The uniform agreement in the emotions of a society is, in its context, called freedom of emotions. This permits a type of thinking that is formal and schematic, and that can be couched in words and sentences and hence communicated without major deformation. The power of establishing independent existences is connected to it emotively. Such thinking is called rational. (49)

Indeed, Nietzsche prefigured this idea by formulating a similar idea about the rationality of thought. In *The Will to Power* he writes: "*Rational thought is interpretation according to a scheme that we cannot throw off*" (WP 522). Like Nietzsche, Fleck considers the notion of causal relations between different phenomena to be such a schematised idea communicable through verbal means. Using these views, we can defend a notion of polyphonic education based on a rational and emotional foundation of knowledge acquisition and decision-making.

It is clear now that thoughts, emotions and practices are interconnected on the one hand and constrained by language and the limitations of verbal communication on the other. There are, however, forms of communication beyond verbal means. These communicative actions are not based on abstraction, univocity and transparency of meaning. Before discussing this matter, let us focus on one important aspect of rationality and rational communication.

EDUCATION, RATIONALITY AND PERSUASION

For Kant, freedom in the "public use of reason" is the basic condition of human rationality. Free access to knowledge, sharing ideas and free communication were Kant's main concerns in this regard. Habermas bases his theory of the public sphere and communication on this Kantian view of reason, rationality and communication. This view of communication tries to reach consensus, since the principle of rationality is considered universal and valid beyond contextual differences. One needs only to discover these principles in order to agree with them. And since any normal mind is capable of discovering rational principles, consensus is possible. Rationality is thus beyond persuasion and is based on rational choice and conviction. However, this view suffers some shortcomings when it comes to explaining the basis of rational convictions.

Besides being scientific, modern education is, we can argue, a part of the public sphere and has to be dominated by rational argumentation and rational choice rather than persuasion. But this is not the case. Though a proponent of rational communication and the rationality of education, in his *Truth and Truthfulness* Bernard Williams refers to several irrational elements like persuasion and seduction at work in educative practices. Consequently, he considers education as an "authoritative form of persuasion"

(2002: 147). We cannot save the rationality of education or change the nature of persuasion by considering education as a "legitimated" form of persuasion (147), since we need a demarcation criterion between legitimate and illegitimate types of persuasive behaviours. Such a criterion will be dependent on cultural contexts, however. From a strictly rationalistic point of view, we cannot claim that some types of persuasion have the truth on their side, their being persuasive notwithstanding; persuasion is considered unwarranted as such. Once the irrationality of essential parts of an activity is agreed, the consistency of its being a rational activity is lost, if we are not ready to extend the notion of rationality so that it encompasses irrational elements of thought.

Indeed, Williams is in agreement with this study in rejecting the purity of rationality. He agrees that "there is little reason to suppose that we can separate a rational from an irrational *agency* of persuasion" (226). Based on these observations, Williams agrees that education is a "form of seduction" (226). Consequently, rational education is out of the question and socio-cultural considerations become the ground of education rather than pure rational reasons. The kind of culture and cultural values, then, become more important for education than theoretical speculations about the value-neutrality of education.

On the other hand, as Fleck and Nietzsche observe, our reason, emotions, passions and drives are deeply interwoven. As embodied human beings, we are conditioned by this interwovenness. An education true to our human conditions should teach us how to make use of them as sources of creativity and vitality, instead of insisting one-sidedly on purity of reason. Purity of reason is indeed a Platonic heritage. Science's insistence on being purely rational shows that it is not free from this long-standing metaphysical heritage.

EDUCATION, VIOLENCE AND IDEOLOGY

Seductive and persuasive aspects of education become clearer if we consider them against the ideological foundation of education. In the previous chapters, we observed that factors like national security and economic competitiveness are presented as leading principles of scientific education. Here, I want to connect these elements with ideological violence at work in scientific education. Scientific education does employ authority over students because it possesses power and is in a position to do so. The legitimacy of this empowerment is limited. The French philosopher Althusser discerned a sophisticated type of ideological violence at work in modern education. Following Gramsci, he found that the basic need of any economic system is to reproduce its own conditions of production, by producing the kind of people who will keep the wheel of production going (Althusser 2001: 87–90). While previous economic systems preserved themselves by naked violence, the modern state has sophisticated ways of using violence, Althusser argues. In modern states, violence has been rationalised, to use a Weberian terminology. According to Althusser, modern state power rests on two kinds of institutions: the "Repressive State Apparatus" and the "Ideological State Apparatus" (96). The former type of institution, like the police, army and law courts, works by violence. The latter, among them institutions of education, functions by ideology. Ideology here is considered as "a way of thinking which is systematically mistaken, a false consciousness" (Hawkes 1996: 4).

Seen from our perspective, current education is based on epistemological violence and persuasion, since it is based on the logic of exclusion. It preserves and enhances the domination of certain social orders. Indeed, distortion is at work whenever we present an activity based on power and ideology as neutral. In other words, ideology disguises cognitive and social processes by enveloping them in claims about value-neutrality. It consciously or unconsciously masks certain interests. The education industry corrupts human nature through systematically distorting the image of knowledge. It conceals the nature of science being dominated by established ideologies and current cultural values.

The educational system starts persuasion from an early age and introduces youngsters into a formalised and schematised power structure that appears natural to them since they have been taught to see it in this way. And the goal of this education is not to advocate truth but to sustain the power system. Esoteric circles of scientists and academics are fully aware of the importance that funding and other social priorities for scientific research have on their academic positions and on education. But they are not truthful enough to admit the influence that unfair competition has on the scientific ideas in school texts—as if these matters have no relevance in the rationale of scientific research.

THE NATURE OF RELATIONSHIPS BETWEEN LEARNERS AND EDUCATORS

As already stated, modern education is related to persuasion, seduction and ideological violence. As an integrated part of the modern social order, education is formalised, schematised and systematised. As argued in Chapter 2, these tendencies are the main characteristics of capitalist rationality. As a result of the rationalisation of education, its seductive and persuasive aspects are masked.

Neither universalism nor the thesis of incommensurability can explain relations between educators and learners, since they are limited to either transparency or incommensurability. Neither can they explain relations between language and the world. Both of them are based only on uniform verbal communication and suffer from shortcomings associated with this form of communication. The relationship between educators and learners, on the contrary, goes far beyond communication through words. Although it embraces this, it is not limited to it. Neither is it limited to theoretical argumentation or abstract knowledge. It needs a variety of means, perspectives and approaches. These can only be provided by the notion of translation. Generally speaking, translation is the basis of human communication in general and communication between educators and learners in particular. It is also the basis of an epistemological pluralism, on the one hand, and relationships between the individual and the world, on the other. In other words, it encompasses the intersubjective dimension of human communication as well as the individual's ability to read and translate the world of objects into the world of concepts and words.

Refusing both monadic relations of incommensurability and total transparency between thought styles without becoming entangled in nihilism demands a new notion of communication. This has to resolve the paradox of communication; thoughts are context-dependent, on the one hand, and communication is possible across paradigms, on the other. The context-dependency of thought shows that "No two historical epochs, no two social classes, no two localities use words and syntax to signify the same things, to send identical signals of valuation and inference. Neither do two human beings" (Steiner 1998: 47). This view distinguishes two kinds of barriers that have to be overcome in order to make communication possible, barriers between different language games and barriers between different individuals within the same language game. There exist, in other words, cultural and individual aspects of communication. Translatability, on the other hand, refers to these boundaries being constructed rather than natural. They can be easily surmounted and are surmounted on a daily basis.

The concept of translation as used here follows thinkers like Davidson and Steiner. Like Davidson, Steiner considers communication and translation identical and writes: "*human communication equals translation*" (49). Translation here is considered as both intra- and inter-linguistic or within and between languages and language uses. It covers, thus, both cultural and individual aspects of communication. Further, it means that translation is "formally and pragmatically implicit in *every* act of communication" (xii). As a result, translation is not confined to written or spoken words. "In this perspective", Steiner writes, "translation is . . . a constant of organic survival. The life of the individual and of the species depends on the rapid and/or accurate reading and interpretation of a web of vital information" (437). Thus, reading, translation and interpretation are basic human activities without which not only is communication impossible but also human survival becomes endangered.

Seen in this light, the relation between two languages is not based on the representational function of statements. There is no correspondence between the words of two paradigms, since words do not mean the same in different language uses. It is, rather, contexts that are translated. Besides, translation and transference of information is partial. There are linguistic elements that do and those that do not lend themselves to translation. This means that, contrary to rational consensus, our relations to others are based on both meaningful agreement and disagreement. Davidson tries to maximise agreement by emphasising the principle of charity, according to which anybody tries to "make maximum sense of the words and thoughts of others" (Davidson 2001: 197). Steiner also bases human relationships on "trust in the 'other'", taking for granted that "there is 'something here' to be learned" (Steiner 1984: 312). The advantages of these views lie in the fact that one does not try to exclude the other or reduce and assimilate him/her into one's own perspective; rather, one offers discursive room to the other. Meaning and identities are not considered to be based on ready-made essences or ideas whose ownership endows one with certain rights. Rather, they are created in meeting with the other and the self. Differences are, therefore, to be recognised, respected and tolerated, since they are a necessary condition of languages working productively. Through agreement and disagreement, individuals resist totalitarian demands of consensus and transparency. The other becomes, as Levinas learns, an ontological entity on which my own identity depends, rather than merely a socially marginalised being. In an educational context, we learn from the other instead of learning about the other. In this sense, the other does not become an object of "*my* comprehension, *my* understanding, *my* narrative, reducing the Other to me" (Todd 2003: 15).

Through translation, thoughts transcend their context of emergence and rise to the level of universality. However, this universality is temporary, since no thought can be universal for ever. New conditions and new translations change the conditions of universality; the universal becomes local and vice versa. In other words, translation is always provisional. Although it aims at a final and consummated stage, this is never reached. This is not to negate durability of thoughts totally. Through translation, the original can express the same idea repeatedly, in different forms and in different times. It becomes re-contextualised and rethought time and gain. The relationship between the original and the translation is, however, interchangeable. In translation different voices meet at the same level, merge and together create a polyphone cognitive space, where meaning and truths are produced and disseminated through shifts in positions and perspectives. Through being reciprocal, translation is educative; through translation different interlocutors learn from each other by alternating the position of being the original. Translation is transformative through being both a constructive and reconstructive process at the same time. This means that it keeps some elements of the original while it uses them in new contexts and creates new meaning. This is an endless process of appropriation through which old elements continue to exist, but in new contexts and re-interpreted. It is continuity in discontinuity, the interplay between identity and alterity. The

Derridaean notion of iterability can function as a complementary element of translatability. This notion refers to repeatability of words and expressions in ever new contexts without there being a fixed essence to be mediated. The context of origin cannot limit or close the meaning of language. Rather, words acquire new meaning by being interpreted and re-interpreted in ever new contexts.

TRANSLATION AND THE WORLD

The question now is: is translation limited to relations between different languages? No. Translation also embraces the relationship between language and reality. As in the case of kinship of languages, kinship between the real world and language manifests itself in translation. This notion of translation is not based on correspondence and analogy. As Benjamin writes: "translation would be impossible if in its ultimate essence it strove for likeness to the original" (Benjamin 1982: 73). On the contrary, since Wittgenstein's *Philosophical Investigations*, we have moved away from image theory and likeness between reality and language. Basically, our relation to the world is based on the ability of the human race as "an artistically creating subject". Seen in this light, the nature of language is translation of one sphere into the other. This means that the relation between humanity and the world is aesthetic by nature. This aesthetic characteristic of human relation to the world belongs to the basic human condition. We have to use language in order to make sense of our world. And this means that we have to connect different spheres of being in a way not given by nature. Humanity has to translate the world of objects into the world of words and expressions. As Nietzsche formulates the issue: "Between two absolutely different spheres, as between subject and object, there is no causality, no correctness, and no expression; there is, at most, an aesthetic relation" (TL). This view of relations between language and reality replaces correspondence of propositions to things by an artistically transformative process of translation of one sphere into another. This process is, of course, mutual. This is the meaning of the metaphorical nature of language suggested by Nietzsche (TL).

Indeed, metaphor means transference. The Greek etymology is from *meta*, implying "a change" and *pherein* meaning "to bear, or carry". In Modern Greek, the word metaphor also means transport or transfer. The important aspect of metaphor in our context is its being a figure of speech in which one class of things is referred to as if it belonged to another class; objects are referred to as if they belonged to words and vice versa. It is significant that a metaphor establishes a relationship between different spheres, but it leaves more to the imagination. A metaphor is a shortcut to meaning. It sets two unlike things side by side and makes us see the likeness between them. It is also a figure of speech in which words and phrases literally denoting one kind of object or idea are used in place of another to suggest a likeness or analogy between them. This process is, however, misconceived as words and objects corresponding. Compared with Socrates, who holds that the language of truth is mathematics and calculability, basing the relationship between words and objects on the notion of metaphor is closer to the way language functions. We do indeed translate one sphere into the other. At the same time, through translation our statements become accountable to the world. The world is, then, the original, or the text. It is the basis of translation. We have no right to distort this original by confusing text and interpretation.

The advantages of such a view of the relation between the world and language is that although the translatability of two spheres is accepted, the world is not reduced to our descriptions or pictures of it, since there is no picturing at all. Language never succeeds in giving an adequate rendering of reality once and for all; there are no completed and closed facts, as in the traditional view of science. In summary, translation is not a methodology of enquiry, or a mode of understanding that can be rejected or accepted; rather, it has to do with our way of being in the world.

TRANSLATION AND EDUCATION

The notion of translation used in this section also draws on Walter Benjamin. The most fruitful point is his distinction between two aspects of any original work: the informative contents and "the unfathomable, mysterious" poetic aspect of the work. This view of translation is applicable to education and educators as well as to the world itself. Analogous to this, any educator's life and conduct have two aspects, a surface possession of certain kinds of information and knowledge, and a poetic depth, the unfathomable bottom of each personality, beyond words and statements. The informative aspect of educators is easily communicable through verbal communication. It just needs verbal means and acts of speech. Since any user of language can use words in a meaningful way, there are always good possibilities of verbal communication. By contrast, the poetic aspect of communication goes beyond the mere ability of language use. It can be "reproduced only if [the translator] is a poet" (Benjamin 1968: 70). Thus, the poetic aspect of the original needs to be transferred to the new context by means other than words. It demands a poetic or artistic outlook on the world. This means the ability to go beyond words and verbal expressions and experience things in their immediacy. Rather than being caught within the confines of verbal expressions, in a poetic aspect things are lived. Besides being creative, this aspect of translation lets the way any individual manifests human nature or love come to the fore.

The point is that although they may possess the same knowledge, different educators manifest their knowledge in different ways. In some, knowledge becomes the excellence and grandeur of life, while in others, life becomes a servant of knowledge. And it is just this aspect of the character of educators that is at issue. The notion of style is useful in this regard. As mentioned, style has two interconnected aspects, a collective and an individual one. Coming together they cover the two aspects of communication mentioned above. The communal aspect of style makes verbal communication between users of a language possible. It also makes communication between different linguistic communities possible. The individual aspect has to do with the poetic aspect of relationships. Any individual educator manifests a special mode or style of understanding distinct from others. It is indeed this mode of understanding that qualifies him/her to be an educator rather than his/her knowledge as such. The poetic aspect of relationship refers to creative resources within each individual. It can be communicated through the kinship of styles. While particular thoughts may mutually exclude each other and, consequently, separate individuals, the kinship of styles relates them. Individual or poetic communication is then more than transmission of information. Once this fact is accepted, the kind of style becomes much more important than its content. Famously, knowledge is intentional, knowledge of an object. While two individuals may intend the same object and their kind of knowledge may be the same, modes of intention may be different and distinguish them from each other. One may aim at possessing beings, while the other is disposed to let beings be the beings they are.

Nietzsche believes that "The purpose of style is to communicate inward states and good style communicates inward states well" (EH, Book 4). Conceived in this way, the poetic aspect of translation reveals inward intentions. At the same time, it enhances a polyphonic community where everybody has her/his own distinct voice and is able to communicate with others on the basis of kinship of styles. Authority takes shape as some become the educators of others because of the excellence of their styles of life and thought, instead of being a ventriloquation instance of an invisible third voice. Besides excellence of thought and style, they possess generosity and strength of love and gift-giving. Socrates and Descartes, for instance, became teachers of humanity and acquired authority because they gave birth to innovative and excellent styles of thought. It is not just transmission of information that makes them timeless. They have attained an "eternal afterlife" thanks to their style of thought continuing to live in succeeding generations. The American essayist and philosopher Ralph Waldo Emerson, who was admired by Nietzsche, also refers to kinship between styles of thought. Addressing the issue in an American context, he makes "transition" the core of his philosophy instead of "tradition". Style and nature become the constant elements of life and the basis on which knowledge is understood and transferred. He sees connections between "internal states" of nature and style when he writes about great writers like Chaucer, Marvell and Dryden: "They impress us with the conviction that one nature wrote and the same reads" (Emerson 1903: 91). This position shows the timelessness of great thinkers, cultures and works. Each work of art, each thinker and culture has, to use Benjamin, a life and an "eternal afterlife". To my mind, while life starts in a context, afterlife transcends this context and becomes universal.

Having this starting point is to believe in the possibility of the continuity and accumulation of knowledge, since kinship of styles can lead to understanding over time and across cultures. Thus, despite transition being the logic of history, the experiences of past cultures and thinkers are not lost for ever. Needless to say, this approach to the question of style is possible only as a part of the inclusive perspective and epistemological pluralism advocated here.

Having translation and interpretation as a starting point in our relationships to each other and to the world, reading, in its widest sense, becomes not only an extremely important educational means but also our major epistemological activity. Reading paves the way for multiplicity of perspectives and interpretations. It also confirms the enigmatic character of existence. Reading is not an arbitrary activity. There is a dialectical interplay between fact and translation/interpretation. We have no right to distort texts by interpretation.

There is a sense of epistemological justice in having interpretation and reading as the main epistemological activities. To ground understanding on interpretation is to give things their due and recognise their existence as they are, without correcting them. Seen in this light, the Platonic two-world model is unjust because it underestimates the world of the senses. Through doing justice to the world, we find our own due place in it and live in harmony with ourselves and with nature. Our knowledge becomes knowledge from within the world, since we become a part of the world. Using interpretation as an epistemological tool makes knowledge transparent to the human race. We are then in a position to take responsibility for our own world, deeds and values.

TRANSLATION AND FACT

The main problem with having reading, interpretation and translation as our main cognitive activities is that modern humanity is formed in the image of the prevailing scientific paradigm, whereby interpretive procedures are either banned or marginalised. Through its close connections with natural sciences analytic philosophy has established an unbridgeable gap between fact and interpretation. The basic step will then be to establish new principles of the organisation of knowledge by establishing the fundamental homology between the facts of natural sciences and philological interpretation.

Seen in this light, although scientific facts are dependent on cultural values and interpretation, they function as thought constraints. Perceived in this way, the notion of fact signifies the boundary of arbitrary thought. Otherwise, arbitrariness and anarchy can corrupt the stringency of thought and the unity of style. Fleck's theory of fact provides a useful analytical tool in this regard. By focusing on its condition of emergence and epistemological function, he considers the notion of fact as "*the signal of resistance* opposing free, arbitrary thinking" (Fleck 1979: 101). This view is consistent with the notions of objectivity and the individual introduced earlier. The active or subjective part of cognition can be presupposed by the knower. These constitutive elements of knowledge are conditioned by the thought style. Once they are postulated, the individual has to carefully and stringently follow their inevitable consequences. These results are termed facts. Thus, the individual is actively engaged in the process of knowledge without arbitrarily manipulating the process. His/her thoughts are constrained by these facts that in their turn are conditioned and constrained by the thought style. This means that interpretation and translation cannot be conceived as arbitrariness of thought or capricious allegations about things. They are, rather, skilful and disciplined penetrations into the nature of things and are based on a careful distinction between interpretation and text, between translation and original. Although translation owes its existence to the original, it creates and recreates, interprets and reinterprets the original time and again. At the same time, it is aware of the fact that the original does not exist for the sake of translation. It is not to be distorted by translation. As Nietzsche puts, interpretation is based on "the art of reading well—of reading facts without falsifying them by interpretation" (A, 52). Seen in this light, there is no unsurpassable boundary between the canonical science of physics and the science of interpretation, or philology. Or, as Nietzsche considers the issue in *Beyond Good and Evil*, physics can be placed in the domain of philology, the science of interpretation, since physics too is a kind of interpretation (BGE, 22). Physics is interpretation or translation of physical phenomena based on careful observation, and philology "teaches" physics "to read well, that is to say, to read slowly, deeply, looking cautiously fore and aft, with reservation, with doors left open, with delicate eyes and fingers" (D, Preface 5), as Nietzsche puts it in *The Dawn*. Starting from interpretation, the interpreter is aware of her/his situatedness, the limits of her/his perspective and the limits of communication. Such an interpreter carefully preserves the balance between imposing order, the creative aspects of thought and the result of such an order. Translation is the ability to shift perspective between original and translation. Through this process we become skilled in looking at our own perspective from that of others and vice versa.

To claim affinities between reading and observation, fact and interpretation is to reverse centuries of development. It demands changes in both educational and social institutions and in categories of consciousness. A basic presupposition is, here, as everywhere, that we abandon the traditional idea of progress, based on the perception of the present as the end of history.

Modern science is indeed just a translation of reality into language. It is not the only or the final form of human knowledge and can consequently be changed and replaced by future forms of knowledge; these forms of knowledge would certainly encompass science and go far beyond it. The next presupposition is to connect the hopeful horizon of the future with a fair analysis of the present and the past—the past in terms of the natural and cultural history of humanity.

FIDELITY AND FREEDOM

The notion of educator reminds one of imitation, homology, analogy, hegemony and likelihood. This way of thinking is true of the traditional notion of educator. The same can be said of the traditional view of translation. Based on a reinterpreted notion of translation, the notion of educator used here is based on apparently contradictory concepts of fidelity and freedom, to borrow two notions from Benjamin. As a good translator, the learner finds the educator worthy of imitation and incorporates the original's mode of signification. He/she does not veil the original's style of life but allows it to be revealed. A good learner lets "pure style", a style common between the educator and the educated, be manifested all the more fully. The educator is important to the learner insofar as the educator has already released the learner from the obligation of conveying an essential meaning inherent in the educator. Rather than becoming the prisoner of style, the learner releases the shared style and mode of signification, incorporated in the educator, by recreating them freely in his/her own context and life.

The notion of translation provides education with a variety of means and approaches such as "paraphrase, graphic illustration, pastiche, imitation, thematic variation, parody, citation in a supporting or undermining context, false attribution (accidental or deliberate), plagiarism, collage and many others" (Steiner 1998: 437). To this catalogue of means we can add notions like reverence, appreciation, admiration, blame, critique, evaluation, affirmation and negation. There is no single kind of relation between educator and educated to be recommended. Educators are to be considered from a variety of perspectives.

Indeed, educators show only the direction. They ease the task of education by showing its beginning and end, a possibility and an actuality at the same time. Indeed, the learner reinterprets and recreates educators according to his/her needs, stage of development and level of knowledge. The educated admires the educator and tries to imitate him/her and find support in him/her for his/her own actions. On the other hand, he/she tries to liberate himself/herself through contest, parody, paraphrasing, criticism and revaluation. Indeed, this is a feasible position towards any great thinker or great historical event. On the one hand, they are monuments of human achievements; they have achieved something of value that has to be revered, preserved and transferred to next generations. But reverence, preservation and transference should not happen uncritically. Any past is to be evaluated, criticised and denied so that new generations can create their values. This is indeed a precondition of coming to terms with the problems of alienation and nihilism. Education consequently becomes a process of both forwarding what is valuable in past and present generations and renewing these values. One cannot emulate or reject a thinker unambiguously. One learns not only from those whom one admires but also from those to whom one is opposed.

10 The Educational Order of Truth

In Chapters 8 and 9, I spelled out some main characteristics of my notion of education. We are now in a position to return to our original issue of truth and education. We can now consider the paradox of truth and its educational implications, taking advantage of the notions of science, objectivity, style and translation as they have been discussed in this study in order to shed light on connections between education and truth. Subjects to be discussed here are characteristics of the educational order of truth and its relation to the notion of education.

In Chapters 2 and 3, I discussed how a one-sided emphasis on objectivism and relativism leads to alienation and nihilism. In order to come to terms with these problems, we have to take into account not only inclusive notions of culture and knowledge and the relationship between them, but also the notion of educational exemplars as the place where these notions meet and interplay. Through this notion the universal can be exemplified in the particular and the particular can be raised to the level of universality. This mode of understanding defends the notion of universality without denying the local aspect of truth; it shows how educational ideas become exemplified in educators and learners. Through enabling us to take account of their educational implication, the notion of educator helps us to consider what each part of the paradox implies and how these parts can go together without entangling us in fruitless contradictions. The problem and the solutions are, then, embedded in the same process. We can thus keep what is universal and connect it with the particular without one excluding the other. Rather, they can be conceived of as constitutive of each other. In order to make this issue clear, I concentrate first on two aspects of truth, its universality and contextuality, and then connect them with the notion of exemplar. In so doing, I retain the notion of truth without becoming dogmatic. I combine defensible aspects of relativism with viable aspects of universalism in a single notion of truth and connect it with the notion of educator. As a result, truth becomes related to the everyday practice of education. Educational practices, on the other hand, receive meaning thorough being guided by truth. This is the meaning of what I term educational order of truth.

UNIVERSALISM

The universal aspect of truth has been discussed by different philosophers, who try to transcend the contextuality of our everyday actions, like that of education, and establish universally compelling truths, valid for all contexts and ages. In order to study the implication of universalism, I choose to dwell on Habermas's view on truth. To begin with, Habermas agrees that life-worlds constitute the framework of our behavioural certainties. These certainties can easily be disputed and questioned. Despite this, he bases his project of the unconditional validity of truth on these behavioural certainties. He makes a distinction between two spheres of the life-world; the action-context of language games and the rational discursive sphere. These two spheres are in perpetual interactions; they are translatable into each other. Having this in mind, Habermas writes:

> Shaken-up behavioral certainties are transformed on the level of argumentation into controversial validity claims raised for hypothetical propositions; these claims are tested discursively—and, as the case may be, vindicated—with the result that the discursively accepted truths can return to the realm of action. (Habermas 2005: 117)

Habermas also emphasises the internal connection between truth and justification. To him, truth is "justified assertion". In fact, he talks of two stages of validity. At the first, validity takes the form of behavioural certainty in the context of everyday behavioural certainties. Whenever these context-dependent certainties are disputed, we enter dialogue and argumentation at the theoretical-rational level of discourses. Contrary to ordinary conversations, this rational discursive sphere is relieved of the burden of action. In this sphere, rational attitudes and reasoning reign; discourses are submitted to the force of good reasons and best rational arguments. Since the order of reason goes beyond the action-context of contingent language games, once we succeed in establishing a context-transcendent validity, a renewed behavioural certainty, through discursive vindication, is also established.

In Habermas's theory of the communicative act, truth is restricted to propositional validity. His "Janus-faced" notion of truth "mediates between behavioural certainty and discursive assertibility" (117). The two-way movement between the context of action and rational discourse is characterised by two stable ends, behavioural certainty and discursive assertibility, and a hypothetical stage in the middle. To Habermas, whenever we use language to reach an understanding, truth is a matter of the validity of our claims and our ethical responsibility for these claims being true. Human beings are participants in argumentation and action on the basis of "intersubjectively shared convictions". Truth claims can be vindicated only discursively and in the context of justification. Behavioural certainties of the context of action become hypothetical propositions which have to go through a Darwinian competition of acquiring the best argumentation in their favour. In the end, the fittest are "redeemed" or vindicated and return to the realm of action and become again behavioural certainty. Habermas speaks in this regard of "the discourse theory of truth", according to which, "a proposition is true if it withstands all attempts to refute it under the demanding condition of rational discourse" (120).

At the root of this process there is, Habermas argues, a "cooperative search for truth" (117). In his theory of truth, these cooperative endeavours and the unconditional validity of truths rest on a shared reality, "a single objective world" or simply "the world". This world is "the intersubjectively shared public space with which everything that is merely subjective can be contrasted" (114). It is in some sense beyond language games and action-contexts. Habermas bases this realist attitude of un-conditionality on critical standards operating in everyday life. To his mind, everyday realism provides the "normative reference point" for our truth claims. Any speaker becomes accountable to his/her validity claims in three regards whenever he/she makes use of language: in regard to the speaker's personal world or expressions of one's personal experiences; in regard to the social world or the speaker's relations to others; and lastly, in regard to the objective world of language's universal pragmatic function to represent something in the world. In general, our validity claims are, according to Habermas, accountable to the world.

There are some serious problems associated with the Habermasian solution to the paradox of truth. First, truth is restricted to propositional validity, to truth as *veritas*. In this sense, truth is scientific and philosophical; it is only discursive. The disclosing aspect of truth, *aletheia*, or artistic truth, is set aside. This bases Habermas' notion of truth exclusively on rational discourses and excludes the perspective of art. As a result, it becomes authoritative, general and abstract. The aesthetic aspect of truth that relates truth to a particular context, like that of education, disappears.

Second, the very distinction between two spheres is problematic. Similar to the positivistic distinction between context of discovery and context of justification, the Habermasian spheres are interconnected and biases in the context of action (or ordinary conversation) influence justificatory endeavours in the rational discursive sphere. Behavioural disputes of the context of action can be transferred to the context of justification and trouble the rational argumentation of "trouble-shooter". Third, the holistic character of the process of justification through argumentation makes it difficult to determine whether a settled dispute uniquely lends validity to just the set of propositions that is disputed. A belief makes sense within a system of beliefs; rejection and affirmation of beliefs occur holistically. This last point is Wittgensteinian. He writes: "what we believe is not a single proposition; it is a whole system of propositions" (1969: § 141). As a result, "All testing, all confirmation and disconfirmation of hypothesis takes place already within a system" (105). The next point is also a Wittgensteinian one: even if all arguments speak for a hypothesis, we cannot be sure that it is "objectively *certain*" or "certainly true". Famously, Wittgenstein sees no connection between truth and Cartesian certainty. We can ask: Even if we reach behavioural and theoretical certainties, are they to be accepted as unconditionally true? Besides, as has been suggested, rationality is not a homogenous notion. The dominating notion of rationality is based on an exclusive male and Western perspective. Generally speaking, any justification takes place within this form of life. We do not possess a meta-language or meta-perspective from which we can look at all perspectives and things.

Habermas rightly emphasises the force of good arguments and the possibility of shifting perspective accordingly. In his ideal world "reaching understanding" is the basis of interpersonal relationships. Participants in communication and language games demonstrate willingness "to shift perspective" on the basis of good arguments. A Habermasian "ideal speech situation" is signified by "openness to the public, inclusiveness, equal right to participation, immunization against external or inherent compulsion, as well as the participant's orientation toward reaching understanding" (Habermas 2005: 118). These characteristics can really create good conditions for public speech, but they cannot resolve the problem of power imbalance embedded in social relations and speech acts. This model will probably work if we replace argumentation and rational discourse by translation. Propositional validity needs to be completed by the disclosive aspect of truth. Rational discursive truths are limited without being connected to artistic truths. In that case, there will be no need of a dichotomy between context of action and context of rational discourse. There is no need for some perspectives to be assimilated or marginalised in order to reach consensus. The otherness of the other and differences in perspectives are preserved as the ground of the productive process of knowledge acquisition. This process is characterised by active participation and creative interaction; the self and the other are co-participants in creating shared meaning through translation.

Keeping with the notion of rationalism, Habermas's solution itself becomes authoritarian, since it demands consensus and certainty. Search for truth or will to truth is considered to be a homogeneous process, where all participants, as actors in behavioural and intellectual realms, cooperate to find out "good reasons", and whenever such reasons are found they accept them unreservedly as universally justified assertions or universal truths. The search for truth is thus stripped of a power struggle, diversity of perspectives and conflicts of interests.

Habermas also presupposes rationality beyond all disputes. Disputes and disagreements are kept at the level of the context of action. At the level of rationality, they are resolved since rational discourse is general and context-independent. Rational discourse is considered universal and the same for all cultures, and all participants are sincerely oriented toward reaching understanding. Accordingly, the relationship between truth and power does not receive due attention.

Contrary to this position, Foucault considers the true/false dichotomy a mechanism of exclusion rather than inclusion. It is not always best reasons that make a certain type of discourse true. The search for truth or the will to truth, as he calls it, following Nietzsche, is not independent of social and historical processes of production, distribution, organisation and legitimatisation of knowledge and discourses. According to Foucault, "Each society has its regime of truth, its 'general politics' of truth: that is, the type of discourse which it accepts and makes as true" (2005: 333). This can be said even of the Habermasian organic community and his ideal speech situation; it has its "regime of truth" and its politics of truth. This means that argumentation and theoretical truth cannot be separated from power and politics. As Foucault emphasises, "truth isn't outside power, or lacking in power" (333). Truth is, rather, constitutive of power and thus in a position of power. The problem is not whether a community does or does not have a politics of truth; living together makes such a politics inevitable. Thus, as in the case of cultural values, we have to focus on the kind of politics rather than affirming or rejecting politics of truth as such. There are certainly inclusive politics that promote human knowledge and exclusive ones that corrupt our understanding.

Habermas emphasises the consensual aspects of truth and aims at reaching consensus. Foucault, on the contrary, puts the emphasis on the mechanisms of exclusion. Other philosophers also highlight the connections between truth, consensus and power. If for Foucault perpetual strife and social struggle replace consensus and harmony, Vattimo calls modern dictatorships "techniques of organising consensus" (Vattimo 2005: 172). Arendt observes "mass manipulation of fact and opinion" (Arendt 2005: 307) in modern states. By focusing on the way language functions, Foucault adds a power dimension to the issue of truth. His notion of discourse signifies mechanisms whereby some ideas take command over humanity and regulate thoughts. A discourse is, broadly speaking, a way of producing knowledge, a way of including certain questions about reality and excluding others. It is a system of statements and a way of describing and classifying people and things and ideas about them. Though discourses emerge out of power/knowledge relations between groups of people, they regulate and constitute these groups.

In Foucault, knowledge, argumentation and power are interwoven. He writes:

> There is no power relation without the correlative constitution of a field of knowledge . . . [T]he subject who knows, the object to be known and the modalities of knowledge must be regarded as so many effects of these fundamental implications of power/knowledge and their historical transformation. (1995: 27–28)

Indeed, Habermas studies institutional mechanisms of coercion through contrasting the notions of the "life-world" and "system", the social milieu and economic and state apparatus, respectively. Seen in this light, the ideological aspect of scientific education lies in the very fact that the system or the state tries to dominate the life-world. As a part of a life-world, Habermas's notion of "public sphere" refers to a vision of undisturbed communication and dialogue. In current circumstances, however, the public sphere is deformed by political and economic interests which try to sanction their own decisions and values (Habermas 1992: 206). Through education the social processes of distortion appear as natural. The point is that the power aspect is not limited just to the context of action. It goes through the whole of human relations and influences actions as well as rational argumentation.

There are also problems associated with everyday reality. Instead of being the basis of common understanding, as in Habermas, everyday reality is, at least as Hannah Arendt sees it, the sphere of the political manipulation of masses. Arendt studies the relationship between truth and politics. Like Habermas, her view of truth is based on distinctions between truth and opinion. She makes a distinction between factual and rational truths. Rational truths (scientific and philosophical truths) do not belong to everyday reality and are not to be distorted or manipulated. In her traditional view, rational truth is "what we cannot change . . . it is the ground on which we stand" (Arendt 2005: 313). Political by nature, factual truths, by contrary, can be manipulated. Arendt considers the everyday (marketplace) and rational spheres as incommensurable. While Habermas thinks of everyday reality as the "normative reference point" for all claims to truth and their discursive justification, the basis of the unconditional validity of truth, Arendt considers the everyday sphere as a sphere of manipulation of factual truths by politics; she regards everyday reality as "the lowest level of human affairs". To Arendt's mind, this is the realm of opinion rather than truth. She maintains that rational truths are hardly communicable to the everyday sphere. Such communication changes the nature of truth and converts it into opinion.

Using Arendt, we can distinguish a serious problem related to Habermas's view of truth, its being limited to verbal communication. As mentioned earlier, this means that his discourse on truth is limited to science and philosophy without taking into account the artistic aspect of truth and aesthetic aspect of our relations to the world and to each other. What matters in educational contexts is, as Arendt, quite similarly to Nietzsche, maintains, truth can "inspire only when it manages to become manifest in the guise of an example" (Arendt 2005: 306). And this non-propositional notion of truth leads us to the notion of educational examples. In order to become useful in education, Habermas's heroic endeavours to establish a universal notion of truth have to be completed by other aspects, such as truth as testimony and disclosure defended by philosophers like Levinas, Arendt and Heidegger.

CONTEXTUALISM

Leaving the universal aspect of truth, it is now time to dwell on the other dimension of the paradox of truth, its context-dependency, or singularity. Vattimo and Davidson are helpful when it comes to understanding this aspect of truth. Like Habermas, Vattimo believes in the power of good argumentation. But his model is not as complicated as Habermas's. Vattimo's starting point is the notion of "dwelling" in specific societies, as opposed to the Habermasian ideal community. Vattimo's main point is that "I can do epistemology, I can formulate propositions that are valid . . . only on the condition that I dwell in a determinate linguistic universe or paradigm" (Vattimo 2005: 172). This means that one cannot consider such epistemologies as universal and stable. According to Vattimo, belonging to a tradition or form of life does not by definition mean passively accepting their authority. The interesting thing about dwelling is that it implies an interpretive belonging that involves both consensus and the possibility of critical activity. Accordingly, we can successfully take part in transformative activities within the paradigm. Vattimo is quite clear about the fact that we can by no means retain a "traditional metaphysical vision of the proposition-thing correspondence" (172), the incontrovertible givenness of an object possessed by a clear and distinct idea and adequately described in a proposition that faithfully reflects the idea verified in the light of rules of correspondence.

Indeed, if we push for universalism based on the traditional notion of rationalism and if we keep a dichotomy between the context of action and that of rationality, we disconnect truth and education, since education always takes place in a context. To my mind, interpretive dwelling in educational contexts explains connections between truth and education much better than Habermasian movement between different contexts. As discussed, education is a translational process characterised by active participation of educators and learners in creating shared meaning. The notion of meaning, as the basis of truth and interpretation, is immanent in the very context of discursive actions of education. Truth here, as will be explained later in this chapter, is manifest in the very notion of educator. Thus, the discourse we need to explain connections between truth and education as well as truth and educator is situated within the same context.

Another way of looking at the relationship between education and truth is, like Davidson, to contextualise truth by linking it to speakers of particular languages at a particular time and particular place. Like Habermas, in Davidson's theory, truth is connected to our "need of communication". It is also connected to meaning and theories of interpretation that language users make use of in their translation of the speech of others and in understanding them (Davidson 2005: 70). In other words, and more precisely, truth is not extra-linguistic; rather, it is situated within specific languages. Truth conditions of statements are thus relative to speakers and time. As a result, this theory of language refuses to formalise language, since to formalise language is not only to reduce individual diversity to general concepts, but also to believe in the context-independency of these general concepts.

Although Davidson relates truth to language, he considers it "as objective as can be" (Davidson 1984: 198). He uses the semantic conception of truth as a basic, theoretical and undefined concept in order to show that we can actually know something of an objective world that is not of our own making. Although Davidson makes use of Tarski's semantic theory[1], he applies it to natural languages rather than formalised ones. The interesting point in this context is that in Davidson, a theory of meaning is "an empirical theory", which means that "it may be tested by comparing some of its consequences with the facts" (Davidson 2005: 72). This means that Davidson's notion of truth has two aspects. Besides an intersubjective aspect, in which agreements between speakers of different languages are involved, truth is related to agreement with reality. The relationship between truth and reality is analogous to that between meta-language and object language, where each one is translatable into the other. This view confirms the view of the relationships between the world and knowledge suggested by this study in Chapter 9.

Davidson's theory of truth leads us to the notion of communication as translation, a further point of convergence with the view advocated by this study—that intersubjective relationships are based on translation. Having translation as the starting point, instead of principles of rationalism, we can argue that it is true that any thought is dependent on a context, but through translation each thought transcends the context of its production and reaches a higher level of universality. In the meeting between translation and the original, new ideas emerge that are not reducible to either of them, but encompass them and become valid in new contexts. Thus, translation is a presupposition of truth, since the relation between knowledge and the world as well as our relation to each other are based on translation. Though an important element in discussions about the universality of truth, translation is not enough to underpin the universality of truth; it is necessary but not sufficient. Besides the logic of translatability, we need another logic, that of showing truth. Some individuals can function as originals, or the basis of translation and interpretation. These individuals qualify themselves for such a privileged position by living certain ways of life and letting truth become manifested in them. Seen in this light, truth becomes a matter of how we should live our lives. As such, truth becomes educationally significant. I shall discuss the educational significance of educators in the next section.

SHOWING TRUTH

Habermas's endeavours to establish the universality of truth and the unconditional validity of true propositions through rational discourse, and

Davidson's endeavour to do the same through translation and interpretation are necessary but not sufficient; they are limited to the linguistic and discursive spheres and do not cover all human practices. They leave out the non-propositional aspect. Truth as testimony and disclosure is an important aspect of truth talk. Husserl, Heidegger, Levinas and Arendt have in different ways explained this aspect of truth. In educational contexts, it becomes crucial. Truth, in this sense, is not only epistemological; it also has aesthetic and ethical dimensions. Truth is closely allied with the human creative actions within a context, like that of our educational practices.

In order to explain the issue in an adequate way, we need the logic of exemplarity, the notion of example and the ways truth is manifested in exemplars. This is a comprehensive way of considering the issue and covers its verbal and non-verbal aspects. In this sense, truth is shown rather than being proved by theoretical argumentation or related to general forms. Showing truth also concerns the relationships between truth and human types as its vehicle. There are two aspects of truth, its artistic/esoteric aspect and its communality.

In this regard, I am in agreement with Arendt when she defends the thesis of showing truth. Her starting point is the distinction between two kinds of truth, philosophical and factual. She espouses the view that "philosophical truth concerns man in his singularity" (Arendt 2005: 305). This means that such a "truth can be neither gained nor communicated among the many" (299). The important point is that truth is communicable by other means than propositional ones. Indeed, Arendt agrees with philosophers like Nietzsche who maintain that truths go beyond discursive communications and are exemplified by the life and conduct of exemplary individuals. Truth becomes connected with living in a certain way. The bearer of truth, or truth-teller, becomes the place where truth can be manifested and exemplified; the person becomes a living example of a certain truth. Such a person, Arendt maintains, owns the privileged position of "truthteller". However, she maintains that rational-philosophical truths are "apolitical by nature". She connects this view to the liberal tradition of North America and James Madison, who maintains that governments rest on opinion rather than truth. To Arendt's mind, the life of citizens is the realm of opinion with rhetoric as an adequate form of speech. The life of the philosopher, by contrast, is related to truth and dialogue as adequate discursive means, she argues. Seen in this light, politics and opinion belong to the same sphere, while philosophy, truth and dialogue have their own distinct sphere. Besides this distinction being Platonic, to consider truth as naturally apolitical is problematic. Arendt's attempts to place political or factual truths in the realm of public opinion and rational truths in the realm of the singularity of truth-tellers does not offer any help. As is the case with many other distinctions, its two domains, rational-philosophical and political-factual, belong to the same life-world. Political-factual truths contaminate rational truths; rational truths are not immune to politics and power struggle. At best, Arendt's attempt to establish a non-political truth grants the philosophical elite's view of truth and rationality a dominant position; it is exclusive.

Arendt is right in claiming that in current cultural contexts truth and politics belong to different spheres. From this we cannot, however, conclude that truth as such has nothing to do with politics. Rather, the position of truth-teller is oppositional, since truth and current politics belong to different spheres and inevitably come into conflict with each other. As a result, the truth-teller's actions become highly political. Consequently, we cannot claim that his/her actions and truths are apolitical. Truth has thus to do with power and politics, but at a very fundamental level. As I will explore later on in this chapter, such a contemporary truth-teller is Nelson Mandela. Before entering this discussion, we need, however, to elaborate how truth can be manifested in individuals. This is needed since it makes the link between the universal and the singular clear. It also links them to the notion of education.

TRUTH AND EXEMPLARS

In this section I concentrate on Hegel and his way of exemplifying a universal truth in the exemplary life of a singular individual, Christ. In Hegel, Christ occupies a special position, the position of truth. Simply formulated and with a risk of misunderstanding, to Hegel's mind, any individual is the exemplification of some idea. Any Christian individual actualises himself through his embodiment in Christ. Christ, in his turn, is the very exemplification of the principle of example, "the reflective 'example of the example'"; he is his own example. In him paradoxical entities converge and God Himself becomes Man; he is the "exemplification" of God in Man. In Hegel, to become exemplified in man is indeed a part of the notion of God. The important point in our context is that "the example of example" is at the same time the truth; it coincides with the Truth.

Zizek highlights the difference between the Platonic view of Ideas and the Hegelian one. Whereas the Platonic view is mimetic and Plato sees "the imitation of imitation" at work everywhere, Hegel sees a point "at which (human) example and (divine) Idea become indistinguishable, a point of 'chiasmic exchange of properties'" (Zizek 1991: 42). Instead of merely imitating, at some point man attains divine properties and vice versa. Taking advantage of this Hegelian way of argumentation, we can claim that any ordinary individual is an "exemplification" of some educational idea. Any educator, on the other hand, contains the unity of universal and particular truths, since properly understood any educator is the place where an educational truth is manifested; he/she is the exemplification of this truth and this truth is lived and lived up to. While any individual is an exemplification of a certain educational ideal, the educator is his/her own example, the example of his/her example which reflects his/her own light upon himself/ herself; he/she is the example of the logic of exemplarity. Any educator is an example toward which all other examples converge and become actualised; they are examples of an exemplar, or educator. The former are within a context, the latter transcends it. At the same time, there is a point of exchange of properties, where learners attain the educator's properties and the truth becomes manifest in their actions. While all other individuals try to become exemplified in the educator, the educator becomes the manifestation of a context-independent truth. He puts forward an example to be imitated by any and all. Indeed, it is a part of the universality of truth to become exemplified in singular individuals, on the one hand, and to elevate a singular truth to a higher level of universality, on the other. Neither educator nor imitators imitate higher truths in a metaphysical sense. They are, rather, the place where the particular and the universal become indistinguishable and the universal becomes manifest without any reference to the abstract sphere of pure ideas. In this way, the paradox of truth becomes conceivable and productive.

A CONTEMPORARY EXEMPLAR

To make these discussions more salient, I use the person of Nelson Mandela as an educational example, an "example of an example". Considered in the light of the logic of exemplarity, he is an exemplary individual, a place where the highest truth of our age is manifested. Undoubtedly, he reflects his own singular truth. His individual truth, however, becomes universal, since he is the vehicle of truths that belong to our age as such. Through reflecting his own example, he manifests a truth that is not limited to his local context; rather, he bears witness to truth and experiences that belong to the spirit of our time and, as such, belong to any and all. While all other individuals can imitate him, he is not imitating anybody since he is his own example; he expands the horizon of life by establishing this example. Through making us think about the truth, he explores our time and makes its conditions known. His position thus contributes to the growth of human knowledge and understanding of the spirit of our age, its problems and their solutions. He is an educator and an exemplary individual.

To my mind, Mandela is the manifestation of the principle of inclusion. In his essay "The Laws of Reflection: Nelson Mandela, in Admiration", Derrida puts the question "Who is Mandela?" and answers that he is "man and philosopher". He shows his admiration for Mandela by writing that Mandela "seems exemplary and admirable in what he thinks and says, in what he does or in what he suffers" (Derrida 1987: 13). By admiring Mandela, we admire the man and the philosopher in him and the ideals he conveys. In him, we admire the principle of inclusion and this admiration enables us to understand this cardinal principle of our time. In so doing, we make these truths our own.

It is important to bear in mind that Mandela becomes a philosopher by virtue of conducting a philosophical life rather than by being a philosopher by profession. In this sense, philosophy means the pursuit of truth. Seen in this light, the "pole star" of philosophy "is truth alone, the naked, unrewarded, unbefriended and often persecuted truth" rather than the occupation of someone with a "well-paid" academic position (Schopenhauer 1910: xxix–xxx). Here, the difference is between two styles of life, one confined to beautiful words, the other devoted to finding harmonic accord between words and deeds. What is characteristic in the former case is the gap between one's speech and one's deeds. Talks about truth and philosophy are in the service of one's career. Truth remains, then, external to one's deeds. In the latter, one not only searches and remains faithful to truth, but also manifests it in the way one lives; words become one with deeds. One's truth becomes, then, immanent in one's life and conduct. While Aristotle (*Nicomachean Ethics*, 1124b, 28) presents this manner of life as a sign of greatness, Socrates (in, for example, *Laches*) and Nietzsche (SE, DS) suggest it as a criterion regarding our need to distinguish between good and bad educators. This issue will be discussed in the next chapter. Here I focus on Mandela as truth-teller.

It is by virtue of being a truth-teller, on the one hand, and manifesting this truth in his struggle, on the other, that Mandela becomes an educator. He not only made the truth about the logic of inclusion visible, but also lived up to its standards. Through his suffering, Mandela threw apartheid into sharp relief against the logic of inclusion. By so doing, he stripped the proper nature of apartheid, the logic of exclusion, and made it subject to moral indignation on a global scale. In the context of this study, using Mandela as educator, we can reveal more subtly organised forms of exclusion. In fact, apartheid was the manifestation of our time's problems in their most naked form, those related to exclusion. The exclusion of people and their perspectives is not a characteristic exclusively related to apartheid, however. There are parallels to be drawn between apartheid and the prevailing epistemological paradigm. As in the case of apartheid, in epistemological contexts people are excluded and marginalised due to their gender, race, ethnicity and lack of power. As, among others, Okruhlik and Harding show, science is based exclusively on the perspective and needs of Western male and empowered social classes. This is indeed to force people into silence and to the margins. As discussed, the current social organisation of knowledge excludes groups of people as well as the perspectives of art and philosophy. By establishing a consensus exclusively based on science itself, it becomes harmful to the growth of knowledge and human flourishing. As discussed, Habermas emphasises "openness to the public" and "general inclusiveness, equal rights to participation, freedom from repression, and orientation toward reaching understanding"

(2005: 119–20) as the presupposition of argumentation and understanding. If we take these criteria as necessary characteristics for a science beneficial to life, then science is badly outdated. We can fairly claim that the worst kind of exclusion is an invisible one. People do not see the logic of exclusion at work in science, since they are educated scientifically. In this educational paradigm, it is objectivity of science that is the case rather than it being exclusive. Mandela revealed the most basic problem of our age, the problem of exclusion. By challenging the logic of exclusion, he established an exemplary logic of inclusion and became its embodiment. Seen from the perspective of this study, Mandela qualifies himself as an educator through being a strong, active and oppositional individual; he does this through his struggle.

Given these circumstances, it is the responsibility of the philosopher-educator, as outlined above, to make the logic of exclusion visible on semantic and epistemic planes. What is needed here is for the gap to be made visible between the continual engendering of discourses about disinterestedness of knowledge and the mechanisms of exclusion at work in the daily practice of science. We have to reformulate the terms of the old quarrel over the relations between knowledge and life. It is not in an outdated discourse about the neutrality of science but in a new discourse about the exclusion or inclusion of different perspectives that we can bring together science, education and truth. Mandela is helpful in this regard. Through this struggle, he negates the logic of exclusion at the first stage. This means that he manifests an opposition to oppressive economic, social, political and educational circumstances that create a marginalised other. At the next stage, he affirms the logic of inclusion. This means not only recognising the other as something independent of social and cognitive disaffiliation, as the "very alterity", as that which signals ontological and epistemological difference. This is to destroy an otherness related to social and cognitive exclusion in order to affirm the other as a necessary constituent of the knowledge of the self.[2]

Through his struggle, Mandela shows the necessity of such a paradigm shift. He signifies the closure of an epoch, the global closure of the violent and naked logic of exclusion. We can make him justice through expanding the logic of inclusion to ever new domains of life. His victory inaugurates, then, a new stage in educating humanity in the logic of inclusion. As this education is based on inclusion of marginalised perspectives, it meets the demand for a strong notion of education advocated here. Such an education becomes the basis of an inclusive notion of science; they support each other reciprocally. This means that Mandela becomes an educator because of the kind of knowledge and truth that he gives birth to.

As was pointed out earlier, there are connections between sorts of truths and their originators. In other words, truths are related to the struggles, failures, victories, needs, circumstances and characters of their originators. An active Mandela gives birth to a different type of truth than, for instance, a relativist Kuhn. This means that neither the notion of truth nor that of education is homogeneous. Rather than being a matter of consensus, they are marked by struggle, contest and dispute. Consequently, we can use Mandela to overcome Kuhnian nihilism. Such a struggle is not only a destructive force, it is also a constructive source of stimulation to ever higher levels of awareness and excellence.

Another characteristic of Mandela that qualifies him as an educator is his healthy life style. In him, human health, in its cultural and physiological sense, becomes truth. He demonstrated incredible strength in resisting the barbarism of our time in its most brutal form. He did not give up due to a healthy manner of life and the wealth of his creative resources. This position is a celebration of life and worthy of being imitated. Philosophers are, Nietzsche maintains, physicians of their time. He also espouses the view that health is the ability to overcome sickness (GS, 2). Mandela the philosopher becomes a good physician of our time by making an accurate diagnosis regarding it sickness. He tried to cure our time through attempting to reverse the destructive energies of the logic of exclusion into an inclusive one. This is a kind of health that we have to acquire again and again, as Nietzsche puts it (GS, 382).

This healthy and inclusive logic does not work only on the level of rational discourse, theoretical argumentation or everyday reality. It encompasses all of them. It functions by manifesting truths that belong to all these spheres. Proactive by nature, such a position enables us to include perspectives of art, philosophy, science and history in the same way that we include gender perspective and the perspectives of marginalised groups. Through these processes, an inclusive style of thought is shaped which frames our educational actions. It is based on inclusive notions of objectivity, science, education, exemplar, culture and a strong notion of individual, as these terms are used here. Indeed, there is an intrinsic connection between these notions; they are constitutive of each other and support each other. In this view of education, there is not a certain set of personal characteristics or ideas to be imitated. Rather, there are a certain logic and style to be acquired. To see the issue in this light is indeed to revolutionise the whole institution of education and renew its basic principles.

By struggling against apartheid, Mandela presented his style of life pedagogically. He showed how we can transfer the weakest aspect of our time, its disease, to a source of vitality and creativity. In the context of this study, this view of truth gets its due through a defence of a pedagogical renewal based on an inclusive notion of objectivity. Seen in this light, truth becomes a part of a complex whole of problems of our age—the problems of education, science, politics, power, translation, interpretation, and epistemological renewal. Truth stimulates us to contest hierarchies of power, the unfair treatment of people and nature, and the realist principle of correspondence between truths and an independent reality in order to create a new organisation of the production and distribution of knowledge.

In addition to global fame in his lifetime, Mandela will certainly obtain an afterlife, a life no longer determined by nature and the limits of his embodiment, but by history, since the afterlife is historical rather than physiological. Consequently, his ideas will also obtain an afterlife and transcend his context of life and action. What originally was valid in a South African context becomes the universal logic of truth, the exemplary truth. Through these processes, he continues to be worthy of imitation; he manifests trans-historical human values. By transcending his context of action, his truth becomes our shared truth and his values become our shared values. Indeed, we already share these values albeit within the framework of our life-world.

Our age's struggle and strife for a better world becomes manifest in Mandela's struggle; he becomes the exemplary individual, an individual who defends human dignity across cultural contexts. Anybody can say of him: "This is the way I wish to be. He is the manifestation of my values." In him our age's dreams of the inclusion of all people, solidarity, and epistemological, economic and political democracy become personified. His struggle can be used as an exemplary struggle to democratise social and educational institutions. Through his exemplary logic of inclusion, we can postulate new cultural and epistemological values which facilitate the human understanding of the natural and social world.

Describing the notion of educator in this way may be considered simplistic and naïve. It may be seen as romanticising a person or exaggerating his/her abilities and virtues. This is not the whole story, however. Problems related to this manner of education will be discussed in Chapter 11. Here, it is enough to mention that constructing a model personality of a human being demands highlighting some characteristics more clearly. But it does not mean indulging in fanciful thoughts about impossible characteristics. We need to recall that the relationship between educators and learners is based on the notion of translation. Translation provides us with a variety of educational means through which the learner can approach the educator. This means that the learner does not passively imitate the other. Being active participants in the process of education, learners are engaged in constructing desired individual and cultural values and characteristics. These characteristics are not ready-made, rigid and nonnegotiable. Indeed, they are contextual; they are created while the process of education goes on. They originate in the common needs of the educator and the learner.

11 Education and the Problem of Authority

In the preceding chapter I connected notions of knowledge and truth with education. These notions were based on a plurality of perspectives and modes of understanding. I also criticised the way exemplars are used in scientific education. The main source of this problem was identified as the exclusive character of paradigms. Education through philosopher-artists was introduced as a solution to the problem of education. The main concern was to find good educators in order to establish a style of life based on harmony between words and deeds. In this chapter I focus on problems related to this educational model—the problem of distinguishing between the good educators and decadent ones. I invite Aristotle, Mill and Nietzsche into the conversation in order to shed light on the problem of education and authority.

PROBLEMS RELATED TO EXEMPLARS

To entrust to educators the role of intellectual leader of an age presents certain difficulties, if it is not understood properly. Paul Feyerabend discusses the relationship between philosophers and laymen in modern societies. His starting point is his notion of "democratic relativism". He not only believes in the equality of different truths, but also engages all citizens in discussions about truth. "Democratic relativism" signifies, contrary to philosophers like Nietzsche, Arendt and Mill, Feyerabend's high esteem of public opinion. Feyerabend's philosophical project is designed to control "objective facts" by "(subjective) public opinion" (Feyerabend 2005: 153). Feyerabend contests the all-knowing "super-experts" or philosophers since they try to prevent lay people from thinking, trying instead to do the thinking in their place. Seen in this way, philosophers as educators not only function as super-experts who "define what it means to know and what is good for society", but they represent an "authoritarian approach" which tries to "shape the world in their own image" (151). Feyerabend recommends instead a democratic approach in order to make sure that super-experts do not impose their narrow conceptions on the masses. He aspires to a state of being in which "everybody has the right to act as a 'wise man'" (149).

In fact, this study approves cognitive democracy and is in agreement with Feyerabend in emphasising the individuals' rights to think and act autonomously; it also encourages individuals' participation in cognitive issues. These are necessary characteristics of any healthy socio-cultural order. Further, it is also desirable for everybody to act "wisely", provided that we consider the notion of wisdom as part of a discourse related to the notion of power and distinguished by inner tension, rather than as a homogeneous notion. Such a society can really function as an educational goal. However, there are serious difficulties connected with democratic relativism. Since connections between relativism and nihilism have been discussed in detail in Chapter 3, there is no need to repeat them here. Here, I refer instead to problems connected with public opinion, conformity and individual freedom. Before doing that, some words about authority and obedience are necessary, since this notion is central to education.

THE PROBLEM OF AUTHORITY AND OBEDIENCE

The notion of education suggested here is non-hierarchical, since authority is not concentrated in educators; it is, rather, placed within the context of education. Seen in this way, power is relational and a matter of negotiation. Obedience and authority are not absolute; they also are relational and positional. Generally speaking, this study is in agreement with Aristotle when he writes: "For who would learn to command well must, as men say, first of all learn to obey . . ." (*Politics*, 1333a). Thus, command and obedience do not exclude each other. They are different sides of the same process. Neither are they problematic as such. They become problematic whenever command or obedience becomes absolute. Seen in this light, authority as such is necessary; it becomes undesirable as soon as it becomes authoritarian. Thus, instead of denying the authority of philosopher-educators, it is wise to concentrate on what kind of educators we need. This cannot be done by theoretical argument. It is an aesthetic issue which demands an examination of exemplary lives of educators. Dealt with in this way, the emphasis is less on particular persons than on their embodiment of historical human types and styles of thought and conduct. They are then accepted or contested together with their manner of life and the truth they convey. This is a genealogical manner of analysis, since it concentrates on constitutive processes of phenomena by looking for their contextual emergence. Considered in this manner, the basic tenet is a correspondence between human types and truths. In this regard, I draw on Nietzsche: "every great philosophy so far has been . . . the personal confession of its author and a kind of involuntary and unconscious memoir" (BGE, 6). This is a productive way of discussing the issue, since thoughts and ideas are extremely influenced by their originators. This issue has already been discussed in detail. Here, I just take from it the unity of subject and object and the identity between doer and deeds; it is thinkers' health and decadence that become truth and deed. Related to this, there is a second point. Educators are not judged by the quantity of their knowledge and expertise; rather, they are judged by their manner of significance, kind of knowledge, skills, life and conduct.

There are always risks of decadent thinkers becoming educators. Nietzsche's approach to educators, typified by David Strauss, is helpful. Nietzsche makes a distinction between the "cultivated philistine", like Strauss, and his/her counterpart, "the genuinely cultured person", like Goethe (DS, 2). Being a typical cultivated philistine, David Strauss demonstrates characteristics that make him a forerunner of the scholarly type occupying academic positions today. They are characterised by several traits. Focused on bookish knowledge, this type of educator is a "walking encyclopaedia", without this knowledge leading to harmony between truths and deeds. Truth remains, then, external to their life. As a result, they are interested in ascetic ideal. Interest in theoretical knowledge, general forms and abstract notions detached from life and beyond human reach is a sign of this style of life. The cardinal characteristic of these educators is, however, their style of exclusive thought and conduct. They exclude epistemological pluralism and declare their own type of education the climax of cultivation and declare themselves as canon and "model writers" (DS, 1). In so doing, they become authoritarian. And this is the problem with current education. In the previous chapter, I discussed the opposite type, a really cultivated educator, by presenting Nelson Mandela as a model educator. Such educators are signified by their inclusive manner of being and frame of mind.

Education is marked by contests between different types of educators, between philosopher-artists and philistines. Feyerabend's critique is relevant to the latter. Trained in the same paradigm and interacting among themselves, they are scarcely able to see the world from other perspectives than their own, which they consider to be true. Since society is organised according to the needs of this human type, they are the judges of culture. Occupying this position, they can determine the good of society and define what knowledge is. They are in a position to shape the world in their own image. As a result, they do not understand those who try to challenge the prevailing order. On the contrary, they resist changes. This mode of understanding leads inevitably to authoritarianism and absolutism, to the overestimation of one's own position. This illusory self-understanding is characterised by a groundless optimism based on fancying oneself in possession of virtues that one does not have. Artist-philosophers are needed to replace this type of educator. Through telling the truth about educators of today, they can teach us how to resist the manipulative efforts of the education industry and the state.

In an educational context, these issues are related to our view of the nature of knowledge, the role of educators, the place of learners, knowledge acquisition and the social organisation of knowledge. Generally speaking, scholarly types demonstrate a Platonic view of knowledge. They consider knowledge a reflection of the external world that has to be passed on unchanged. As a result, educator-scholars are considered to be transmitters of ready-made truths. Students are seen as empty vessels. The scholarly type often uses paradigm as a source of authority and becomes its ventriloquist in order to silence the voices of learners.

In an education based on the notion of educator as used here, authority and obedience are not closed notions; they are produced in the process of education. They are based on a reciprocal interaction between equally distinguishable individuals who share a common aim. Being the end and the beginning of the process of education, the educator shows the way toward what is humanly possible by her/his exemplary life. The educator stimulates the learner's creative resources and the learner tries to reach this aim by following the educator's example. As a result, they create a common orientation of mind. As their actions are based on love and their inner drives, authority and obedience are based on mutual love and friendship between the two. The difference between these types of obedience is related to the character of the individuals and educational aims involved in the process. Through deeply personal relationships, the true educator discerns the learner's needs and talents. There is a sense of kinship between the two. The learner looks for what she/he loves most and strengthens those aspects of his personality. The educator gives the learner a sense of personal integrity, when otherwise he/she would have to construct an identity out of an amalgam of different elements, like celebrities and sport stars. This type of education leads to a harmony between the exterior and interior aspects of one's personality, between knowledge and action.

THE PROBLEM OF PUBLIC OPINION

Feyerabend's fascination by public opinion is a source of problems rather than solutions; it places him among the super-experts whom he criticises, since to subjugate the individual to public opinion is a source of conformity; public opinion can easily become tyrannical, intolerant and authoritarian. Cognitive democracy does not necessarily mean making public opinion the judge of culture and cognition. Since Plato, philosophers have been aware of the dangers of public opinion. For Plato, the ignorant public opinion of ancient Athens was the cause of the traumatic death of Socrates, the man whom Plato considered the most virtuous human being. The very distinction between knowledge and opinion has provided a way of avoiding the tyranny of public opinion. Aristotle encourages us to let truth come before public opinion by writing that "to care less for truth than for what people will think, is a coward's part" (*Nicomachean Ethics*, 1124b28). In this study, I defend an inclusive notion of knowledge, without equalising knowledge and public opinion. This notion of knowledge is democratic, since it includes any perspective worthy of being included. On the other hand, it is selective and distinguishes between different values and beliefs; it does not yield to public opinion or any other external source of authority.

Nietzsche's dislike of public opinion is well-known. Nietzsche's view of democracy can, however, create misunderstandings. To avoid this risk, I prefer to refer to John Stuart Mill instead. In his *On Liberty*, Mill discusses the "the tyranny of the majority" and the influence of public opinion upon individual freedom. When "society is itself the tyrant", he argues, "it leaves few means of escape" (1974: 63). Mill also talks of the "enslavement of the soul itself" (63), whereby repressive mechanisms are internalised by the oppressed. It goes without saying that, since the time of Mill, forms of tyranny have become more and more complicated and techniques of oppression and manipulation have become more and more sophisticated. Covert and overt forms of tyranny demand consensus and use public opinion as an effective tool. They often invent some abstract social cause in order to present their own interests as the interests of humanity. Nazi Germany demonstrated a case of herd-like behaviour connected with manipulation of public opinion. The dangerous thing is that a majority of scholars and academics of our day are in the service of such states.[1] Behind a mask of academic freedom, scholars are really governed by states and multinationals. Such a climate has an oppressive effect on the individual. Consequently, there is an acute need of opposition to the oppressive power of public opinion. This can be offered by art and philosophy.

Through manipulating public opinion, patterns of conduct and modes of understanding have been internalised that are inimical to human flourishing. This can be said of countries with sophisticated tools of manipulation as well as of those dominated by naked dictatorships. To make the social mechanisms behind these phenomena visible is an acute educational task. Equipping the individuals with inner sources of resistance and enabling them to take control of their lives at all levels are also important educational ends. To have the individual's capacity of resistance as a reference point is to oppose the social mechanisms of mental and material suppression. In order to resist social and cultural oppressive powers, we need a strong notion of the individual. And this demands educators like Mandela who link their lives with humanity and give us means of resisting the manipulative efforts of states, religions and the culture industry.

DANGERS RELATED TO CULTURAL EXAMPLES

Risks related to educators are, as argued in the previous section, based on their becoming authoritarian. There are also risks related to cultures functioning as educators. A comparison between the original ideals of a culture and their practical results is a good criterion to judge cultures. This is a genealogical style of analysis and leads us back to the contextual emergence of current ideals. In fact, these ideals emerged in the soil of the Enlightenment; the Enlightenment has functioned as the educator of the modern age, since the intellectual make-up of Western man and current educational and cultural institutions are mainly the result of the Enlightenment's ideals. In the context of this study, two main characteristics of the Enlightenment are important. This culture not only declared an opposition to all authorities but also demonstrated a strong support for rationality and objective knowledge. These ideals have acquired a global dimension through the global domination of Western culture. Worldwide dissemination of scientific knowledge through liberal education has been linked to the Enlightenment's commitment to social progress and the promise of liberating the individual from authoritarianism. In sum, the establishment of a progressive and democratic social order has been the declared aim of the Enlightenment. As discussed earlier, the sum consequence of modern culture has been the alienation of humanity in the face of an impersonal and dehumanised social order. Two world wars, the rise of Nazism and the herd-like behaviour at its root, have shown that the achievements have been the opposite of true individualism. Conformity has been the actual result of scientific culture. Colonialism showed another aspect of scientific culture. Most recently, global warming has brought to the fore issues that endanger life due to a heartless use of technologies based on science.

The emergence of positivism in the field of theory of knowledge and the subsequent awareness of its being illusory has been a disappointment from an epistemological point of view. Thus, the Enlightenment has, its high ideals notwithstanding, functioned as a bad educator. There must be some intrinsic characteristics that make this the case.

Indeed, the Enlightenment's failure to fulfil its promises has led to a historical disappointment bluntly formulated by Adorno and Horkheimer. They ask: "Why is mankind, instead of entering into a truly human condition, sinking into a new kind of barbarism?" (Adorno and Horkheimer 1972: xi). Although this question has profound legitimacy, one could say that it is not the right question or, at least, that it is not put in the right way. One could instead pose the question in this way: Given modern circumstances and the modern education industry, why not barbarism? Or, formulated more clearly, why is barbarism inevitable, given the kind of education we are going through? We have already discussed the logic of exclusion at the heart of modern culture. Accordingly, a certain human type, Western scientific man, has been associated with the ideals of the Enlightenment, as the only human type capable of accomplishing these ideals. Consequently, he is the norm and unquestionable aim of all education. Such logic leads inevitably to violence in different shapes; it can manifest itself in the shape of steady ongoing epistemological violence or more naked forms of physical violence, but the logic is the same.

The Enlightenment's close alliance with traditional notions of science and objectivity has been a source of problems. As a result many of the problems discussed in relation to science can be connected to the wider context of the Enlightenment. In his early writings on education, Nietzsche had already discerned and warned about an "approaching barbarism". Using genealogical analysis, he identified the "soil" of barbarism by tracing its origin to the rational tradition of Hegel (ULH, 8). He takes issue with Hegelianism regarding the use and abuse of history. Hegelianism tried to educate youths by reducing history to pure knowledge or the science of history. Nietzsche saw connections between scholarly culture and barbarism, since this culture tried to subdue life to abstract knowledge.

Nietzsche defines barbarism in opposition to cultivation rather than civilisation. This is a fruitful distinction. Indeed, atrocities of our time are either stimulated by or take place among more or less civilised peoples. These people may naively believe in some ideology or are manipulated by others, as was the case with Germans during the time of the Nazis, but the consequences are the same. Under present circumstances the more civilised a people or a state is, the more destructive the power at its disposal. Indeed, the huge dangers that are threatening humanity today are in the hands of "educated" people. In fact the "educated" part of the world is now exploiting the uneducated part on a scale that clearly contradicts our high ideals of humanism.

This is not to refuse the dreams of the Enlightenment categorically. The Enlightenment can still be used as educator, given a critical appraisal of its aims, means and demands. There are, of course, aspects of the Enlightenment that can function as exemplary monuments and release creative modes in us, like its refutation of authorities external to man. There are also aspects to be revered, preserved and transferred to coming generations, like stringency of enquiry. The most important task is, however, to combine these two aspects with a critical appraisal of this culture. The main criticism, as was discussed in previous chapters, has to be a critique of scientific knowledge. Only in this way does the Enlightenment become a true educator. In order to do this we need educators who signify the closure of an epoch and the beginning of a new one: the closure of the epoch of exclusion and the beginning of an epoch of inclusion. Such a task demands changes in the individual as well as on cultural planes. This issue will be discussed in the next chapter.

12 The Nature of Educational Renewal

In the preceding chapters, radical educational changes were suggested. In this chapter, I shall try to clarify these changes. Cultural values and individual characteristics, I argued, are constitutive of knowledge. The prevailing technical-scientific cultural climate and atomistic individualism give rise to a kind of knowledge that leads humanity into alienation and nihilism, since these tendencies are based on the logic of exclusion, on the one hand, and mask the active part of the individual in cognition, on the other. Such a situation makes cultural and educational changes inevitable. Since both cultural values and individual characteristics are constitutive of cognition, changes suggested here have two interconnected sides, one pedagogical and one cultural. They are interchangeable and should be considered different aspects of the same process; each of them would be fruitless without the other. While cultural changes improve the social organisation of science, individual ones make the individual capable of taking advantage of an inclusive organisation of knowledge. Cognitive democracy establishes equality between different perspectives and maintains inclusion as a principal cognitive norm. Individual rigour and strength, on the other hand, is needed to enhance such an organisation of knowledge and make it durable. In the coming sections, I shall spell out some main characteristics of changes suggested by this study.

CULTURAL CHANGES

Continuity ensures that patterns of behaviour are effective. Through sanctioning certain patterns of behaviour and modes of knowledge and forbidding others, cultures establish habitual ways of acting and become constitutive of human nature. As argued earlier, Aristotle has shown the importance of habitual repetition and prolonged patterns of knowledge and behaviour. Through being repeated, behaviours penetrate deep into the human psyche and influence human nature. Being constitutive of human nature, cultures can improve or deteriorate it. Through genealogical analysis, we have traced the contextual emergence of modern technical-scientific culture back to the Enlightenment. We have also recognised that this culture continues to operate in the present through scientific education. We have argued that this continuity creates some serious social and epistemological problems. The question is, how can we disrupt these influences and release ourselves from the burden of the past? How soon can human nature be changed and what kinds of change are desirable?

Although heirs of the Enlightenment, Marx and Nietzsche, each in his own way, mark discontinuity in the tradition of the Enlightenment. They offer tools for analysing modern culture and its relation to human nature. Primarily, Marx pushes for changes in social configurations constitutive of knowledge and human nature. As has been said, for him the nature of man is his labour. As such, human nature is historical. This means that the kind of organisation of labour is constitutive of human nature. For Marx, it is the type of production and distribution of commodities that signify the main traits of any community, its thoughts and knowledge; the relationship here is the notorious relation between base and superstructure. But this relation is not one-way; there is a mutual relation between the type of man, his knowledge and the type of production. According to Marx, it was the emergence of private property that determined the step toward modern capitalism. This means that not only are human beings deprived of the ownership of their nature or labour, but also their way to insights into constitutive elements of knowledge is blocked by ideological presentations of this state of affairs.

From this starting point, it is easy to conclude that through changing social organisation of human labour, man reclaims his nature. This means a move away from reified human nature. Consequently, man becomes one with his nature and inner creative resources. This also means reverence and love of nature and human dignity; these elements become the new cultural values. Since cultural values are constitutive of knowledge, such a change can also lead to changes in the constitution of human knowledge. In the long run, radical changes in human nature are to be expected. This is a process of increasing self-consciousness and the improvement of human knowledge. In this sense, the growth of knowledge in general and individual self-consciousness in particular become dynamic sources of liberation. Indeed, awareness that both commodities and intellectual values are products of human activities is a presupposition of individual and cultural freedom. As already discussed, this awareness is nihilistic; it negates old values. This is an important step, since liberation is impossible within the boundaries of old values. Nihilism is, however, temporary. Humanity overcomes it as soon as processes which lead to the abstraction of human labour and knowledge and transform them into exchangeable entities are brought into the light and replaced by new ones.

The Marxian solution has, however, it own limitations. It is not inclusive enough. Famously, Marx's starting point was labour conditions in manufactures. As a result, labour related to household did not receive his due attention. Since domestic labour is by and large related to women, Marx's analysis of the condition of labour in capitalist societies is basically based on masculine labour. Feminist thinkers have analysed some shortcomings related to Marxism. Shulamith Firestone, for instance, argues that the Marxian solution excludes the "psychosexual" perspective (Firestone 1970: 6). And this, according to Firestone, is the root of the failure of all social revolutions. She suggests her own solutions based on including the gender perspective on social revolutions. She develops "a materialist view of history based on sex" (6). In spite of its shortcomings, the Marxian emphasis on power-relations is important. By changing the power relation between genders, classes and social groups, a cultural renewal leads to the inclusion of the perspectives of oppressed people and women in the constitution of knowledge. This inclusion contributes much to changes in the nature of cultural values and, consequently, in human knowledge. Through inclusion becoming a basic cognitive value, the way is also paved for the inclusion of the perspectives of philosophy, art and history. A post-revolutionary culture is a strong culture based on the inclusion of new values, problems and perspectives that cover humanity as a whole. It provides the general intellectual climate for plurality of perspectives. It is democratic and based on cognitive pluralism. Needless to say, such a revolution is a cultural one and has nothing to do with revolutions in the traditional sense. It thus needs other means than ordinary revolutions. This leads us to the educational and individual aspects of changes.

EDUCATIONAL CHANGES

Although enlarged by inclusion of a sexual dimension, Firestone's solution is Marxian and shares the political nature of his solution. A reference to Nietzsche adds a further dimension to this solution. Nietzsche's approach to politics is different from that of Marx. Although he, like Marx, was against the exploitation of humanity by private interests, he did not share the Marxian view of the importance of politics for human liberation. For Marx economic exploitation and mental suppression could be eliminated by means of politics. Nietzsche was concerned with the educational improvement of humanity and asked: "How should a political innovation be sufficient to make men once and for all into happy inhabitants of the earth?" (SE, 4). In my opinion, this is a very important question and should be taken seriously. It points out that individuals must participate in cultural processes if they are to reach long-standing results. Nietzsche underestimates, however, the weight of social changes and overestimates the importance of educational revolution. The failure of Marx and Nietzsche to achieve any radical change in the condition of humanity can be explained by their emphasising only one aspect of change, either social or educational. Marxism failed totally to create its utopian society because it considered states and collectives as the agents of social change and the individual was set aside. Instead of conscious individuals, it was a conscious class and the strong state that was the pivotal point of this theory. Marxism neglected the importance of educational revolution. Neither has the educational revolution that Nietzsche expected happened, since it was separated from social changes. The social and cognitive condition of humanity today is the same or in some respects worse than the time of Nietzsche and Marx. The social and mental repressive mechanisms are more sophisticated and stronger today than a century ago.

To consider Nietzsche as categorically apolitical is, however, to misconceive him. His educational theory engages politics albeit in a nonconventional way. He really wants to change things and this engages him inevitably in politics, although, for him politics is not the main arena for achieving cultural changes. In fact, he does not reject politics categorically; rather, like Plato, he gives the philosopher-educator the right to "make use of whatever political and economic states are at hand" for his "project of cultivating and education" (BGE, 61). This view places him quite close to the pragmatists, though he cannot be conceived as one of them. Marx was not alien to the role of philosophy in changing the world either. Famously, his thesis eleven sees changing the world instead of merely interpreting it as the task of philosophy. Marx emphasised a self-conscious class becoming a state and the agent of change. He believed in a collective solution and social practice. For Nietzsche, education is a process of individual formation and transformation. He tried to limit the influence of the state on education and assigned authority to philosophers instead. By so doing, he released educators from the task of maintaining a particular social order.

Using Marx and Nietzsche, we can reach a comprehensive solution based on both collective and individual engagement. Indeed, these two thinkers were aware of the interconnectedness of social and educational changes. The anti-capitalistic tendencies in Nietzsche are usually underestimated. He considers the spirit of capitalism to be the dominant spirit of his age. In *Richard Wagner in Bayreuth* he repeatedly attacks the "brutal greed for profit of the owners; the hollowness and thoughtlessness of a society that thinks of the people only in terms of how they can be beneficial" (RWB, 4). Nietzsche was really aware of the fact that achieving radical changes in a single area of social life is impossible "without at the same time introducing innovation everywhere" (4). Indeed, educational changes are aimed at reaching improvement in the condition of humankind through changes in the cognitive conditions of the individual. Seen in this light, scientific revolutions become a part of an educational renewal. Contrary to the current situation, this kind of revolution becomes a part of conscious human efforts to improve our cognitive conditions rather than being imposed on the scientific community. These revoloutions are a result of philosophical-oppositional actions and are considered in the much wider context of a culture rather than in isolated scientific communities. Quite close to the

Marxian view of the matter, Nietzsche connects individual prosperity to social and cultural circumstances:

> We cannot be happy as long as everything around us is suffering and inflicts suffering on itself . . . we cannot be even wise as long as all humanity has not entered the competition for wisdom and led the individual to life and knowledge in the wisest possible manner. (RWB, 4)

Such a statement illustrates a holistic view of society and the interconnectedness of changes in different domains of life. Both Marx and Nietzsche use history as a source of knowledge about both the present and human conduct in general. They connect knowledge to action and praxis in history. They conceive history as distinguished by a struggle between antagonistic forces. For Nietzsche, history signifies a struggle between slaves and masters—two kinds of thought and behaviour, both in society and within the individual. For Marx, the struggle is between owner and oppressed classes. While for Marx it is production and distribution of material commodities, for Nietzsche it is the production and distribution of knowledge that determines the main characteristics of a society. These points of view converge, however, in demanding radical changes in the social organisation of labour and of knowledge. These changes presuppose radical changes in our perception of our own nature and the nature of our cognitive activities. The production and distribution of knowledge and commodities can be accomplished differently in different cultural contexts. Because current social circumstances are unfavourable to a desirable organisation of production by mind and hand, they have to be changed for the better. The important thing is that these changes are radical enough to become the new nature of humanity.

CHANGES AND THE INDIVIDUAL

As was discussed earlier, Nietzsche shares the Marxian characteristic of not being essentialist. They were in agreement about the variability of human nature. We have used Marx to explain the cultural aspects of an educational renewal. Nietzsche is helpful regarding the individual aspects of such a renewal.

Seen from a Nietzschean perspective, human nature is marked by heterogeneity rather than homogeneous unity. It contains opposite drives. Nietzsche emphasises the weight of individuals' active participation in whatever concerns their lives. To his mind, human nature can become one thing or another depending on the individual's inner strength or weakness. On several occasions, he compares us with animals. "In man *creature* and *creator* are united" (BGE, 225), he writes. While the creature or animal side can live in the present, limited to the egoistic needs of the day, the creator side is distinguished by the ability to see beyond individual life toward what is eternally justified in man and in life. Seen in this light, possibilities of changing human nature lie in its openness, complexity and enormous potential for development: it encompasses the span between two extreme ends of human existence, animal and man. An important aspect of education is that it constitutes inner strife. Its aim is to overcome the animal aspects of our existence and transfer these latent energies into human creativity. This is not only a characteristic of humanity, and as such related to culture's inner strife, but also of each individual. More pertinently, humanity is eternally open to change and development. This openness has two interconnected aspects, a cultural and an individual.

To be clear, to Nietzsche's mind, human nature is love (GS, 363). Love, in its turn, is an inner source of creative human resources. The utmost aim of education should be to bring up a human type that acts out of love. Thus, the dividing line is between those creative individuals who act out of love and those whose actions are imposed by external circumstances. These two human types signify the master and the slave manner of living, respectively. A shift from the slave manner to the master manner primarily demands radical changes in production and the distribution of knowledge. Acting out of love and the ability to see beyond individual life gives rise to a notion of objectivity that is in line with natural human needs rather than being beneficial only for a certain group; under such circumstances the interests of the individual coincide with those of humanity. Such an individual is a healthy one who knows how to shift perspectives and use art, science and philosophy as complementary perspectives.

From a Nietzschean perspective, objectivism is the root of modern asceticism. As a result, it is not love that is manifested in human actions. It is, rather, *ressentiment* and revenge. Before going further, it is worth reflecting on the notion of revenge. In Nietzsche, revenge is not only the central trait of nihilism, but also the essence of metaphysics. Consequently, he connects freedom from nihilism and metaphysics to delivery from the spirit of revenge. Nietzsche wrote, in *Thus Spoke Zarathustra*, that "the highest hope" of humanity is deliverance from *"revenge"* (Z, II, "On the Tarantulas"). In order to know what he means by revenge, we have to refer to *Zarathustra,* where it is emphasised that revenge is: "the will's ill will against time and its 'it was'" (Z, II, "On Redemption"). Heidegger explicates the Nietzschean notion of revenge: "Revenge is the will's aversion to time, and that means the ceasing to be, its transience" (Heidegger 1999: 73). Blanchot also relates revenge to hatred of the transient (Blanchot 1999: 125). Revenge becomes, then, the essence of metaphysics, since metaphysics dislikes the transient world of the senses and invents a world of eternal ideas as the true world. And this, as Michel Haar (1999: 14) argues, is the ground of nihilism. Freedom from revenge is thus freedom from nihilism and this is possible through an educational renewal based on a re- conceptualisation of the notion of objectivity, where the active part of the individual in cognition is recognised.

Like the emergence of revenge, the emergence of private property and the social order based on it has deprived man of being master over his own nature, his labour. In both cases, the individual is deprived of something deeply personal and is subjugated to external powers. In the first case, it is the ideal of priests or the will to abstract truth that master humanity, and in the second, it is another abstract universal entity, money. The reduction of the individual and labour to abstract entities goes hand in hand with the transferring of categories of consciousness into mental idols.

Although Marx considers classes to be the agents of change, he is aware of the role played by the individual. He also has individual liberation in sight. In Marx, historical development is a movement toward "free individuality". Under such circumstances, humanity acquires great abilities to promote the "conscious reorganisation of society" (Marx 1959: 88). According to Marx, human liberation is "the domination of individuals over chance and circumstances" (Marx 1973: 117). Nietzsche also defends the sovereignty of the individual. He presents a new notion of progress. As a result of this kind of progress, "Man becomes more profound, mistrustful, 'immoral', stronger, more confident of himself—and to this extent 'more natural'" (WP, 123), instead of coming closer to abstract and general truths. In such humanity, nature and strength become deeds and the individual acts, will to power. To become "more natural" means to be released from revenge and the hold of oppressive social mechanisms and act out of love, inner drives and human nature. In both writers, destruction and construction are closely connected. Such a strong notion of the individual corresponds to an inclusive notion of objectivity. By these two aspects of change coming together, the needs of theory and the needs of organism are united.

A STRONG NOTION OF THE INDIVIDUAL

Cultural and educational changes discussed here pave the way for a strong type of individual. This notion is important, since the kind of individual is central to knowledge and truth. I have already discussed the main characteristics of such an individual, characteristics that are not naturally given and have to be acquired through education. These characteristics were identified as the ability to make use of different perspectives, be critical of one's own paradigm, look at one's own perspective from the prism of the others, possess a rigorous manner of argumentation and own the ability to resist the manipulative powers of collectives and states. This notion of individual needs further clarification. Traditional views share a weak notion of the individual, since in these theories the individual is reduced either to a transcendental subject or to saleable labour power. These abstractions obscure the individual's vision and block his/her understanding of his/her actual state of being. Liberation involves the individual's awareness of the real conditions of life and his/her own abilities, possibilities and limitations. Such awareness and the concomitant ability to use it in the service of self-formation is the basis of individualism as the term is used here. Marx gives us a clue to keeping the balance between individualism and egoism. He makes a distinction between the individual as a necessary ingredient of an exchange economy and the individual as the basic constituent of human liberation. The first notion is nothing more than an atomistic notion of individualism. The individual is considered an abstract entity and a part of bourgeois ideology. In this sense, the individual egoistically concentrates on his/her own interests and is separated from community. This kind of individualism is indeed anti-individualism because it is based on a transcendental notion of subject rather than actual individuals. While in theory the transcendental individual enjoys freedom, real individuals are oppressed by the actual circumstances of bourgeois society; they are constrained by the conditions of the principle of universal saleability. Through the process of education, the individual is made current or saleable. In science, too, the empirical subject collapses into a transcendental subject. The realm of the transcendental subject is that of abstract objects and theories. Traditional objectivity corresponds to the transcendental subject. Objectivism replaces human interests and the transcendental subject replaces the empirical subject.

A reference to Kant sheds light on this matter: In Kant the human subject, like all other entities, can be conceived in two different ways. One is the human subject as thing-in-itself. In this sense, the human subject has a transcendental form. In this capacity, the subject is beyond the flux of empirical representations. From this transcendental position, the human subject imposes on the world of objects a self-legislated scheme of its own *a priori* categories. The other form of human subject is the empirical subject, a thing-for-us. It is important to keep in mind that what Kant establishes is the transcendental subject and not the empirical subject. The transcendental subject has nothing to do with contingent social circumstances; it belongs to the realm of *noumena,* a demigod and inhabitant of the realm of things in themselves. The Kantian transcendental subject is an unhistorical subject; it is an eternal abstraction of human nature, rather than a real individual. At the same time, the empirical subject is objectified and reduced to an object of a transcendental thing-in-itself. Through this distinction the Kantian notion of knowledge becomes authoritarian and repressive instead of being liberating.

Contrary to Kant, education has to do with empirical individuals, individuals who live and work in contingent contexts of life-worlds; they are conditioned by language, gender, sex, class and cultural affiliations. The educational changes advocated here are meant to lead to the liberation of this type of individual. Seen in this light, there is a connection between social reality, the notion of the individual and his/her form of consciousness. In other words, different social configurations are constitutive of different individual characters. Accordingly, improvement of the latter demands changes in the former. Since prevailing educational discourses distort social reality and justify different forms of social domination, radical changes in their make-up are necessary. This means preferring a possible social order to the actual one. This possibility is a source of change and of individual participation. Accordingly, the individual and his/her environment change each other reciprocally.

Corresponding to the strong notion of the individual, there is a strong notion of educator. Such an educator embraces the weak notions of educator, like those of scientific exemplars and cultural monuments, by including some of their main problems in his/her own repertoire. By so doing, this type of educator has the strength to overcome their shortcomings and give the individual the strength to choose his/her own way among a plurality of ways and acquire a style of his own. The educator, then, becomes the initiator of perpetual changes.

Conclusions

In the present study, I have focused on scientific education instead of science teaching. Having this starting point, my concern has been what happens to us as human beings at a time when science is both the form and the content of education. Looking at science education in the light of its practical implications, I identified alienation and nihilism as the inevitable consequences of an education scientific in form and content. Having this in mind, I argued for a strong notion of education as an alternative to the prevailing educational system and as a solution to these problems. Taking this notion of education as my starting point, my task has been to rethink not only the notion of education, but also of truth, objectivity and science. These notions have thus been explored in close connection with each other. Such connections pose difficulties. The main one is the paradoxical nature of the connection between education and truth; while education is context-dependent, we consider truth to be universal. How can they go together? Contrary to traditional ways of thinking, according to which truth is either independent of cultural contexts or totally dependent on them, my argument has been that the contextual and the universal are necessary constituents of truth. Human beings are active participants in all acts of cognition. As such, they are embodied and act within different contexts. Traditional epistemologies choose to disregard this, but we cannot escape from it. Suppression of the active role of the human agent in knowledge is indeed the basis of alienation.

The contextual emergence of knowledge does not mean a total lack of human communication or cognitive relativism; this position leads to nihilism. Based on objectivism and relativism, respectively, alienation and nihilism constitute two different stages of the same process. By adhering to "what is the case" and ignoring human participation in cognition, objectivism leads to reified consciousness. Though products of the human mind, objectified ideas appear as alien forces to humanity and start to master us; we become alienated from our world. An awareness of the man-made nature of these truths, on the other hand, leads to nihilism. The positivistic view of science, with its emphasis on "what is the case", was presented as a source of alienation. Kuhnian questioning of science, on the other hand, was blamed as a source of nihilism.

In my discussions of objectivity, I put the emphasis on the logic of inclusion as the basis of this notion, instead of exclusion. Contrary to old epistemologies, according to which truth is used to exclude different perspectives on the world, I use the very same notion in order to overcome the narrowness of the perspective of local values, relativism and individual egoism; it is used to enhance the universal aspect of education, knowledge and human problems. At the same time, I have tried to avoid dogmatism and absolutism associated with the traditional notion of universal truth. Accordingly, the paradoxical nature of truth becomes a central issue. The main concern has been to give a satisfactory explanation to the tension between universal and local aspects of truth. I propose a solution based on sensitivity to each term of this paradox. I am suggesting an orientation toward connections between this paradox and its educational-practical implications, since truth is immanent in the process of education rather than imposed on it from outside. This approach enables me to present a solution to the issue on the same level as the one at which the problem emerges. This is the main difference between what I am suggesting and prevailing epistemological paradigms that consider truth to be a formal and external source of legitimacy. Based on epistemological pluralism and bearing its ground of legitimacy within itself, I termed this epistemology inclusive epistemology.

The prevailing educational paradigm is based on the traditional notion of scientific objectivity conceived as correspondence between thoughts and objects. This notion leads either to objectivism or to relativism. Contradictory as it may seem, objectivism and relativism presuppose each other. Objectivism creates an illusion of a reality independent of the human mind, language and knowledge. A representational notion of language, an essentialist view of meaning, where meaning is considered as constant based on a natural bond between words and objects, constitute a basic presupposition of objectivism. Science is presented as the single objective picture of the world independent of scientists' gender, beliefs and cultural values. The individual scientist, it is presupposed, discloses only pre-given facts. The esteem of these facts depends on their dependence on a universal abstract truth. Through these processes human knowledge appears as de-personalised and a totally alien force. As a result, the individual becomes alien to his/her world. To explain these phenomena, I made use of Marx's notion of alienation; there are parallelisms between objectivism and mechanisms behind the prevailing market economy. Marx identifies human nature with our labour. Through the mechanisms of market economy human labour becomes detached from the human subject and takes the form of a commodity, owned by capital. Since labour is nothing less or more than human nature, such a process leads to our alienation from our own nature. Within such a social structure, money is the highest universal abstract value. All other commodities, including human labour, are exchangeable into money. Indeed, human labour and its products have to become reified and emerge as alien forces to human beings in order to become exchangeable in money.

Conclusions 177

In such a world, social relations are also reified. Emerging as objective forces, they appear as if they are nature itself.

Because this process is hidden from the individual, an awareness of the man-made nature of these values leads inevitably to traditional truths losing their value and, consequently, to a crisis of values. And this is the advent of nihilism. My argument has been that there is a connection between nihilism and relativism. Relativism is defended by a wide range of philosophers and philosophical tendencies. In this study, the focus has been on Kuhn's criticism of science and scientific education as well as on Feyerabend's notion of scientific relativism. Kuhnian studies in the history of science reveal the paradigmatic character of science and scientific education. This insight shifts the focus from a formal logical analysis of scientific theories' structures to contextual analyses of science. Since objectivity has traditionally been conceived as truth independent of contexts, the revelation of its dependency on cultural contexts provoked a crisis in philosophy of science. Studies in the actual practices of scientists also revealed, contrary to the traditional notion of science, the irrational elements embedded in science. Unable to present a new notion of truth, Kuhnian science studies declare truth as redundant. As a result, nihilism becomes inevitable. Against this view, it was argued that we are in need of truth talk; we need a normative notion of truth in order to make sense of our cognitive activities. This truth is, however, diametrically different from the metaphysical notion of truth. It is based on both propositional *(veritas)* and non-propositional or aesthetic *(aletheia)* notions of truth. These two aspects of truth and knowledge are recurrent themes of this study.

Nihilism has not been rejected or confirmed unambiguously. We are concerned here with a much more complicated phenomenon than one that can simply be rejected or affirmed. Indeed, given present circumstances, nihilism is not only inevitable but also necessary. Scientific man needs to become aware of the shaky grounds of the current notion of scientific objectivity in order to overcome his naive faith in metaphysical truths. And this awareness comes via nihilism. Nihilism has two faces. It can either stimulate creative human resources or lead to resignation and despair. Correspondingly, there is an active or creative and a passive or reactive nihilism. The former stimulates creativity; by rejecting the old values and creating new ones, the individual takes control of his/her values. This demands strong and healthy individuals, individuals who are able to make use of a plurality of perspectives in matters of cognition. In reactive or passive nihilism, the individual first questions the ground of science and then the ground of his/her own existence without being able to create new grounds. Consequently, the supposedly stable foothold is lost and the individual is resigned to despair and passivity. His/her action becomes reactive. Instead of acting from innermost love, the individual reacts to external stimuli and develops a pattern of behaviour marked by vengeance and revenge. Using Kant, Schopenhauer, Nietzsche and Marx, I argued that unsurpassable lines between the subject and the object are artificial; making our own bodies the object of knowledge, we become subject and object at the same time. The fact that human nature is man's labour or his ability to create means that man is not only an artist by definition, but is also one with his actions and deeds. To see science from the perspective of art and both of them from that of life is thus an important step away from alienation and nihilism. Since, seen in this way, life becomes creative in humanity and human labour becomes an expression of our nature, we become one with our actions.

Negative nihilism was discussed as a sickness in modern scientific education that has to be cured. Education is, then, a therapeutic process of overcoming and curing nihilism. It was suggested that, in order to overcome nihilism, radical changes in the notions of objectivity, truth, science and education are needed.

The traditional notion of objectivity is a weak one, since it doesn't distinguish between cultural values beneficial to the growth of knowledge and those which block such growth; it defends a value-neutrality thesis, which means a one-sided refutation of all cultural values. As a result, it doesn't do justice to cultural values. It is also based on the single perspective of the European male and empowered classes and excludes the perspective of women and other marginalised people. Art, history and philosophy are also marginalised. Detached from its contexts of production and use, science is justified by elements internal to science; it is considered from the perspective of science itself. By making science its own judge, internalist epistemologies block the way for a critical appraisal of science. They justify science by its use of mathematics, its methods of observation and experimentation. According to this view, there is a single universal perspective, a single universal class of knowers and a single universal true picture of the world. The social organisation of knowledge and society has also to be based on this single perspective, since it is true by virtue of its correspondence with the natural order of the world. Not only are these claims not in line with the actual state of affairs, but also they limit the scope of human knowledge. Knowledge is diminished, narrowed and limited to the point of view of a small group of human beings. While, in reality, scientific education is extremely paradigm-based, internalist epistemologies claim independence from paradigms and social circumstances. Moreover, they make individuals merely a means in the service of science. This is indeed to use violence in a very sophisticated way. To exclude perspectives of women and marginalised social groups is to practise epistemological violence. Education is used as an instrument to enhance and preserve the logic of exclusion. I have argued that in order to overcome these limitations there needs to be an inclusive notion of objectivity. Through its logic of inclusion, this notion functions as a ground for human liberation from nihilism and alienation.

On the one hand, the inclusive notion of objectivity recognises the role played by cultural values in cognition. On the other hand, it recognises the active role played by the knower in all acts of cognition. It is based on distinguishing between cultural values favourable to the growth of human knowledge and those unfavourable to it, instead of denying them categorically. It also distinguishes between different types of individual characteristics, those which contribute to the growth of knowledge and those which block it. These characteristics are the basis of respectively strong and weak individuals—individuals who are able to make use of a plurality of perspectives and those who are not.

Inclusive epistemology draws on standpoint epistemology. It is in agreement with the view that epistemological standpoints are not neutral; they belong to men, women, and different cultures and bear the stamp of these positions. To make it clear, a distinction has to be made between inclusion and assimilation. Inclusive epistemology is based on the inclusion rather than assimilation of perspectives of women and marginalised people, on the one hand, and those of philosophy, history and art, on the other. While assimilation dissolves differences, inclusion preserves them. As a result, inclusion makes use of a plurality of perspectives in matters of knowledge and understanding. Not only is each subject viewed from different points of view, but also each perspective is looked at through the prism of other perspectives. This epistemology demands strong individuals, individuals who are able to make use of this plurality of perspectives, to look at their own perspective from that of others and shift perspective whenever it is needed. Such individuals also possess the ability to use the stringency of scientific argumentation, artistic creativity and philosophical critique in relation to the world and to each other. They also gain perspective on their own age through looking at it from a historical perspective.

I also make a distinction between a strong or progressive notion of culture and a repressive or weak one. A strong culture enables the individual to take advantage of a plurality of perspectives in his/her cognitive activities. A weak culture, on the other hand, is based on the principle of exclusion. Strong and weak cultures advocate different values. While strong cultures are a framework for values which strengthen knowledge, like solidarity, openness, reverence for nature and human dignity, equality between genders and people with different cultural and geographical backgrounds, weak or authoritarian cultures demand hierarchical authority and consensus. A strong culture encourages marginalised perspectives to take an active part in the production and use of knowledge. In addition to acknowledging the perspectives of women and marginalised peoples, it creates a cultural climate beneficial to the flourishing of the perspectives of art, philosophy and history. Such a cultural climate gives birth to a science quite different from the prevailing one. In such a climate not only do different perspectives get their due, but they also contribute, each in its own way, to the growth and flourishing of human knowledge. Each of these perspectives enriches science in its own way. While those of women and marginalised people widen the social base of science, those of art and philosophy extend its cognitive foundation. Together, they cover a broad range of cultural and epistemic values. Such a science then grows strong; it can also rightly ascertain its universality. Educated in this style of thought, the individual is able to look at his/her own perspective from the perspective of others; the perspective of art is used to look at the perspective of science and vice versa.

Corresponding to the inclusive notions of objectivity and knowledge, there is an inclusive notion of science. This notion of science is based on reading and interpretation as major cognitive activities. Having this notion of science as a standpoint, an inclusive notion of fact based on plurality of perspective, rigour of argumentation and transparency of the active part of the knower is within reach. This notion of fact is based on the awareness that our horizons of interpretation are always actively created rather than being naturally given. Thus, the focus is placed equally on these starting points of cognition and on the end results of these presuppositions, elements that have to be accepted passively given certain starting points. The exchangeability of active and passive elements of cognition shows that we have to establish our starting points time and again. Consequently, we reach different facts depending on different starting points.

This means awareness of the groundless ground of science. To be able to withstand this awareness demands strong individuals. Such individuals are aware the no final footholds exist; paradigms or forms of life are not to be considered as the ground of knowledge. We have to create and recreate such grounds perpetually. This means that instead of there existing pre-given facts to be discovered once and for all, we have to invent interpretations time and again. Indeed, notions of fact and interpretation do not exclude each other. The positivistic distinction between these notions is a mark of weak notions of fact and weak individuals. There is no knowledge outside interpretation, since the relationship between humanity and the world is based on translation or interpretation. Weak individuals need things to be determined beforehand, however, and the positivistic notion of fact provides them with footholds. These footholds are, however, illusory.

Fully aware of the interdependence of fact and interpretation, strong individuals are able to use the notion of fact as a thought constraint. Through the strong notion of the individual, the notion of interpretation becomes reinterpreted. It is not conceived as an arbitrary activity. In this style of interpretation, truth is a normative notion that guides our interpretive practices and style is a regulative notion that creates unity among a diversity of perspectives and a plurality of interpretations; both notions are constitutive of knowledge. Each individual has to give style to his/her life and knowledge; he/she has to use this style as a signpost to orientate. At the root of this insight is an awareness that human agency takes an active part in the process of knowledge which is, in turn, constitutive of the object of knowledge.

Avoiding the traditional dichotomy between relativism and absolutism, we need a new notion of communication. This notion of communication is, I argued, based on translation. Indeed, translation and interpretation, I argued, are identical. Translation is not only the basis of relations between different paradigms; it is also the basis of relations between users of the same language. Further, the relation between the human world of concepts and the world of objects is also based on translation. This means that, contrary to Socrates, the language of knowledge is not that of mathematics and calculation, but that of metaphors. This is a significant characteristic of strong individuals, who are able to communicate across paradigms. By means of translation, paradigms and individuals are able to share ideas across times and cultures.

Rejecting the incommensurability theory and its belief in monadic paradigms, I emphasised the possibility of communication without reducing it to consensus or rational transparency. This notion of communication is based on translation. The basic presupposition here is that life is dialogic by nature. Translation is thus a perpetual process based on meaningful understanding and misunderstanding. Notions of responsibility for the other and trust that there is something to be learned from the other make this relation a basis for reciprocal exchange of ideas. We also have to be oriented to maximise the understanding of the other. The notion of translation used here is not based on the representational notion of language or the essentialist view of meaning. There is no eternal meaning to be communicated; rather, meaning is created at the meeting point between the original and the translation. Since the relation between the original and the translation is variable, meaning is created in a variety of ways. They encompass such activities as appropriation, transformation, critique, refutation and confirmation. As is the case with all communication, relations between different paradigms have to be based on telling, listening, connecting, mutual understanding and transformation in each individual and his/her surroundings.

The notion of translation used here encompasses all kinds of communication, verbal and non-verbal. While the traditional view of translation is based just on transaction of information between the original and the translation, the notion of translation used here goes beyond the informative contents of the original. Indeed, it is not too hard to communicate the informative aspect of the original, since this aspect is limited to the means of verbal communication. Any original contains, however, a poetical aspect, or style. In this regard, the translator must be a poet, that is, have a poetical outlook on the world, in order to be able to transmit this dimension of the original; this is an inclusive notion of translator. While the words and expressions of the original are context-dependent, its poetic aspect reaches far beyond its context of production and use. It is indeed related to its "afterlife", a life beyond ordinary or biological lifetimes and thus eternal. It stimulates creative resources within the translator. Through new translations of the original, the same story can be told again and again. Translatability reveals kinship between different languages. Seen in this light, the essence of language is its translatability. Translation then becomes the basis of culture and knowledge.

Analogously to translation's two different aspects, there are two aspects of truth. Besides its informative content, there is an aspect of truth that cannot be communicated by means of words and verbal communication; it has to be shown through the life and the conduct of educators. Seen in this light, any educator is an example of a truth. This aspect of truth is communicable through non-verbal means of communication, like the kinship of styles. One has to obtain the proper disposition for it. The notion of educator used here refers to a variety of phenomena. Besides exemplary individuals, paradigms and cultures can also function as educators. Considered in isolation, each of these notions has its own limitations. Paradigms are, for instance, limited to the informative aspect of education and technical skills; they have nothing to do with truth. Indeed, examinations, standard problems, laboratory procedures and other educational procedures shape the mind of novices in the image of science. Paradigms have a regulative function and use the individual instrumentally.

Past cultures can provide us with monumental examples of cultural excellence, but they cannot exemplify their greatness in the present by themselves. They are in need of being exemplified in real life. A strong notion of education connects different types of educators and exemplifies them in a single individual. Such an individual is the space where truth is manifested. On the one hand, she/he is dependent on the context of a life-world. On the other hand, she/he transcends this context through constituting an educational example that can be followed by any and all human beings. Analogous to translation, any educator has an informative aspect that is context-dependent. This aspect can easily be imitated by whoever is able to use a language and take part in language games. Any educator has, however, an aesthetic aspect that is available to those who demonstrate kinship of style with the educator.

In the context of contemporary life, Nelson Mandela is such an individual. The most interesting thing about him is not his knowledge of life and its conditions, but his style and his truth, the truth of problems that need to be revealed and recovered. He is admirable in his struggle against apartheid, or the spirit of exclusion. In the context of contemporary life, mechanisms of exclusion are at work everywhere, in social, epistemological and cultural contexts. On the other hand, there is an ongoing struggle for inclusion. Truth manifests itself in revealing the logic of exclusion, on the one hand, and our need of inclusion, on the other. Mandela demonstrated the logic of exemplarity of truth by becoming engaged in a struggle for inclusion and against exclusion. His struggle transcends the context of his lifetime and becomes a manifestation of universal aspects of truth. Thus, through him we learn the true nature of our time and become engaged in a struggle against its narrow-mindedness and egoistic individualism. Mandela signifies a range of cultural values beneficial to the growth of knowledge. [1]

The relationship between educators and learners is analogous to translation. It is positional and relational. It is based on a network of means like fidelity, freedom, critique, reverence, refutation, acceptance, parody, travesty, and so on. Since there is no eternal essence to be transmitted, any individual has to be able to create unity among this variety of means through his/her unique style.

The learner interprets and reinterprets, translates and retranslates the educator in order to reach a point where the kinship of styles is revealed and the learner establishes her/his own style, becomes independent of the educator and goes beyond him/her. Although there is a process of identification at work, the learner does not become identical to the educator; she/he is always distinct in a nuanced way. Although education is based on the confirmation of kinship of style, it tolerates, respects, recognises and includes differences as well. Thus, it creates a balance between the contextuality and universality of knowledge and truth. By being transferred from one individual to another, from one context to another, knowledge acquires its own life and becomes independent of each. At the same time, it is dependent on both, on their differences and kinships. While differences refer to the context-dependency of truth, kinship refers to context-independent aspects of truth and education.

To avoid dangers related to this notion of education, I proposed the logic of inclusion as a criterion. In fact, the social and cultural situations of our time demand such a criterion. On the one hand, a growing number of individuals and social groups claim their own perspectives on matters of knowledge and education. On the other hand, due to the exclusive logic of the current scientific paradigm, huge obstacles block their way. And this creates frustration and despair. Education has to ease the inclusion of people, teach them to live together across differences and help them to find a purpose in their lives. Education does this by encouraging their contribution to the constitution of knowledge and recognising their active part in it. By so doing, education becomes based on reverence, love and care. It prepares active individuals who can take control of circumstances, instead of being servants of them. The criterion of inclusion is as applicable to individuals as to cultures and the educational canon. In the case of individual exemplars, it refers to their ability to make use of the perspectives of art, history and philosophy. It also considers their ability to use the view-point of the other as a critical perspective on their own. In the case of cultures, it is connected to principal values. Either these values are inclusive and broaden the basis of knowledge and contribute to the universality of science and human understanding by including different perspectives, or they are exclusive and narrow the scope of knowledge to the local interests of certain groups and limit the growth of knowledge and block human understanding.

Judged by this criterion, the disadvantage of weak or scientific exemplars is their being based on the single perspective of the prevailing scientific paradigm. They are limited to the informative aspect of education and technical efficacy, without being able to take into account the aesthetic aspects of the relationship between educators and pupils. Other examples of weak educators can be found in the scholarly type that dominates the academic world of the day. Their work is basically exclusive. The example of the Enlightenment provides us with another way of working exclusively; this culture is based on a Western notion of reason and rationality. Indeed, these perspectives share the characteristic of being scientific in the weak sense of the term. This science is monophonic, since it is based on the local interests of Western man. As a result, it is not only unable to sufficiently explain the global aspect of knowledge and truth, but also tries to preserve and enhance the domination of a single type of knower. The strong or healthy notion of educator does not simply reject these notions. On the contrary, it encompasses some of their most interesting aspects and problems without being limited to any of them. Strong exemplars are not based on a single perspective. Rather, they are oriented to inclusive human interests.

The view of education defended here contests the traditional notion of education in still another aspect, authority. Here, authority is not fixed, centralised and external to the process of education. The aesthetic character of this kind of authority means that it is immanent in educational practices. Based on the notion of translation, it not only eases the transmission of knowledge, but also does it in an artistic manner. This means that the distinctiveness of learners' perspectives is preserved and enhanced.

It goes without saying that in order to establish the notions of education and the individual defended above, radical cultural and educational changes are needed. My arguments, therefore, have been that educational and cultural renewals presuppose each other. An inclusive culture, an inclusive notion of objectivity, a strong notion of education and a strong notion of the individual are interconnected as aspects of the same phenomenon. Indeed, since these notions presuppose each other, one is impossible without the other. In order to establish these notions we need changes on a broad front of both cultural and individual institutions. The main contention here is, however, that pedagogical renewal is a primary precondition of cultural renewal.

Notes

NOTES TO THE INTRODUCTION

1. There are many ways in which scientific approaches to education are at work today—in, for example, notions and practices of school management, the assessment of learning, applications of psychological theories. As a more extended illustration, I focus here on the area of aesthetic learning.
    "Discipline-based art education" offers a good example of a scientific notion of education being applied to the arts. This educational paradigm is reductionistic in at least two basic respects. First, it presents and teaches the arts as different formalized disciplines quite similar to scientific ones. Based on scientific notions of rationality, the writers of "National Standards for Art Education", for instance, (http://www.artteacherconnection.com/pages/standards.htm, access April 16, 2007), demonstrate not only an obsession with the standardisation of the arts and art education, but also present a view of the arts as propositional knowledge. Although there are references to art production and practical skills, the overall emphasis is on students' knowledge of aesthetic ideas, materials and contexts. Knowledge, in its turn, is considered as abstract knowledge based on an ultimate reality. Generally speaking, knowledge, truth and beauty are assumed to be general conceptions independent of culture and life contexts. Students are supposed to receive this type of knowledge from sources outside the context of their life-world. Basically, the systematisation of art, its standardisation and schematisation, so characteristic of the current educational paradigm, are helping to reduce art to a science of art, where theoretical knowledge of art is placed high above art itself. A second reductionist aspect of the prevailing educational paradigm is the reduction of art to works of art. As I will argue, although works of art are an essential part of what art is, to reduce art to works of art is to misconceive it and to generate a narrow conception of art education. Based on discipline-based art education, "music education as aesthetic education" presents a scientific interpretation of music education. Here also, music is reduced to a "formal discipline of study" (Regelski 2005: 224). Critics of discipline-based music education like Elliot (1995) and Regelski (2005) suggest a shift of focus from abstract knowledge and aesthetic theories to praxial philosophy. I shall not try to follow these writers. My concern is at a more general level. In this book I focus partly on art as a critical perspective on science. More generally, I am concerned with the consequences of an education being scientific through and through. I suggest radical shifts in educational principles through redefinition of key notions like objectivity, fact and truth.

2. An important point has to be mentioned about my approach to the divide between modern and post-modern philosophers. I do not oppose or endorse unequivocally those who advocate the idea of a post-modern condition, like Jean-Francois Lyotard. The same can be said of my stand toward those who reject such an idea, like Habermas. Instead of excluding one group and including the other in my story, my attempts have been aimed at bringing together viable aspects of the two in order to construct an inclusive notion of knowledge. From the former I take the ideas of questioning the notion of universal rationality and of an absolute notion of reality. At the same time, I, like the latter, insist on truth and objectivity. Traditional notions of reality and reason as well as a representational notion of language are to be questioned, since they function as the basis of reified systems of knowledge. Following Nietzsche and Heidegger, post-modern thinkers have taken this task seriously. My concern, however, is not this questioning as such. Rather, I am concerned with the issue of how we can transfer this reconstructive consciousness into a constructive force. By not taking this task seriously, we perpetuate nihilism as a state of mind.

NOTES TO CHAPTER 1

1. Famously, there are a diversified variety of theories of truth—correspondence, coherence, pragmatic, semantic, redundancy and so on. To discuss all of them is far beyond my competence and the space available here. I am concerned here mostly with the correspondence theory of truth in contrast with a genealogical one. Other theories are not discussed in detail. They will be discussed only if they can shed light on my main discussions.
2. In this regard, I draw on Jose Medina and David Wood, who consider that the debate on truth "has taken a new and distinctive turn in contemporary philosophy: *a normative turn*" (Jose Medina and David Wood 2005: 1).
3. There are, of course, different kinds of relativism. Relativism means different things in epistemology, ethics, aesthetics, semantics and so on. While in epistemology relativism is related to beliefs and belief systems, in ethics it is related to moralities. In aesthetics it is the notion of taste and in semantics the notion of meaning that is basic. There are, however, some common traits in different brands of relativism. All relativistic theories relativise a central notion like truth or knowledge, moral values, beauty, taste, or meaning to particular frameworks like the individual subject, a form of life, a paradigm, a conceptual scheme or a language. We can thus distinguish different kinds of relativism by the object they make relative. Moral relativism, for instance, relativises moral values. Epistemological or cognitive relativism asserts the relativity of knowledge. In this context it is cognitive relativism and the relativity of truth that is at issue. Semantic relativism is also involved. Cognitive relativism brings to the fore a variety of concepts, such as rationality, truth and knowledge. It implies the relativity of both rationality and knowledge because they are associated with the concept of truth. The framework to which truth is relativised is a paradigm or conceptual scheme and the theoretical framework of a scientific community. Cognitive relativists do not only assert that different cultures or communities have different views about which beliefs are true and that different communities operate with different epistemic norms, criteria of truth and standards of rationality but also that no one set of epistemic norms is metaphysically privileged over any other. Or no standpoint is uniquely privileged over all others. Semantic relativism relativises the notion of meaning to language uses.
4. Another influential theory of truth, to name but one, is the descriptive view of truth. This theory separates the factual from the normative and considers

the true as merely a descriptive predicate. This view of truth is based on a distinction between fact and value. As will be discussed, such a clear cut distinction is deeply problematic. Cultural values are constitutive of cognition and there is no knowledge independent of cultural contexts.

NOTES TO CHAPTER 2

1. It is no accident that in an apparently secular culture like that of Sweden, together with "Western humanism", "ethics born by Christian tradition" (Skolverket: 3) is still one of the basic values upon which the school curriculum rests. My source in this regard is *Curriculum for Compulsory School System, the Pre-school Classes and the Leisure-time Centre Lpo 94*. The whole text is available at www.skolverket.se.
2. Because human labour is the same as human nature, human alienation from human labour or creativity amounts to self-alienation.

NOTES TO CHAPTER 3

1. For instance, the educational system, educators and scholars demonstrate an amazing indifference to wars and atrocities that took place during the last century and go on in the present. However, the decisive role of scientific education, scientific research and related technologies in this regard cannot be denied. Generally, what we know, say and do is directly influenced by science and scientific education; these things have a crucial role in what we have become and in our understanding of history and the world. Indifference to these events, their cause and results is nothing but a passive form of nihilism.

NOTES TO CHAPTER 5

1. The shift of focus is from an action-centred notion of morality, where the primary question is "What should I do?", to an agent-centred morality where the primary question is "What sort of person should I be?" Correspondingly, the notion of truth is related to the notion of life. Seen in this light, to live up to one's own standards, one has to go through a process of purification.
2. The tragic or artistic thought style was found among the Greeks, who made it their way of understanding the world. It can now become enriched and more extended through incorporating new forms of knowledge unavailable to the Greeks. Through incorporating diverse forms of knowledge and perspective it upholds a healthy order where knowledge and life receive their due. It becomes more inclusive.
3. This is to oppose Dewey where he makes a distinction between "artistic" and "esthetic", where artistic "refers primarily to the act of production and 'esthetic' to that of perception and enjoyment" (Dewey 1934: 46). These two conceptions are connected to the artist and the audience, respectively. This distinction becomes, however, problematic in the "age of reproducibility of the work of art", as Benjamin puts it. It is especially problematic with regard to virtual artworks that are based on information technology and the Internet, because there are no clear-cut lines between production and reception. These notions increasingly merge in a reciprocal interactivity between the work and the audience, where the audience's manipulative efforts become a part of the creative process. This kind of art gives birth to new problems and possibilities that cannot be explained in terms of the distinction between

production and perception. It reshapes the issue of creativity as the privileged realm of professional artists and makes it available to wide ranges of anonymous users. This participatory mode of understanding art may weaken the authority of the artwork and the traditional notion of the artist as genius, but it strengthens that of art as such; it affirms the notion of art as the general human ability to create and produce. An example of the work becoming a process of creation shared by the artist, the work and the audience is Seiko Mikami's "Molecular Clinic 1.0". This work is based on molecular biology's view of the molecular composition of liquids, solids and gases. According to this theory, we can create innumerable varieties of each entity by manipulating its molecular combination. Mikami has exhibited a virtual spider on the Internet, which presumably lives in the ArtLab server. As a part of the artwork, participants manipulate the spider's molecular combination. By so doing, they affect the informative contents of the work and give birth to unpredictable varieties of the spider and its environment. This work does not only exhibit an essential trait of our age, the unpredictability of the results of our manipulative activities, but also questions the notion of artwork as the authentic production of a particular artist. Nor is the audience the passive admirer and consumer of such a production. Such a view of art and artwork is a move away from alienation. This is also an inclusive way of understanding art; the perspective of audience is included in that of the artwork. It shows the impact of history and contemporary technological development on our understanding of art. It is within the framework of current historical circumstances and technological development that works of art become the co-production of the artist and the audience and are understood accordingly. Within the same framework, past art is given an afterlife by the present. This is done through new understanding and interpretations. Technological development is one side of a process whose other side is changes in the categories and conceptions through which art is understood. Besides being inclusive, this mode of understanding art is non-essentialist. Art can be understood differently in different historical contexts. The human ability to create, the practice of art in its broadest extension, remains, however, the only constant element, a trans-historical realm of human activity. This understanding of art corresponds to the inclusive epistemology defended in this study.

4. Dewey relates the necessity of artistic perspective to its ability to go beyond verbal means. He writes: "Art expresses, it does not state: it is concerned with existences in their perceived qualities, not with conceptions symbolized in terms" (Dewey 1934: 84).

5. As Fleck observed, creative researchers have a unique use of language. But their individual language uses undergo a process of normalisation as scientific novelties become common knowledge and are incorporated in the body of handbooks and school texts (Fleck 1979: 118–24). Science texts transfer a common language or a language of reified conceptions rather than creative scientists' unique language uses. And this language is presented as the single language of science. As Kuhn shows, this type of language use emerged as a part of the current scientific paradigm.

NOTES TO CHAPTER 7

1. In our context, the notion of illusion renders *Schein*, which also means "appearance", "semblance" and "seeming". In Kant also illusion translates *Schein*, where he defines dialectic as "a logic of illusion" (CPR A239/B350).

His concern is however the study and critique of transcendental illusions, a result of Reason's perpetual attempts to move beyond possible experience.
2. The question can be raised how can we expect people simultaneously to have a critical view of things and to build a ground of understanding on illusions? However, the illusory character of grounds of knowledge does not mean that we can change them arbitrarily or presuppose whatever we wish. Styles of thought are indeed thought constraints and harness the arbitrariness of thought. And herein lays the importance of the unity of individual and cultural styles. Unity of style enables thought rigorously to follow ways of argumentation and interpretation once starting points of thought are presupposed and determined. Indeed, by presupposing these starting points, thought binds itself to accept what follows. Much of the result is already embedded in the presupposition and agreed in advance. By providing starting points, styles equip us with points of reference for judging thoughts and ideas. We do not need to refer the legitimacy of a fact to transcendental forces. Our commitment to our own undertakings provides grounds enough for such legitimacy and critique.
3. See, for instance, National Research Council (2003) and (1999).

NOTES TO CHAPTER 10

1. Through his semantic conception of truth, Tarski establishes a semantic relationship between expression in an object language and expression in a meta-language. The brilliance of his solution lies in the fact that the tangible semantic relation between expression in an object language and expression in a meta-language replaces the traditional and problematic relation of correspondence between language and the world, between facts and words. The point is, however, to show how this relationship extends beyond language into the world.
2. The interesting point in this context is Levinas's criticism of the Western metaphysical tradition and his critical reading of the history of philosophy. He criticises the Western metaphysical tradition for trying to assimilate "the other", or the difference, into "the same".

   For Levinas, the relationship to the other is based on the notion of responsibility. This means that I am responsible for the other by definition and "responsibility for the other precedes every decision, it is before the origin" (Levinas 2005: 265). Responsibility for the other is, in other words, always already there. My relation with the other always starts with responsibility; I cannot refuse it. In Levinas's theory there is an asymmetrical ethical relation between me and the other. Strictly considered, for Levinas, I am responsible for the other, but not vice versa.

   We can come to terms with this Levinasian asymmetry by appeal to notions of dialogue and translation. We have already emphasised the dialogical nature of life. It also was emphasised that my relation to the other is based on translation. The other is thus not a passive observer; rather, he/she is a co-participant in dialogue, translation. Thus, she/he bears the same responsibility toward me. Indeed, I become the other in relation to another I and that I, in its turn, is responsible toward me. Responsibility toward each other is thus mutual. The other becomes a responsible other instead of being an authoritative other.

NOTES TO CHAPTER 11

1. I am in agreement with Nietzsche and Marx when they relate education to the true needs of the individual rather than states. Famously, Nietzsche sees no common interest between the individual and the state. He relates the state categorically to barbarism. He would agree with Marx that the current barbarism of wars and the destruction of the environment originate in the fact that human relations are reified by modern states functioning as the agents of the labour market in making mankind saleable. But while Marx would argue that there are interim forms of the state necessary for the cause of educational changes, Nietzsche would argue that there is no state or political party whatsoever which has the cause of culture as its concern. This Nietzschean view may need some modifications. However, his point, in *On the Future of Our Educational Institutions*, that modern states undermine an education targeted at the cultivation of people, since they are interested in the speedy production of "the servants of the day" (FE, 63) is to be taken seriously. The same can be said of his points that modern education not only subordinates the individual to abstract truths, but also undermines the autonomy of individuals before the state. This education is aimed at individuals' "unconditional obedience" to the state by different means like "excessive examinations" (FE, 31). To avoid this, this study suggests a replacement of the leadership of the state by that of philosophers and educators.

NOTES TO THE CONCLUSIONS

1. Indeed, Gandhi and Martin Luther King also demonstrate the same spirit of inclusion and thus can be used as educators. They have not only inspired whole nations but humanity as such. They honoured the past, celebrated the present and looked at the future of humanity. Apartheid and Hitler appeared as the opposite, as the spirit of exclusion.

Bibliography

AAAS (1989) *Science for All Americans*, Washington: AAAS.
Abell S. K. (2007) *Handbook of Research on Science Education*, Mahwah, New Jersey: Lawrence Erlbaum Associates Publisher.
Acampor C. D. (2002) "Nietzsche Contra Homer, Socrates and Paul", in *Journal of Nietzsche Studies* 24, pp. 25–53.
Adler, M. J. (1994) *Art, the Arts, and the Great Ideas*, New York: Simon Schuster.
Adorno, T. W. (1998) *Critical Models, Interventions and Catchwords*, New York: Columbia University Press.
———. (1997) *Aesthetic Theory*, Minneapolis: University of Minnesota Press.
———. (1964) *The Jargon of Authenticity*, London: Routledge.
Adorno, T. W., and Horkheimer, M. (1997) *Dialectic of Enlightenment*, London: Verso.
Alcoff, L. M. (2005) "Reclaiming Truth", in *Truth: Engagements Across Philosophical Traditions*, ed. J. Medina and D. Wood, Oxford: Blackwell Publishing, pp. 336–49.
Allison, D. B., ed. (1999) *The New Nietzsche*, Cambridge, MA: MIT Press.
Althusser, L. (2001) *Lenin and Philosophy and Other Essays*, New York: Monthly Review Press.
Ansell-Pearson, K., ed. (1991) *Nietzsche and Modern German Thought*, London: Routledge.
Appel, F. (1999) *Nietzsche Contra Democracy*, Ithaca: Cornell University Press.
Appiah, K. A. (1994) "Identity, Authenticity, and Survival: Multicultural Societies and Social Reproduction", in *Multiculturalism: Examining the Politics of Recognition*, ed. A. Gutman, Princeton: Princeton University Press, pp. 107–63.
Arendt, H. (2005) "Truth and Politics", in *Truth: Engagements Across Philosophical Traditions*, ed. J. Medina and D. Wood, Oxford: Blackwell Publishing, pp. 250–314.
———. (2003) *The Portable Arendt*, London: Penguin Books.
Aristotle (2001) *Metaphysics*, in *The Basic Works of Aristotle*, R. McKeon ed., New York: The Modern Library, pp 681-926.
———. (2001) *Nicomachean Ethics* in *The Basic Works of Aristotle*, R. McKeon ed., New York: The Modern Library, pp 927-1112.
———. (2000) *Politics*, Chapel Hill and London: University of North Carolina Press.
———. (1984) *Poetics*, in *The Complete Works of Aristotle*, revised Oxford translation, 2 vols., ed. J. Barnes, Oxford: Princeton University Press.
Armour-Garb, B. C., and Beall, J. C., eds. (2005) *Deflationary Truth*, Chicago: Open Court.
Athearn, D. (1994) *Scientific Nihilism*, Albany: State University of New York Press.

Bibliography

Audi, R., ed. (1995) *The Cambridge Dictionary of Philosophy*, Cambridge: Cambridge University Press.
Babich, B. (1994) *Nietzsche's Philosophy of Science*, Albany: State University of New York Press.
Babich, B., and Cohen, R. S., eds. (1999) *Nietzsche, Theories of Knowledge and Critical Theory*, 2 vols, Boston: Kluwer Academic Publishers.
Bakhtin, M. (1986) *Speech Genre and Other Essays*, Austin: University of Texas Press.
———. (1984) *Problems of Dostoevsky's Poetics*, Minneapolis: University of Minnesota Press.
———. (1981) *The Dialogical Imagination*, Austin: University of Texas Press.
Beardsley, M. (1958) *Aesthetics: Problems in the Philosophy of Criticism*, New York: Harcourt, Brace and Company.
Benhabib, S. (2002) *The Claims of Culture: Equality and Diversity in the Global Era*, Princeton: Princeton University Press.
Benjamin, A., ed. (2005) *Walter Benjamin and Art*, London: Continuum.
Benjamin, W. (1997) *Charles Baudelaire*, London: Verso.
———. (1982) *Illuminations*, London: Fontana Press.
Benner, D., and English, A. (2004) "Critique and Negativity: Towards the Polarisation of Critique in Educational Practice, Theory and Research", in *Journal of Philosophy of Education* 38, no. 3, pp. 409–28.
Bergson, H. (1911) *Creative Evolution*, New York: H. Holt and Company.
Bingham, C. (2001) "Gadamer and Derrida on Authority", in *Educational Theory*, pp. 265–72.
———. (2001) "I am the Missing Pages of the Text I Teach: Gadamer and Derrida on Teacher Authority", in *Philosophy of Education* 2001, S. Rice, K. Alston et al eds., Urbana, Illinois: Philosophy of Education Society, pp. 265-72.
———. (1998) "The Goals of Language, the Language of Goals, Nietzsche's Concern with Rhetoric and Its Educational Implications", in *Educational Theory* 48, no. 2, pp. 229–41.
Black, M. (1962) *Models and Metaphor*, Ithaca: Cornell University Press.
Black, P., and Atkin, J. M., eds. (1996) *Changing the Subject: Innovations in Science, Mathematics and Technology Education*, London: Routledge.
Blackburn, S., and Simmons, K., eds. (1999) *Truth*, Oxford: Penguin Books.
Blanchot, M. (1999) "Nietzsche's Experience of the Eternal Recurrence", in *The New Nietzsche*, ed. D. B. Allison, Cambridge, MA: MIT Press, pp. 121–27.
Blondel, E. (1991) *Nietzsche, the Body and Culture: Philosophy as a Philosophical Genealogy*, Stanford: Stanford University Press.
Bloom, H. (1994) *The Western Canon: The Books and School of the Ages*, New York: Harcourt Brace and Company.
Bowie, A. (2003) *Aesthetics and Subjectivity: From Kant to Nietzsche*, New York: Manchester University Press.
Bradbury, M., and McFarlane, J., eds. (1976) *Modernism: A Guide to European Literature 1890–1930*, New York: Penguin.
Brobjer, T. H. (2004) "Nietzsche's Reading About Eastern Philosophy" in *Journal of Nietzsche Studies* 28, pp. 3–36.
Bybee, R. W., and DeBoer, G. E. (1994) "Research on Goals for the Science Curriculum" in *Handbook of Research on Science Teaching*, ed. D. L. Gabel, New York: Macmillan Publishing Company, pp. 375–87.
Caranfa, A. (2006) "Voice of Silence in Pedagogy: Art, Writing and Self-Encounter", in *Journal of Philosophy of Education* 40, no. 1, pp. 85–103.
Chalmers, A. F. (1990) *What is This Thing Called Science? An Assessment of the Nature and Status of Science and Its Methods*, Milton Keynes: Open University Press.
Clark, M. (1990) *Nietzsche on Truth and Philosophy*, Cambridge: Cambridge University Press.

Cohen, S. (1998) *Passive Nihilism: Cultural Historiography and Rhetoric of Scholarship*, London: Macmillan Press.
Cohen, R. S., and Schnell, T., eds. (1986) *Cognition and Fact: Materials on Ludwik Fleck*, Dordrecht: D. Reidel Publishing Company
Comay, R. (2005) "Materialist Mutations of the Bilderverbot", in *Walter Benjamin and Art*, ed. A. Benjamin, London: Continuum, pp. 32–59.
Cooper, D. E. (1985) "On Reading Nietzsche on Education", *Journal of Philosophy of Education* 17, no. 1, pp. 119–26.
———. (1983) *Authenticity and Learning: Nietzsche's Educational Philosophy*, London: Routledge and Kegan Paul.
Curd, M., and Cover, J. A., eds. (1998) *Philosophy of Science: The Central Issues*, London: W. W. Norton and Company.
David, M. (2005) "Truth as the Primary Epistemic Goal; a Working Hypothesis", in M. Steup and E. Sosa ed., *Contemporary Debates in Epistemology*, Oxford, Blackwell Publishing, pp. 296-312.
———. (2001) "Truth as Identity and Truth as Correspondence" in *The Nature of Truth: Classic and Contemporary Perspectives*, ed. M. P. Lynch, Cambridge, MA: MIT Press, pp. 683–704.
Davidson, D. (1984) *Inquiries into Truth and Interpretation*, Oxford: Clarendon.
———. (2005) "Truth and Meaning", in *Truth: Engagements Across Philosophical Traditions*, ed. J. Medina and D. Wood, Oxford: Blackwell Publishing, pp. 69–79.
———. (2001) *Inquiries into Truth and Interpretation*, New York: Oxford University Press.
Davis, W. B. (2004) "Zen After Zarathustra: The Problem of the Will in the Confrontation Between Nietzsche and Buddhism", in *Journal of Nietzsche Studies* 28, pp. 89–138.
De Caro, M., and Macarthur, D., eds. (2004) *Naturalism in Question*, London: Harvard University Press.
Deleuze, G. (1999a) "Active and Reactive", in *The New Nietzsche*, ed. D. B. Allison, Cambridge, MA: MIT Press, pp. 80–106.
———. (1999b) "Nomad Thought", in *The New Nietzsche*, ed. D. B. Allison, Cambridge, MA: MIT Press, pp. 142–69.
Derrida, J. (2005) "The End of the Book and the Beginning of the Writing", in *Truth: Engagements Across Philosophical Traditions*, ed. J. Medina and D. Wood, Oxford: Blackwell Publishing, pp. 207–24.
———. (1992) *The Other Heading: Reflections on Today's Europe*, Bloomington: Indiana University Press.
———. (1988) *Monoculturalism of the Other, or The Prostesis of Origin*, Stanford: Stanford University Press.
———. (1987) "The Laws of Reflection: Nelson Mandela, in Admiration", in *For Nelson Mandela*, ed. J. Derrida and M. Tlili, New York: Seaver Books.
———. (1982) "White Mythology: Metaphor in the Text of Philosophy" in *Meaning of Philosophy*, Chicago: University of Chicago Press.
———. (1976) *Of Grammatology*, Baltimore: John Hopkins University Press.
Descartes, R. (1988) *Selected Philosophical Writings*, Cambridge: Cambridge University Press.
Desideri, F. (2005) "The Mimetic Bond: Benjamin and the Question of Technology", in *Walter Benjamin and Art*, ed. A. Benjamin, London: Continuum, pp. 61–72.
Dewey, J. (1934) *Art as Experience*, New York: Capricorn Books.
Duckworth, E., Easley, J., et al. (1990) *Science Education: A Minds-On Approach for the Elementary Years*, London: Lawrence Erlbaum Associates.
Dupré, J. (2004) "The Miracle of Monism", in *Naturalism in Question*, ed. M. De Caro and D. Macarthur, London: Harvard University Press.

———. (2001) *Human Nature and the Limits of Science*, Oxford: Clarendon Press.
Duschl, R. A. (1994) "Research on the History and Philosophy of Science", in *Handbook of Research on Science Teaching*, ed. D. L. Gabel, New York: Macmillan Publishing Company, pp. 443–65.
Eiland, H. (2005) "Reception in Distraction", in *Walter Benjamin and Art*, ed. A. Benjamin, London: Continuum, pp. 3–13.
Elgin, C. (2005) "Word Giving, Word Taking" in *Truth Engagements Across Philosophical Tradition*, J. Medina and D. Wood ed., Oxford: Blackwell Publishing, pp. 270-286.
Elliot, D. J., ed. (2005) *Parxial Music Education*, Oxford: Oxford University Press.
———. (1995) *Music Matters: A New Philosophy of Music Education*, New York: Oxford University Press.
Emerson, R. W. (1903) *The Complete Works*, vol. 1, Cambridge, MA: Riverside Press.
Fenves, P. (2005) "Is There an Answer to the Aestheticizing of the Political?", in *Walter Benjamin and Art*, ed. A. Benjamin, London: Continuum, pp. 108–20.
Feyerabend, P. (2005) "Notes on Relativism", in *Truth: Engagements Across Philosophical Traditions*, ed. J. Medina and D. Wood, Oxford: Blackwell Publishing, pp. 146–56.
———. (1987) *Farewell to Reason*, London: Verso.
Firestone, S. (1971) *Dialectic of Sex; the Case for Feminist Evolution*, New York: Morrow.
Fiske, J. (1991) *Reading the Popular*, London: Routledge.
Fleck, L. (1979) *Genesis and Development of a Scientific Fact*, Chicago: University of Chicago Press.
Foucault, M. (2005) "The Discourse on Language and Truth and Power", in *Truth: Engagements Across Philosophical Traditions*, ed. J. Medina and D. Wood, Oxford: Blackwell Publishing, pp. 315–35.
———. (2001) *Fearless Speech*, ed. J. Pearson, Los Angeles: Semiotext(e).
———. (2000) *Essential Works of Foucault 1954–1984*, New York: Penguin Books.
———. (1995) *Discipline and Punish*, New York: Vintage Books.
Freeman, K. (1983) *Ancilla to the Pre-Socratic Philosophers*, Cambridge, MA: Harvard University Press.
French, P. A., and Howard, K. W., eds. (2003) *Meaning in the Arts*, vol. 27, Boston: Blackwell Publishing.
Gabel, D. L., ed. (1994) *Handbook of Research on Science Teaching*, New York: Macmillan Publishing Company.
Gadamer, H. G. (1986) *The Relevance of the Beautiful and Other Essays*, Cambridge: Cambridge University Press.
Garrison, J. (2001) "Integrating Art/humanities and Science/Engineering" in *Philosophy of Education 2001*, S. Rice, K. Alston et al, eds. Urbana, Illinois: Philosophy of Education Society, pp. 36-40.
Geyer, F., ed. (1996) *Alienation, Ethnicity, and Postmodernism*, Westport, CT: Greenwood Press.
Giarelli, J. (2001) The Education of Eros and Collateral Learning in Teacher Education" in *Philosophy of Education 2001*, S. Rice, K. Alston et al, ed. Urbana, Illinois: Philosophy of Education Society, pp. 285-287.
Gilmartin, D. (1994) "Scientific Empire and Imperial Science: Colonialism and Irrigation Technology in the Indus Basin", in *The Journal of Asian Studies* 53, no. 4, pp. 1127–49.
Glissant, E. (1997) *Poetics of Relation*, Ann Arbor: University of Michigan Press.
Goudsblom, J. (1980) *Nihilism and Culture*, Oxford: Blackwell Publishing.
Grander, M., James, G. G., et al. (1990) *Toward a Scientific Practice of Science Education*, London: Lawrence Erlbaum Associated Publishers.

Groff, P. S. (2004) "Al-Kindii and Nietzsche on the Stoic Art of Banishing Sorrow", in *Journal of Nietzsche Studies* 28, pp. 139–73.
Gutman, A. (1994) *Multiculturalism: Examining the Politics of Recognition*, Princeton: Princeton University Press.
Haar, M. (1999) "Nietzsche and Metaphysical Language", in *The New Nietzsche*, ed. D. B. Allison, Cambridge, MA: MIT Press.
Habermas, J. (2005) "Richard Rorty's Pragmatic Turn", in *Truth: Engagements Across Philosophical Traditions*, ed. J. Medina and D. Wood, Oxford: Blackwell Publishing, pp. 109–29.
———. (1999) "On Nietzsche's Theory of Knowledge: A Postscript from 1968", in *Nietzsche, Theories of Knowledge and Critical Theory: Nietzsche and the Sciences I*, ed. B. Babich and R. S. Cohen, pp. 209–23.
———. (1994) "Struggle for Recognition in the Democratic Constitutional State", in *Multiculturalism: Examining the Politics of Recognition*, ed. A. Gutman, Princeton: Princeton University Press, pp. 107–48.
———. (1992) *Postmetaphysical Thinking; Philosophical Essays*, Cambridge: Polity Press.
———. (1985) "Questions and Counterquestions", in *Habermas and Modernity*, ed. R. Bernstein, Cambridge, MA: MIT Press.
———. (1972) *Knowledge and Human Interests*, London: Heinemann Educational.
Hank, C. (2005) "Incommensurability and Educational Research" in *Philosophy of Education 2001*, S. Rice, K. Alston et al, eds. Urbana, Illinois: Philosophy of Education Society, pp. 225-236.
Hans, J. S. (1992) *Contextual Authority and Aesthetic Truth*, Albany: State University Of New York Press.
Hansen, B. (2005) "Benjamin or Heidegger: Aesthetics and Politics in an Age of Technology", in *Walter Benjamin and Art*, ed. A. Benjamin, London: Continuum, pp. 73–93.
Harding, S. (1998) *Is Science Multicultural? Postcolonialisms, Feminisms, and Epistemologies*, Indianapolis: Indiana University Press.
———., ed. (1993) *The "Racial" Economy of Science: Toward a Democratic Future*, Bloomington: Indiana University Press.
Härnqvist, K., and Burgen, A., eds. (1997) *Growing Up with Science: Developing Early Understanding of Science*, London: Jessica Kingsley Publishers.
Harr, M. (1999) "Nietzsche and Metaphysical Language", in *The New Nietzsche*, ed. D. B. Allison Cambridge, MA: MIT Press, pp. 5–36.
Havas, R. (1995) *Nietzsche's Genealogy: Nihilism and the Will to Knowledge*, Ithaca: Cornell University Press.
Hawkes, D. (1996) *Ideology*, London: Routledge.
Hedfors, E. (2005) *The Reading Of Ludwik Fleck: Questions of Sources and Impetus*, Stockholm: KTH Architecture and the Built Environment.
Hegel, G. W. F. (1977) *Phenomenology of Spirit*, Oxford: Oxford University Press.
Heidegger, M. (2005) "On the Essence of Truth", in *Truth: Engagements Across Philosophical Traditions*, ed. J. Medina and D. Wood, Oxford: Blackwell Publishing, pp. 243–57.
———. (2003) *The Essence of Truth*, New York: Continuum.
Heidegger, M. (2002) *On the Essence of Truth: On Plato's Cave Allegory and Theaetetus*, London: Continuum.
———. (1999) "Who is Nietzsche's Zarathustra?", in *The New Nietzsche*, ed. D. B. Allison, Cambridge, MA: MIT Press, pp 64–79.
———. (1992) *Parmenides*, Bloomington: Indiana University Press.
———. (1991) *Nietzsche*, vol. 4, San Francisco: HarperCollins.

———. (1987) *Nietzsche*, vol. 3, San Francisco: Harper & Row Cop.
———. (1977) *Basic Writings*, New York: Harper and Row.
Hickman, L. A. (2001) "Philosophical Tools for Technological Culture", in *Philosophy of Education 2001*, S. Rice, K. Alston et al, eds. Urbana, Illinois: Philosophy of Education Society pp. 25-35.
Hickman, R., and Huckstep, P. (2003) "Art and Mathematics in Education", in *Journal of Aesthetic Education* 37, no. 1, pp. 1–12.
Higgins, C. (2003) "Teaching and the Good Life: A Critique of Ascetic Ideal in Education", in *Educational Theory* 53, no. 2, pp. 131–54.
Hilleesheim, J. (1973) "Nietzsche Agonists" in *Educational Theory* 23, no. 4, pp. 343–53.
Hodge, J. (2005) "The Timing of Elective Affinity: Walter Benjamin's Strong Aesthetics", in *Walter Benjamin and Art*, ed. A. Benjamin, London: Continuum, pp. 14–31.
Holma, K. (2007) "Essentialism Regarding Human Nature in the Defence of Gender Equality in Education", in *Journal of Philosophy of Education* 41, no. 1, pp. 45–57.
Hornsby, J. (2001) "Truth: The Identity Theory", in *The Nature of Truth: Classic and Contemporary Perspectives*, ed. M. P. Lynch, Cambridge, MA: MIT Press, pp. 663–81.
Hutchins, R. M. (1936) *The Higher Learning in America*, New Haven: Yale University Press.
Hylton, P. (2007) *Quine*, New York: Routledge.
———. (1990) *Russell, Idealism, and the Emergence of Analytic Philosophy*, Oxford: Clarendon.
James, W. (2005) "Pragmatism's Notion of Truth", in *Truth: Engagements Across Philosophical Traditions*, ed. J. Medina and D. Wood, Oxford: Blackwell Publishing, pp. 26–38.
Jefferson, A., and Robey, R., eds. (1996) *Modern Literary Theory: A Comparative Introduction*, London: B. T. Batsford.
Johnson, J. S. (1998) "Nietzsche as Educator: A Re-examination", in *Educational Theory* 48, no. 1, pp. 67–84.
Kant, I. (1996) *Critique of Pure Reason*, Indianapolis: Hackett Publishing Company.
———. (1970) "An Answer to the Question: 'What is Enlightenment?'" in *Kant's Political Writings*, ed. Hans Reiss, Cambridge: Cambridge University Press.
Kaufman, R. (2005) "Aura, Still", in *Walter Benjamin and Art*, ed. A. Benjamin, London: Continuum, pp. 121–47.
Kaufmann, W. (1974) *Nietzsche: Philosopher, Psychologist, Antichrist*, Princeton: Princeton University Press.
Kertz-Welzel, A. (2005) "In Search of the Sense and the Senses: Aesthetic Education in Germany and the United States" in *Journal of Aesthetic Education* 39, no. 3, pp 102–14.
Kessler, S. J., and McKenna, W. (1978) *Gender: An Ethnomethodological Approach*, Chicago: University of Chicago Press.
Kierkegaard, S. (2005) "Truth, Subjectivity and Communication" in T*ruth Engagements Across Philosophical Tradition*, J. Medina and D. Wood, ed. Oxford: Blackwell Publishing, pp. 48-60.
Koopman, C. (2005) "Art as Fulfilment: On the Justification of Education in the Arts", in *Journal of Philosophy of Education* 39, no. 1, pp. 85–97.
Kuhn, T. S. (2000) *The Road Since Structure*, Chicago: University of Chicago Press.
———. (1998a) "Logic of Discovery or Psychology of Research", in *Philosophy of Science: The Central Issues*, ed. M. Curd and J. A. Cover, London: W. W. Norton and Company, pp. 11–19.

———. (1998b) "Objectivity, Value Judgement, and Theory Choice", in *Philosophy of Science: The Central Issues*, ed. M. Curd and J. A. Cover, London: W. W. Norton and Company, pp. 102–18.

———. (1977) *The Essential Tension*, Chicago: University of Chicago Press.

———. (1970) *The Structure of Scientific Revolutions*, Chicago: University of Chicago Press.

———. (1957) *The Copernican Revolution: Planetary Astronomy in the Development of Western Thought*, Cambridge, MA: Harvard University Press.

Lakatos, I. (1978) *Philosophical Papers*, Volume 1: *The Methodology of Scientific Research Programs*, Cambridge: Cambridge University Press.

Lakoff, G. (1995) *Moral Politic*, Chicago: Chicago University Press.

Lampert, L. (2001) *Nietzsche's Task: An Interpretation of Beyond Good and Evil*, New Haven: Yale University Press.

———. (1993) *Nietzsche and Modern Times: A Study of Bacon, Descartes, and Nietzsche*, New Haven: Yale University Press.

———. (1987) *Nietzsche's Teaching: An Interpretation of "Thus Spoke Zarathustra"*, New Haven: Yale University Press.

Landry, D., and MacLean, G., eds. (1996) *The Spivak Reader*, London: Routledge.

Laudan, L. (1998a) "Commentary: Science at the Bar—Causes for Concern", in *Philosophy of Science: The Central Issues*, ed. M. Curd and J. A. Cover, London: W. W. Norton and Company, pp. 48–54.

———. (1998b) "Demystifying Underdetermination", in *Philosophy of Science: The Central Issues*, ed. M. Curd and J. A. Cover, London: W. W. Norton and Company, pp. 320–53.

Levinas, E. (2005) "Truth of Disclosure and Truth of Testimony", in *Truth: Engagements Across Philosophical Traditions*, ed. J. Medina and D. Wood, Oxford: Blackwell Publishing, pp. 261–70.

———. (1996) *Basic Philosophical Writings*, Bloomington: Indiana University Press.

Levisohn, J. A. (2001) "Inclusion and Objectivity: Helen Logino's Feminist Theory of Science Inquiry", in *Philosophy of Education 2001*, S. Rice, K. Alston et al, eds. Urbana, Illinois: Philosophy of Education Society, pp. 333-45.

Longino, H. E. (1998) "Value and Objectivity", in *Philosophy of Science: The Central Issues*, ed. M. Curd and J. A. Cover, London: W. W. Norton and Company, pp. 170–91.

Losee, J. (1993) *A Historical Introduction to the Philosophy of Science*, Oxford: Oxford University Press.

Lynch, M., ed. (2001) *The Nature of Truth: Classic and Contemporary Perspectives*, Cambridge, MA: MIT Press.

Malmberg, A. (2005) "The Work of Art in the Age of Ontological Speculation: Walter Benjamin Revisited", in *Walter Benjamin and Art*, ed. A. Benjamin, London: Continuum, pp. 93–102.

Maloney, D. P. (1994) "Research on Problem Solving: Physics", in *Handbook of Research on Science Teaching*, ed. D. L. Gabel, New York: Macmillan Publishing Company, pp. 327–54.

Margolis, J. (2005) "Relativism and Cultural Relativity", in *Truth: Engagements Across Philosophical Traditions*, ed. J. Medina and D. Wood, Oxford: Blackwell Publishing, pp. 182–96.

Martin, R. M. (1987) *The Meaning of Language*, Cambridge, MA: MIT Press.

Marx, K. (1998) *Economic and Philosophic Manuscripts of 1844*, New York: Dovers Books of Western Philosophy.

———. (1973) *On Society and Social Change*: Chicago: University of Chicago Press.

———. (1971) *The Grundrisse*, New York: Harper & Row Publishers.

———. (1954) *The Eighteenth Brumaire of Louis Bonaparte*, Moscow: Progress.
Marx, K. and Engels, F. (1975) *Collected Works*, Volume 3, London: Lawrence Wishart.
———. (1975a) "On the Jewish Question", in *Collected Works*, vol. 3, by K. Marx and F. Engels, London: Lawrence Wishart.
———. (1975b) "Comments on James Mill", in *Collected Works*, vol. 3, by K. Marx and F. Engels, London: Lawrence Wishart.
Marx, K., and Engels, F. (1975) *Collected Works*, vol. 4, London: Lawrence Wishart.
McDowell, J. (2005) "Towards Rehabilitating Objectivity", in *Truth: Engagements Across Philosophical Traditions*, ed. J. Medina and D. Wood, Oxford: Blackwell Publishing, pp. 130–45.
McMullin, E. (1998) "Rationality and Paradigm Change in Science", in *Philosophy of Science: The Central Issues*, ed. M. Curd and J. A. Cover, London: W. W. Norton and Company, pp. 119–38.
Medina, J., and Wood, D., eds. (2005) *Truth: Engagements Across Philosophical Traditions*, Oxford: Blackwell Publishing.
Merleau-Ponty, M. (2005) "Perception and Truth, from 'an Unpublished Text,'"Cézanne's Doubt'and 'Reflection and Interrogation'", in *Truth: Engagements Across Philosophical Traditions*, ed. J. Medina and D. Wood, Oxford: Blackwell Publishing, pp. 197–206.
Meszaros, I. (1975) *Marx's Theory of Alienation*, London: Merlin Press.
Mill, J. S. (1974) *On Liberty*, London: Penguin Books.
Mitzes, J. J., and Wandersee, J. H. (1997) "Reform and Innovation in Science Teaching: A Human Constructivist View", in *Teaching Science for Understanding: A Human Constructivist View*, ed. J. J. Mitzes, J. H. Wandersee and J. D. Novak, London: Academic Press, pp. 29–92.
Mitzes, J. J., Wandersee, J. H., and Novak, J. D., eds. (1997) *Teaching Science for Understanding: A Human Constructivist View*, London: Academic Press.
Morris, R., ed. (1989) *Science Education Worldwide*, Paris: UNESCO.
Mullarkey, J. (2006) *Post-Continental Philosophy: An Outline*, New York: Continuum.
National Research Council (2003) Evaluating and Improving Undergraduate Teaching in Science, Technology, Engineering, and Mathematics, Washington, DC: National Academies Press.
———. (1999) *Transforming Undergraduate Education in Science, Mathematics, Engineering, and Technology*, Washington, DC: National Academy Press.
Nehamas, A. (1999) *Virtues of Authenticity*, Princeton: Princeton University Press.
———. (1985) *Nietzsche: Life as Literature*, Cambridge, MA: Harvard University Press.
Nietzsche, F. W. (2007) *The Dawn of Day*, New York: Dover Publication.
———. (1996) *Beyond Good and Evil*, trans. D. Smith, Oxford: Oxford University Press.
———. (1995) *The Birth of Tragedy*, New York: Dover Publication.
———. (1995) *David Strauss, the Confessor and the Writer*, in *Unpublished Writings from the Period of Unfashionable Observations*, Stanford: Stanford University Press, pp. 3–82.
———. (1995) *On the Utility and Liability of History for Life*, in *Unpublished Writings from the Period of Unfashionable Observations*, Stanford: Stanford University Press, pp. 83–168.
———. (1995) *Richard Wagner in Bayreuth*, Stanford: Stanford University Press.
———. (1995) *Schopenhauer as Educator*, in *Unpublished Writings from the Period of Unfashionable Observations*, Stanford: Stanford University Press, pp. 175–233.

———. (1995) *Unpublished Writings from the Period of Unfashionable Observations*, Stanford: Stanford University Press.
———. (1992) *The Case of Wagner*, trans. W. Kaufmann, in *Basic Writings of Nietzsche*, New York: Modern Library, pp. 601–54.
———. (1992) *On the Genealogy of Morals*, in *Basic Writings of Nietzsche*, New York: Modern Library, pp. 437–600.
———. (1986) *Human, All Too Human*, Cambridge: Cambridge University Press.
———. (1982) *The Antichrist*, in *The Portable Nietzsche*, New York: Penguin Books, pp 565–656.
———. (1982) *Ecce Homo*, in *The Portable Nietzsche*, New York: Penguin Books.
———. (1982) *Nietzsche Contra Wagner*, in *The Portable Nietzsche*, New York: Penguin Books, pp 661–683.
———. (1982) *Thus Spoke Zarathustra*, in *The Portable Nietzsche*, New York: Penguin Books, pp.103–439.
———. (1982) *Twilight of the Idols*, in *The Portable Nietzsche*, New York: Penguin Books, 463–563.
———. (1979) *Philosophy and Truth: Selections from Nietzsche's Notebook of the Early 1870's*, New Jersey: Humanities Press.
———. (1979a) "The Philosopher: Reflections on the Struggle Between Art and Knowledge" in. D. Breazeale, ed. *Philosophy and Truth; Selections from Nietzsche's Notebook of the Early 1870's*, New Jersey: Humanities Press, pp. 1-58.
———. (1979b), "On Truth and Lying in an Extra-Moral Sense", in D. Breazeale, ed. Philosophy and Truth; *Selections from Nietzsche's Notebook of the Early 1870's*, New Jersey: Humanities Press, pp. 79-100.
———. (1979c) *Ecce Homo; How One Becomes What One Is?*, Harmondworth: Penguin Books.
———. (1976) *The Portable Nietzsche*, trans. W. Kaufmann, New York: Penguin Books.
———. (1974) *The Gay Science*, New York: Vintage Books.
———. (1910) *The Will to Power*, New York: Vintage Books.
———. (1909) *On the Future of Our Educational Institutions* in *The Complete Works of Friedrich Nietzsche*, New York: Gordon Press.
Nochlin, L. (1994) *The Politics of Vision: Essays on Nineteenth Century Art and Society*, London: Thames and Hudson.
Norris, C. (2004) *Epistemology: Key Concepts in Philosophy*, London: Continuum.
Novak, J. (1977) *A Theory of Education*, Ithaca: Cornell University Press.
Nussbaum, C. M. (1997) *Cultivating Humanity: A Classical Defence of Freedom in Liberal Education*, Cambridge, MA: Harvard University Press.
Nussbaum, J. (1997) "History and Philosophy of Science and the Presentation for Constructivist Teaching: The Case of Practical Theory", in *Teaching Science for Understanding: A Human Constructivist View*, ed. J. J. Mitzes, J. H. Wandersee and J. D. Novak, London: Academic Press, pp. 165–94.
Ogden, C. K., and Richards, I. A. (1946) *The Meaning of Meaning: A Study of the Influence of Language upon Thought and of the Science of Symbolism*, London: Kegan Paul, Trench, Trubner and Co.
O'Hear, A. (1988) *The Element of Fire, Science, Art and the Human World*, London: Routledge.
Okruhlik, K. (1998) "Gender and the Biological Science", in *Philosophy of Science: The Central Issues*, ed. M. Curd and J. A. Cover, London: W. W. Norton and Company, pp.192–209.
Ostrow, S. (2005) "Rethinking Revolution and Life: The Embodiment of Benjamin's Artwork Essay at the End of the Age of Mechanical Reproduction", in *Walter Benjamin and Art*, ed. A. Benjamin, London: Continuum, pp. 226–47.

Owen, D. (2002) "Equality, Democracy, and Self-Respect: Reflections on Nietzsche's Agonal Perfectionism", in *Journal of Nietzsche Studies* 24, pp. 113–31.
Patke, R. S. (2005) "Benjamin on Art and Reproducibility: The Case of Music", in *Walter Benjamin and Art*, ed. A. Benjamin, London: Continuum, pp. 185–208.
Peters, M., Marshall, J., and Smeyers, P., eds. (2001) *Nietzsche's Legacy for Education: Past and Present Values*, London: Bergin Harvey.
Plato (1997a) *Complete Works*, Indianapolis: Hackett Publishing Company.
———. (1997b) *Republic*, Hertfordshire: Wordsworth Editions.
Polanyi, M. (1997) *Personal Knowledge: Toward a Post-Critical Philosophy*, London: Routledge.
Popper, K. (1998) "Science: Conjecture and Refutation", in *Philosophy of Science: The Central Issues*, ed. M. Curd and J. A. Cover, London: W. W. Norton and Company, pp. 3–8.
———. (1972) *Conjectures and Refutation: The Growth of Scientific Knowledge*, London: Routledge and Kegan Paul.
Putnam, H. (2000) *The Threefold Cord: Mind, Body, and the World*, New York: Colombia University Press.
———. (1975), *Mathematics, Matter and Method: Philosophical Papers*, vol. 1, Cambridge: Cambridge University Press.
Quine, W. V. (1998) "Two Dogmas of Empiricism", in *Philosophy of Science: The Central Issues*, ed. M. Curd and J. A. Cover, London: W. W. Norton and Company, pp. 280–301.
———. (1981) *Theories and Things*, Cambridge, MA: Harvard University Press.
———. (1969) "Epistemology Naturalized", in *Ontological Relativity and Other Essays*, New York: Colombia University Press, pp. 69–90.
Rapaport, H. (1997) *Is There Truth in Art?*, Ithaca: Cornell University Press.
Reed, D. R. (1965) *A Theological Reading of Hegel's Phenomenology of Spirit, with Particular Reference to Its Themes of Identity, Alienation and Community*, Lewiston: Mellen University Press.
Regelski, T. A. (2005) "Curriculum Implications of Aesthetic versus Praxial Philosophy", in *Parxial Music Education*, ed. D. J. Elliot, Oxford: Oxford University Press, pp. 219–48.
Reitz, C. (2000) *Art, Alienation and the Humanities: A Critical Engagement With Herbert Marcuse*, Albany: State University of New York Press.
Richards, I. A. (1936) *The Philosophy of Rhetoric*. Oxford: Oxford University Press.
Ricoeur, P. (1977) *The Rule of Metaphor*, Toronto: Toronto University Press.
———. (1965) *History and Truth*, Evanston: Northwestern University Press.
Rivkin, J., and Ryan, M., eds. (1998) *Literary Theory: An Anthology*, Oxford: Blackwell Publishing.
Rorty, R. (2005) "Representation, Social Practice, and Truth", in *Truth:, Engagements Across Philosophical Traditions*, ed. J. Medina and D. Wood, Oxford: Blackwell Publishing, pp. 99–108.
———. (1979) *Philosophy and the Mirror of Nature*, Princeton: Princeton University Press.
Russell, B. (1959) *The Problems of Philosophy*, Oxford: Oxford University Press.
Sallis, J. (1995) *Double Truth*, Albany: State University of New York Press.
Sartre, J. P. (1972) *The Psychology of Imagination*, London: Methuen.
Schacht, R. (1994) *The Future of Alienation*, Urbana: University of Illinois Press.
———. (1983) *Nietzsche*, London: Routledge.
Schmitt, F. F., ed. (2004) *Theories of Truth*, Malden: Blackwell Publishing.
Schmitt, R. (2003) *Alienation and Freedom*, Oxford: Westview Press.

Schopenhauer, A. (1910) *The World as Will and Representation*, London: Kegan Paul, Trench, Trubner and Co. Available at http://www.archive.org/details/theworldaswillan01schouoft.
Sedgwick, R. P., ed. (1995) *Nietzsche: A Critical Reader*, Oxford: Blackwell Publishing.
Sellars, W. (1997) *Empiricism and the Philosophy of Mind*, Cambridge, MA: Harvard University Press.
———. (1963) *Science, Perception, and Reality*, London: Routledge.
Shusterman, R. (1989) *Analytic Aesthetics*, Oxford: Basil Blackwell.
Simmons, E. L. (1991) *What Incommensurability Claims Means: A Study of Ludwik Fleck's Contribution to the Incommensurability Debate*, Notre Dame: UMI Dissertation Service.
Simpson, R. D., Koballa, T. R., et al. (1994) "Research on the Affective Dimension of Science Learning", in *Handbook of Research on Science Teaching*, ed. D. L. Gabel, New York: Macmillan Publishing Company, pp. 211–34.
Sini, C. (1985) *Images of Truth: From Sign to Symbol*, New Jersey: Humanities Press.
Skolverket, (1994) *Curriculum for Compulsory School System, the Pre-school Classes and the Leisure-time Centre Lpo 94*, Stockholm: Skolverket.
Smith, P. (2001) *Cultural Theory: An Introduction*, London: Blackwell Publishing.
Solomon, R. C., and Higgins, M. (2000) *What Nietzsche Really Said*, New York: Schocken Books.
Standish, P. (2001) "Learning *from* Levinas: The Provocation of Sharon Todd", in *Philosophy of Education 2001*, S. Rice, K. Alston et al, eds. Urbana, Illinois: Philosophy of Education Society, pp.75-77.
Steiner, G. (1998) *After Babel: Aspects of Language and Translation*, Oxford: Oxford University Press.
Steup, M., and Sosa, E. (2005) *Contemporary Debates in Epistemology*, Oxford: Blackwell Publishing.
Stickney, J. (2005) "Teaching and Learning in Wittgenstein's Philosophic Method" in *Philosophy of Education 2005*, Burbules, N. C. , Howe, K. R. et al, eds. Urbana, Illinois, Philosophy of Education Society, pp. 299-307.
Story, J. (1993) *An Introductory Guide to Cultural Theory and Popular Culture*, New York: Harvester/Wheatsheaf.
Strong, T. B. (1975) *Friedrich Nietzsche and the Politics of Transfiguration*, Berkeley: University of California Press.
Stroud, B. (2004) "The Charm of Naturalism", in *Naturalism in Question*, ed. M. De Cario and D. Macarthur, Cambridge, MA: Harvard University Press.
Szego, C. K. (2005) "Praxial Foundation of Multicultural Music Education", in *Parxial Music Education*, ed. D. J. Elliot, Oxford: Oxford University Press, pp. 196–218.
Taylor, C. (1994) "The Politics of Recognition" in *Multiculturalism: Examining the Politics of Recognition*, ed. A. Gutman, Princeton: Princeton University Press, pp. 25–73.
Todd, S. (2003) *Learning from the Other: Levinas, Psychoanalysis, and Ethical Possibilities in Education*, Albany: State University of New York Press.
———. (2001) "On Not Knowing the Other, or Learning *from* Levinas", in *Philosophy of Education 2001*, S. Rice, K. Alston et al, eds. Urbana, Illinois: Philosophy of Education Society, pp.67-74.
Tomlinson, J. (1999) *Globalization and Culture*, Oxford: Polity Press. Tubbs, N. (2005) "Philosophy of the Teacher", *Journal of Philosophy of Education* 39, no. 2, special issue.

Vattimo, G. (2005) "The Truth of Hermeneutics", in *Truth: Engagements Across Philosophical Traditions*, ed. J. Medina and D. Wood, Oxford: Blackwell Publishing, pp. 168–80.
———. (1988) *The End of Modernity*, Cambridge: Polity Press.
Warnock, M. (1976) *Imagination*, London: Faber.
Weber, M. (2002) *The Protestant Ethic and the Spirit of Capitalism*, New York: Routledge.
Westerlund, H., and Juntunen, M. L. (2005) "Music and Knowledge in Bodily Experience", in *Parxial Music Education*, ed. D. J. Elliot, Oxford: Oxford University Press, pp. 112–22.
White, J. (2006) *Intelligence, Destiny and Education: The Ideological Roots of Intelligence Testing*, London: Routledge.
White, R. T. (1988) *Learning Science*: Oxford: Basil Blackwell.
Williams, B. (2002) *Truth and Truthfulness: An Essay in Genealogy*, Princeton: Princeton University Press.
Wilshire, B. (2002) *Fashionable Nihilism: A Critique of Analytic Philosophy*, Albany: State University of New York Press.
Wimsatt, W. C. (2007) *Re-Engineering Philosophy for Limited Beings*, Cambridge, MA: Harvard University Press.
Wittgenstein, L. (1969) *On Certainty*, New York: Harper Torchbooks.
———. (1968) *Philosophical Investigations*, Oxford: Oxford University Press.
Wolterstorff, N. (1980) *Works and Worlds of Art*, Oxford: Claredon.
Woolnough, B. E. (1994) *Effective Science Teaching*, Buckingham: Open University Press.
Xie, Y., and Shauman, K. A. (2003) *Women in Science*, Cambridge, MA: Harvard University Press.
Young, J., ed. (2005) *Aesthetics: Critical Concepts in Philosophy*, vol. 3, London: Routledge.
———. (1992) *Nietzsche's Philosophy of Art*, Cambridge: Cambridge University Press.
Zizek, S. (1993) *Tarrying with the Negative: Kant, Hegel, and the Critique of Ideology*, Durham: Duke University Press.
———. (1991) *For They Know Not What They Do: Enjoyment as a Political Factor*, London: Verso.
———. (1989) *The Sublime Object of Ideology*, London: Verso.
Zuidervaart, L. (2004) *Artistic Truth: Aesthetics, Discourse, and Imaginative Disclosure*, Cambridge: Cambridge University Press.

Index

A
Absolutism: 5, 6, 10, 21, 23, 130, 161, 176, 180
Active elements of thought: 113, 115, 118
Adorno T. W: 35, 60, 61, 96, 99, 164
Aletheia: 99, 100, 110, 146, 177
Alienation: and nihilism 13, 15, 37, 43–8, 55–7, 66, 1675; and education 14, 35; and objectivism 24, 35; theories of 36; and knowledge systems 36, 41, 45, 58; and scientific education 37, 64; Marx's theory of, 38–40; and modern society 38; and positivism 49; and modernity 57; and commoditisation of science 85; and truth 100, 104
Althusser, L: 133–4
Apartheid: 155, 157, 182, 190n 1
Arendt, H: 149, 152–3, 159
Aristotle: 63, 94, 103, 112, 126, 155, 159, 160, 162, 166
Art: as perspective 74, 95–7, 111, 171, 178, 179, 180, 183; as perspective on science 77–8, 97; relation with science 92–5; and tradition 96; and history 96; and life 98, 116; and truth 99–100; and philosophy 101–03; and education 108; of education 108; of tragedy 109–10; and ground of knowledge 111–12, 118; of reading 141; work of 96, 100, 110, 140, 187 n3; art education 185 n1;
Authority: and education 159; and obedience 160, 162; hierarchical 179; as immanent in education 184; of artwork 188 n1

B
Bakhtin, M: 3, 4, 33, 77, 125, 129
Beardsley, M: 6, 87, 93
Benjamin, W: 137–38, 140, 142, 187
Bybee, R. W: 25, 59, 60

C
Canon: 125, 129; authority of 130; educational 183
Canonical: science 49, 64, 141; tradition 125; names 125; works 125;
Capitalism: 30, 167, 169
Cognitive democracy: 120, 160, 162, 166
Cognitive pluralism: 12, 23, 101, 168
Colonialism: 86, 164
Communication: 2, 3, 4, 6, 15, 135; verbal 101, 138, 149, 182; rational 130–32; and translation 135, 151, 180; paradox of 135

D
Davidson, D: 136, 150–52, 161, 186 n2
Derrida, J: 22, 126, 137, 154
Descartes: 8, 25, 26, 27, 30, 35, 65, 69, 71, 87–8, 126, 139
Dewey, J: 97, 187 n. 3, 188n.4
Dupré, J: 26

E
Education: as therapy 11, 116; and truth 23, 25 60; and science 24, 25, 27 42; systemisation of 29; and methodology 30; and culture 34; and alienation 35, 36, 3, 43, 56; and translation 43, 57, 138, 142; and nihilism 47, 56, 58; and art 95; and educators 119, 124; rationality of 132; and

persuasion 133; and change 169; and the individual 171–3; and love 171; and politics 169; and national security; 52, 54, 116, 119, 129, 132

Educational revolution: 27, 168, 169

Educational paradigm-shifts: 27–8, 30, 51

Educator: 15, 28, 78, 90, 120, 122, 124, 127, 134, 139, 142, 147; Cultures as educator 122–24; history as 124; great works as; 124–25; relations with learners 126, 129, 130–35, 142, 144, 158, 162, 182, 183; and truth 126, 153, 154, 155, 182; and authority 159, 160, 162; weak notion of 184; strong notion of 184

Elgin, C: 104–05

Emerson, R. W: 139

Enlightenment: 28, 31, 32, 57, 164, 165, 167, 184

Ethics; 12, 183 n 3, 187 n 1; protestant 27; rational 28; and epistemology 103; and knowledge 103, 105

Exclusion: 3, 11, 28, 130; criterion of 84–5; principle of 77; epistemic 87; and truth 99; logic of 134, 155, 156, 157

F

Feyerabend, P: 17- 20, 61, 162, 177

Firestone, S: 168

Fleck L; 13, 50, 60, 62, 64, 75, 80, 91–2, 106–09, 113–14, 131–33, 141, 188n5

Foucault M: 126, 148

G

Genealogy: 12, 24; of education 7; of scientific education 28; of objectivist account of science 25

Genealogical: 10 analysis 12, 13, 25, 26, 64, 115, 160, 165, 166; studies 63, 112

Gadamer, H. J: 100, 101

H

Habermas J: 17, 20, 101, 126, 132, 145–51, 155, 186n2

Harding, S: 7, 80–3, 87, 98, 126, 155

Hegel W F: 38, 75, 153, 165

Heidegger, M: 22, 46, 90–1, 99, 100

History: 12, 64, 74, 75, 79, 81, 94, 114, 117, 170; of thought 12, 27, 85, 126; of science 21, 30, 50, 177; of education 27; of philosophy 76; as open-ended 123; as educator 124; as perspective 157, 179, 183; as struggle 170; Hegelian notion of 38, 165

I

Inclusion: of perspectives 3, 81; of diverse views of knowledge 5; and exclusion 11, 82, 93, 148; demand for 28; and epistemic democracy 81; criterion of 84–85, 168; of marginalised people 85, 87, 168; of women 85; of non-Westerners 8; regimes of 117; principle of 154; logic of 155–56, 176, 178, 183; as cognitive norm 166; notion of philosophy and art 168; and assimilation 179; struggle for 182; spirit of 190n1

Inclusive: notion of universality 4; values 4, 86; notion of truth 21, 99; notion of science 68, 83, 97; notion of objectivity 81–83; epistemology 83, 176, 179; notion of canon 125; style of thought 109, 117; organisation of science 105; perspective 90, 102

Individual; role in cognition 14, 25, 36, 56, 69, 83, 107, 169; and plurality of perspectives 14; and truth 22; and alienation 36, 43, 56; and knowledge 37, 43, 56, 57, 59, 64, 79, 82, 92; and universal saleability 41–42, 163; and nihilism 47, 57; strong notion of 56, 172–74; and education 61, 169; and objectivity 83, 105; and thought style 107–08; weak notion of 108; and collective 110, 116; exemplary notion of 152, 153–4,158; and humanity 171

J

James, W: 22, 103

K

Kant: 1, 37, 40, 47, 69–5, 90–91, 117, 173, 177

Kierkegaard, S: 104

Kuhn T: 12, 21, 26, 33, 45, 49–5, 61–2, 64, 69, 74, 75, 76, 80–2, 85, 91–2, 120–21, 157, 177, 188n5

L

Laudan, L: 52–5
Levinas, E: 136, 149, 152, 189n2
Longino, H: 79–80

M

Mandela, N: 11, 153, 154, 155, 156, 157, 158, 161, 163, 182
Marx, K: 10, 13, 38–9, 40.3, 47, 63–5, 89, 162, 168, 169, 170–77, 189n 1, 190
McDowell, J: 19
McMullin, E: 52–4
Merleau-Ponty, M: 100
Metaphor: 94, 137–8, 181
Methodology: Cartesian 26, 30; and knowledge 25; of science 64; and philosophy 87
Mill, J. S: 159, 163
Moral: 29, 71; responsibility 83, 103; and epistemology 104; indignation 155; relativism 186n3

N

Nietzsche, W. F: 1, 10, 11, 12,, 39, 42–3, 47, 54, 57, 58, 61–9, 72–7, 83, 89, 91–2, 94, 97, 102, 106, 108, 109, 110, 111–13, 123, 124, 126, 131–33, 137, 139, 141, 148, 149, 152, 155, 157, 159, 160–3, 165–69, 170–72, 177, 186n 2, 189 n1
Nihilism: and alienation 1, 13, 14, 44, 46, 56, 57, 58, 64, 66, 68, 104; as lack of transcendence 2, 46, 47; and relativism 5, 44, 47–8, 160; negative notion of 11, 52, 68, 102; and the death of God 32, 47, 58; and knowledge 37; and self-consciousness 37, 56; and individual 43, 47, 57; and objectivism 45; passive notion of 46; and scientific education 47, 74, 58–9; solution of 46; and Kuhnian view of science 49, 52, 53, 55, 62, 68–9, 175; the inevitability of 55; against itself 55; and science 56; as liberating force 57; and the theoretical reason 58; and truth 60, 66; and ascetic ideal 61, 92; and human nature 62, 63, 64; and *the* meaning 130; and metaphysics 171

O

Objectivism: 20, 21, 23, 35, 78, 82, 127, 144, 171, 173, 175, 176; and cultural values 82; and relativism 176
Objectivity: traditional notion of, 14, 18, 176; inclusive notion of 14, 78, 83, 178; and truth 19; and modern science 24; and scientific method 24, 26; and nihilism 46, 68; of science 52, 59; and diversity of perspectives 77; and communality of science 80; weak notion of 82, 101, 178; strong notion of 82

P

Paradigm: 1, 2, 4, 9, 46, 48, 53, 150, 182; of truth 19; and relativism 21–22, 52; educational; 27–28; and scientific relativism 48; and scientific education 51, 177, 178; reticulation model of 52–3; historical character of 53; and individual 55; and education 61, 63, 120, 125; and exemplars 120, 122; as general intellectual climate 122; transformation of 150
Passive elements of thought: 113, 114, 131
Philosophy: as perspective 8, 14, 60, 78, 87, 90, 168, 179, 183; and science 6, 18; traditional notion of, 25, 46; modern notion of 30; and art; 95, 101, 102, 149, 155; of science 49, 62, 80, 87; Firs 87, 88, 89; scientific notion of 87; as critical thought 88, 91, 117; as profession 88; a priori 88–9; reduced to science 88; and foundation of science 89, 91, 101, 117; and education 89, 102; and cultural values 118; and truth 155; and change 169; praxial 185n 1
Plato: 12, 25, 77, 112, 153, 162
Platonic: philosopher-king 18, 20; Ideas 47, 113, 115, 153; two-world model 71, 140; rationality 76; Forms 114; Socrates 126, 130
Platonism: 22, 26, 76

206 Index

Popper, K: 26
Positivism: 30, 45, 49, 50, 57, 58, 61, 72, 164
Public sphere: 132, 149
Putnam, H: 17, 19, 22

Q

Qiune, W. V: 6, 18, 48–9, 50, 74, 87, 88, 89, 93

R

Ramus P: 30, 31
Rationalism: 29, 70, 77, 130, 131, 147, 150, 151
Rationality: 26, 29, 31; and metaphysics 31; and education 34, 132–133; different types of 77, 130; of thought 132
Relativism: 20, 177, 186n; and absolutism 13, 144; democratic 20, 159; as ideology 23; scientific notion of 48; Kuhnian notion of 52; cognitive 186n 3; moral 183 n 3; semantic 186 n 3
Revolutionary science: 50, 45, 54
Ricoeur, P: 17, 19, 91, 100–01
Rorty, R: 18, 20
Russell, B: 19, 87

S

Sellars W: 33, 116
Schacht, R: 36–37
Science; 6, 7: and educational problem 1; as form and content of education 1, 6, 7, 8, 32; and education 1, 6, 25, 35, 60, 61, 63, 119, 121; global notion of 6; as perspective on itself 7; teaching 7, 33, 34, 51, 62; and methodology 8, 26, 27; and art 8; and philosophy 18, 56, 87, 88, 89, 91, 117; and truth 19, 24–5; history of 21; genealogy of 25; and rationality 34, 42; as the measure of all things 33; and culture 34; and life 42; and paradigm 45, 48, 51; and nihilism 49, 55; and alienation 68; and the world 62; and ascetic ideal 61; and art 56, 90–95, 97, 101, 102, 117, 178; and culture 68; and cultural values 79–4; objectivity of 83; and epistemology 88; and ideology 90; and analytic philosophy 140; and interpretation 141; and exclusion 156; and positivism 175; as norm 93–94; social organisation of 107–108; the problem of 69, 73–4; gay notion of 77; Kuhnian image of 50; positivistic account of 68; pedagogical notion of 35; revolutionary 50; normal 50;
Scientific education: 7, 8, 9, 24, 25, 27, 28, 29, 30–7, 43–4, 47, 49, 51, 52, 57, 59, 60, 61, 63, 68, 118, 119, 120, 149; the emergence 28; the problem of 31; and truth 6, 60, 62; and nihilism 58, 60, 63, 64, 66
Scientific revolutions: 21, 45, 50–2, 154, 169
Socrates: 3, 58, 126, 130, 138, 139, 155, 162, 181
Steiner, G: 135, 136, 142
Style: 10, 14, 24, 47, 61; of thought 27, 30, 31, 34, 47, 115, 117, 125, 137; as organisational principle 104–06; as a regulative concept 14, 106, 180; as aesthetic organisational principle 106, 108, 109; as the constraint of thought 107; cultural aspect of; 107; individual aspect of 108, 109; and education 108; and culture 109; tragic notion of 109; as harmony of illusions 113; kinship of 135, 140, 182, 183; of life 155, 161; inclusive notion of 157; scientific thought style 63, 107;
Subject: 25–6; and object 26, 28, 64–5, 66, 69, 70–3, 79, 94, 137, 160, 178; and cognition 35, 69, 71; transcendental notion of 173; empirical notion of 73

T

Translation: 2, 3, 6, 9, 47; and universality 3, 4, 6, 9, 15, 47, 136; and understanding 4; as the link between humanity and the world 94, 137–38, 180; as the link between the universal and the local 23; as the basis of human communication 135; and communication 135, 151, 180–81; and education 138–40; and fact

141; and educators 141, 158, 182; and rational communication 147, 150; as the presupposition of truth 151

Truth: and epistemic violence 2; and education 4, 5, 133, 150; and tradition 5 as a normative notion 5, 102, 180; orders of 17; correspondence theory of 17, 19, 98; identity theory of 19; and science 19–20, 62, 97, 98, 99, 107, 110; a weak notion of 21; an inclusive notion of 21; our need of 22; and morality 39; performative aspect of 23; and nihilism 55, 58, 60, 64, 66, 104; and scientific education 59–60; and ascetic ideal 61, 116; and inclusive epistemology 83, 85; and art 87, 96, 97; ethical aspect of 90; will to 92; and work of art 96; propositional notion of 93, 145; unity of 98; aesthetical notion of 99, 100, 101, 110; poetic notion of 100–01; performative notion of 103; as aletheia, 99, 100, 110, 146, 177; as veritas 99, 100, 104, 110, 146, 177; as testimony 104, 149, 152; metaphysical 115, 116, 177; truth telling 126, 127, 152, 155; educational order of 144; discourse theory of 146; and power 147–48; and politics 149; and interpretation 150–51; showing truth 151–52; and exemplars 152–54, 155, 158, 160–61, 182; and public opinion 152, 162

U

Universalism: 2, 5, 13, 17, 18, 20, 21, 23, 46, 86, 134, 145; and localism 21, 23; scientific 98; and relativism 144; and rationalism 150

V

Vattimo, G: 22, 30, 31, 148, 150

W

Weber, M: 28–29, 31
White, J: 30–1, 125
Williams, B: 132–33
Wittgenstein, L: 22–3, 33, 50, 54, 64, 68, 93, 103, 111, 120, 137, 146, 147

For Product Safety Concerns and Information please contact our EU
representative GPSR@taylorandfrancis.com
Taylor & Francis Verlag GmbH, Kaufingerstraße 24, 80331 München, Germany

www.ingramcontent.com/pod-product-compliance
Lightning Source LLC
Chambersburg PA
CBHW070724020526
44116CB00031B/1620